Foreword by Ken Ham

A Question of

Created or evolved?

Origins

Shelby MacFarlane

WINEPRESS WP PUBLISHING

© 2005 by Shelby MacFarlane. All rights reserved.

WinePress Publishing (PO Box 428, Enumclaw, WA 98022) functions only as book publisher. As such, the ultimate design, content, editorial accuracy, and views expressed or implied in this work are those of the author.

No part of this publication may be reproduced, stored in a retrieval system or transmitted in any way by any means—electronic, mechanical, photocopy, recording or otherwise—without the prior permission of the copyright holder, except as provided by USA copyright law.

Unless otherwise noted, all Scriptures are taken from the Holy Bible, New International Version, Copyright © 1973, 1978, 1984 by the International Bible Society. Used by permission of Zondervan Publishing House. The "niv" and "New International Version" trademarks are registered in the United States Patent and Trademark Office by International Bible Society.

Photo Credits for Cover:
    Picture of male mountain gorilla: courtesy of Margaret Willms Sonnenberg
    Picture of students and teacher: courtesy of Mary Drouillard
    Picture of miniature dachshund: courtesy of Mary MacFarlane
    Picture of baby: courtesy of Brian Schick
    Landscape: Shelby MacFarlane

Printed in Korea.

ISBN 1-57921-763-X
Library of Congress Catalog Card Number: 2004096790

I wish to dedicate this book:
To all "my kids" who read, critiqued, drew illustrations,
and prayed over its pages.
To all their parents, my fellow teachers, friends, and administrator who
prayed for me and encouraged me to write it.
To Roger VanDorp, whose vision prompted me to teach the course
which generated this book.
To my family, who lived with a part-time wife and mother for six years.
However, most of all, I dedicate this book to the great I AM,
who clearly is revealed in all His creation.

Shelby MacFarlane
Oakland Christian School
Auburn Hills, Michigan

TABLE OF CONTENTS

FOREWORD

Shelby MacFarlane has a burden to reach young people with the foundational message of the importance of the book of Genesis and to equip them to be able to defend their faith. To accomplish this, curricula for all ages is desperately needed in the Christian world for Christian schools, home schools, church and family programs.

As a teacher with many years of experience, Shelby has put together a wealth of information to compile a high school level curriculum that will equip young people to more effectively face this evolutionary indoctrinated world.

There is no doubt that the creation/evolution/age of earth issues are at the cutting edge of the spiritual battle today over the authority of God's Word. Evolution/millions of years have become the major stumbling blocks to today's people being receptive to the Gospel of Jesus Christ.

It is one thing to train young people in Christian/home schools to know what they believe about the Bible, but it is another thing to train them to be able to defend their faith using real science so that they can combat the belief of evolution masquerading as science.

It is my hope and prayer that more people like Shelby will be raised up to write an abundance of curricula so that there will be a plethora of materials available to train a new generation grounded solidly in the Word of God.

Ken Ham
President
Answers in Genesis

PREFACE

In studying origins, it is important to note that the evolutionist and the creationist examine the same evidence. **What is different is the world view from which they begin.** While creationists study the evidence from the perspective that the universe is a result of intelligent action, evolutionists accept only a materialistic explanation of the world around them. The evolutionist constantly seeks to explain everything in terms of random mechanistic processes. **Thus, these world views are obviously, diametrically opposed.**

It is also important to understand that the battle is **not** about science. Science requires direct observation of a phenomenon or the ability to test hypotheses and theories and get reproducible, consistent results. Since no human was there to witness the formation of the stars, the Earth and its first inhabitants, and no one is able to reproduce these events in a laboratory, a study of origins cannot rightly be called a science. **Thus, the controversy is not between religion and science but between two different philosophies**.

It is then not a question of who is biased but of what bias one possesses. Both groups "religiously" adhere to their belief systems. While most people believe this to be true of creationists, many do not know that it is also true of evolutionists. This is demonstrated by a statement made by Professor Richard Lewontin in *The New York Review* (January 9, 1997, p. 31) "Billions and Billions of Demons."

> We take the side of science (here equated with materialism) *in spite of* the patent absurdity of some of its constructs, . . . *in spite of* the tolerance of the scientific community for unsubstantiated just-so stories, because we have a prior commitment, a commitment to materialism . . . . Moreover, that materialism is an absolute, for we cannot allow a Divine Foot in the door.

Obviously, to Professor Lewontin, facts are secondary to what he considers the correct world view. To him, what is important is a strict adherence to a materialistic explanation of origins.

Finally, it is crucial to understand that while neither creationism nor evolution is science, there is much circumstantial scientific evidence available in the natural world to be examined. The question is which philosophy does this evidence logically support? The purpose of this book is to present some of that evidence and let the reader decide.

CRITICAL THINKING

Before beginning, it would be well to do a short study on critical thinking. After all, the evolutionist and the creationist examine the same evidence. What is different is the world view from which they begin. While emotion has a place in science, commitment to a certain viewpoint does not make it true. To examine any evidence and interpret it correctly demands a willingness to make objective judgments based on facts and reasons, not merely on emotions or a philosophy. Critical thinking is the ability to do this instead of relying on emotion and prior belief.

One of the first important steps to take is to **define terms carefully**. Vague or poorly defined terms can be misleading and cause confusion. For example, evolutionists often define evolution as "change over time." Since change does occur, the creationist would seem to have no reason to argue with this. However, this definition is too broad and vague. It does not explain how this change occurs—is it due to a loss or to a gain of genetic information? Or is it a combination of both? Also, how extensive is the change? Is it referring to change within genus or species? Or does the change extend further to the phylum level and beyond? These are the issues that divide evolutionists and creationists. Therefore, in making any study of origins, it is important to see how a term is defined and if the definition changes from time to time to suit the needs of a particular writer. If it does, the writer is committing the error of logic called **equivocation**. It is important to make sure that a scientist and/or author is defining his terms precisely and consistently.

Another important step to take is to examine the evidence carefully and come to a conclusion **based on the facts**. It is very poor science, indeed, to study a group of facts that point to a logical conclusion, and then because of a pre-existing bias, attempt to explain away these facts. For example, if an anthropologist finds an obviously human fossil such as a human arm or leg bone in rock he believes is very

old, it would be illogical for him to assume it is not human simply because it does not fit his preconception of where human bones should be found. If he does, this individual is basing his interpretation of the evidence on his preconceptions rather than on the facts. Perhaps, based on this new evidence, he should change his preconceptions and look for other explanations. Individuals who habitually ignore evidence that points to a different conclusion are **suppressing evidence**, another fallacy of logic.

A third step in critical thinking is to avoid **circular reasoning**. Circular reasoning is using two ideas to validate each other: making the assumption that idea A is true because of idea B and that idea B is true because of idea A, without validating either idea through an independent source. For example, if an individual remarks that he is reading a good book and is asked why it is good, he might reply, "I just like it." He may later remark that he likes the book he is reading because it is a good one. If he does, he is guilty of circular reasoning. He has not established any independent facts about the book that merit it being called "good." It is simply good because he likes it, and he likes it because it is good. (To be completely accurate, he would also have to be careful to define precisely what he means by "good" and "like.")

It is also important to avoid **overgeneralization**, a fourth step. Simply because a fact holds true in a specific circumstance does not mean that it is true on a broader scale. For example, even if several red-headed girls and boys have fiery tempers, this does not mean that all redheads do, or even that a bad temper is a common trait among redheads. Similarly, even though there is ample evidence to show that change occurs at the genus and species level, there is no reason to believe that it extends all the way to the kingdom level, unless there is widespread, clear proof that it does.

A fifth step in critical thinking is to **be willing to test and analyze both one's own and other people's assumptions**. It is also important to state the assumption in a way that can be either proved by the evidence or disproved by contrary evidence, if it exists. Scientists call this the **principle of falsifiability**. Again, as in defining terms, preciseness is crucial. In

forming a hypothesis, the scientist must, in a sense, predict not only what will happen but also what will not happen. For example, evolutionists generally believe that every living thing on Earth evolved from a single-celled organism that arose by spontaneous generation from inorganic materials in the Earth's atmosphere. From this "primitive" cell came, first of all, simple organisms such as aerobic bacteria and yeasts, etc. Later insects, fish, amphibians, reptiles, mammals, and finally man evolved. If this theory were true, the evolutionist would predict that the insects and simple plants should show up in very old rock formations. Then fish, amphibians, reptiles, etc. should show up in successively younger rock. A creationist, on the other hand, would predict that representatives of most of the phyla should show up in very early rock, since he believes they were created at relatively the same time. Obviously, the structure of the fossil record—the same evidence for both groups—should support or refute one or the other hypothesis.

It is also important to recognize an error of logic called "**Straw Man**." Individuals who commit this error distort their opponent's argument and then attack the distorted argument. For example, an individual might comment that it is important to remove able-bodied men and women from the welfare roles. If another person replies that welfare is necessary to support the old, the young, and the sick, he has distorted his opponent's argument, since his opponent did not mention taking them from the welfare roles. In a sense, Straw Man is one of the main arguments in the creation-evolution controversy. Evolutionists are often heard stating that creationism is religion while evolution is science, and, therefore, creationism should be prohibited from the public schools because of the separation of church and state mandated in the constitution. In reality creationism deals with scientific facts, as will be demonstrated in the following chapters.

Finally, it is important to keep in mind that even if the reasoning process is entirely correct, **if the assumption upon which it is based is incorrect, the conclusion will also be incorrect.**[*]

---

[*] This is by no means a comprehensive explanation of critical thinking. For additional details, please check with your local public library.

CHAPTER 1

HISTORY OF EVOLUTION

INTRODUCTION

There is much confusion and controversy today over how life on Earth began. Many scientists believe that the Earth and all living things are here as a result of intelligent design. Others feel that all living things exist as a result of random mechanistic processes. In this book we first will study the theory of evolution and how it developed. Then we will look at the theory of creation and discuss why many scientists still believe it today. Evolutionists believe that the first cell formed spontaneously and that all living organisms evolved from that one cell. Who were the men whose ideas came together to form the theory of evolution? What kinds of information did they study in developing their ideas?

SECTION 1: TYPES OF ROCK

Vocabulary words to know: igneous rock, sedimentary rock, and metamorphic rock

One of the first things which scientists examined was the rock layers that cover the surface of the Earth. Thus, it is important to understand the different types of rock and the processes that formed them. There are three basic types of rock: igneous, sedimentary, and metamorphic. **Igneous rocks** form when processes within the earth melt existing rock. While underground, this molten rock is called magma. As the rock reaches the surface, it often comes out with an explosive force; this is called an eruption. Eruptions spew molten material out onto the Earth's surface, forming volcanoes. On the Earth's surface the molten material is called lava.

As the magma and lava cool and harden, they form igneous rock. Igneous rock that is exposed to the wind, sun, and rain gradually will erode, forming particles of rock or sand. If these rock particles gradually build up under water, the upper layers of material can force much of the water out of the lower layers. Gradually the lower layers of material can harden, forming a rock very much like concrete. This is **sedimentary rock**. Both igneous and sedimentary rock later can be subjected to further pressure by upper rock layers. This pressure, along with heat, may not melt them. Instead, they undergo physical and chemical changes while remaining solid. This process forms another type of rock which is called **metamorphic**. (Because the Earth is a dynamic planet, the forces that shape these rocks are continuous, and each type of rock can be changed into another in a continuous rock cycle.) Of these three types of rock, the sedimentary rock is generally the most important to scientists studying origins because it contains the fossils which they examine in an attempt to understand how life on Earth began. See examples in figure 1-1.

Igneous rock from a volcanic eruption

Shale, a sedimentary rock—note the layering

Figure 1-1 *Pictures of sedimentary, igneous and metamorphic rock samples*

Metamorphic rock—a piece of marble, changed by heat and pressure from limestone

SECTION 2: THE GEOLOGIC COLUMN

People and words to know: William Smith, Charles Lyell, and geologic column

Scientists began serious study of these different types of rocks in the late eighteenth century. By studying how sedimentary rocks came together and comparing their relative positions in several places, a man named William Smith managed to put together the first **geologic column**. Smith was an English surveyor who had the opportunity to study layers of sedimentary rock that had been exposed in the digging of an industrial canal in the British Isles. He began to make diagrams of the rock sequences and of the fossils he found in them. He then combined this information with information he gathered from several other places including mines, stone quarries, and road cuts. **Using this data he made a chart of the rocks in his region, designating the bottom layers as the oldest and the top layers as the youngest.** Smith sent copies of his work to many other geologists. When they saw how effective the list was for arranging information, they began to produce geologic columns for their regions also. Although many men worked on individual geologic columns, the man most responsible for the one we use today

is a Scotsman named **Charles Lyell** (1797–1875). Lyell was a lawyer, but he was fascinated by geology. He traveled widely, observing rock formations in many locations. He also spent much of his time gathering and organizing information from other scientists. By the late nineteenth century, Lyell had developed a geologic column that is very similar to the one used today. He examined rocks in different locations and determined through the character of the rocks and the fossils that they held that they were of the same age. This is referred to as **correlating the rocks**. Lyell also used local geologic columns from around the world to help in his formation of one large column. He gave the same names to rocks of the same apparent age from all parts of the world. He also assigned ages to these rocks that were much older than scientists in the past had believed them to be. Thus, the geologic column was born and became the sole method of dating rocks and fossils until the twentieth century. It is still the primary method used today.

QUESTIONS FOR REVIEW

1. What are igneous, sedimentary, and metamorphic rocks?
2. What is the geologic column and for what is it used? (See Figure 1-2 below)

GEOLOGIC TIME SCALE				
ERA	PERIOD	EPOCH	Duration (In millions of years)	Beginning (Millions of years ago)
Cenozoic	Quaternary	Holocene	10,000 ago to the present	
		Pleistocene	2.5	2.5
		Pliocene	9	12
		Miocene	14	26
	Tertiary	Oligocene	12	38
		Eocene	16	54
		Paleocene	11	65
Mesozoic	Cretaceous		70	135
	Jurassic		55	190
	Triassic		35	225
Paleozoic	Permian		55	280
	Caroniferous	Pennsylvania	40	320
		Mississippian	25	345
	Devonian		55	400
	Silurian		25	425
	Ordovician		75	500
	Cambrian		100	600

Figure 1-2 *Geologic Time Scale Chart. This chart is very similar to the one developed by Lyell. You will notice the dates assigned to each period or epoch are given in millions of years. Thus, the Cambrian period of the Paleozoic era began, according to this chart, over 3.6 billion years ago.*

SECTION 3: DEVELOPERS OF EVOLUTIONARY THEORY

Vocabulary words and concepts to know: principle of uniformity, use and disuse of organs, inheritance of acquired traits, vestigial, natural selection, and adaptation

Although some theory of evolution has existed for thousands of years, only in the past two hundred years have scientists made a concerted effort to develop a workable one. During this time, several individuals made contributions to these studies.

Charles Lyell

Charles Lyell's work helped make the theory of evolution possible. Lyell published a book called *Principles of Geology*. In it he postulated his **principle of uniformity**. This stated that "the present is the key to the past." In other words, the processes that shape the world today are the same processes that shaped the world in the past. He believed these processes had operated at the same rate in the past as they do in the present. He made no allowance for the possibility of a major catastrophic occurrence, such as a worldwide flood, helping to form the rock strata and the fossil record. Thus, Lyell believed the Earth had to be very old so there would be enough time for the formation of the deep layers of existing sedimentary rock. Since a great deal of time is necessary for evolution to occur, an old Earth was absolutely necessary for the theory.

Lamarck

Another individual who made a contribution to the theory of evolution was Jean Baptiste de Lamarck. He published two books, *Philosophie Zologique* and *Animaux sans Vertebres*. In them he explained his theory of evolution. Lamarck's theory was based on his belief in two biological processes which he called the **use and disuse of organs and the inheritance of acquired traits**. Lamarck believed that organisms adapted to their environment by changing their existing organs or developing new ones. This change in use of an existing organ or development of a new one is an **acquired trait**. If an environmental change led to the **disuse** of an organ, it gradually would disappear because it was no longer needed.

Photo in public domain

On the other hand, if an organ was gradually used more heavily, it would become more prominent in succeeding generations. Lamarck also believed that these acquired traits could be passed on to the organism's offspring. This he called **the inheritance of acquired traits**. Thus, each generation could benefit from the useful structures produced by earlier generations, and evolution could proceed.

Lamarck illustrated his theory by explaining how giraffes got their long necks. He theorized that early giraffes might have had much shorter necks because they ate mainly grass. However, if grass became scarce due to a drought, the giraffes might have had to stretch their necks to reach the leaves on the trees. He believed the more they stretched, the longer their necks became. The giraffes then passed the trait of "long neckedness" on to their offspring. In this way organisms could change in response to changes in their environment. Lamarck also believed in spontaneous generation of some simple species.

Lamarck's ideas were accepted by many in his day, but later his theories were proved to be false. However, his belief concerning the fate of disused organs still is accepted today. Modern scientists call organs **vestigial** if they appear to be reduced in size and have no obvious function.

Figure 1-3 *An illustration of Lamarck's hypothesis of how the giraffe developed its long neck. Drawing by A. St. Arno.*

Charles Darwin

Both Lamarck and Lyell influenced Charles Darwin (1809–1882). While still a young child, Darwin developed a keen sense of observation and a passion for collecting specimens. These skills remained an extremely important part of his life and prepared him for his work as a natu-ralist. By the time he

Photo in public domain

was twenty, he had learned much about the natural world around him. However, at this time he already had given up medical studies and was preparing for the ministry, although he was not particularly inter-ested in either profession. Thus, when he was offered a job as naturalist on a ship called the *H.M.S. Beagle*, he accepted. The *Beagle* was going on a voyage of discovery and exploration around the world.

Darwin took with him several books on geology. Lyell's *Principles of Geology* was one of the most im-portant. As he read, he became convinced that the Earth was very old. While in South America, he saw an earthquake raise the ground several feet and felt that mountains could be built the same way over a

long period of time. He also found fossils of marine animals high in the mountains and realized that those rocks must have formed under water.

It was on the Galapagos Islands that Darwin began to formulate his theory of evolution. On the islands he saw animals that were like those of the South American continent, but different in some respects. As he traveled to Australia, the oceanic islands, and the Far East, he witnessed more ex-amples of plants and animals that were similar but not exactly alike, although they lived in similar environments. For example, on the Galapagos Is-lands, Darwin discovered thirteen different types of finches, whose beaks and feet were different from each other. These finches were also different from finches on the mainland.

Figure 1-4 *An illustration of some of the va-rieties of finches that live on the Galapagos Islands. It is likely they all came from one original type of finch. Drawing by Amber St. Arno.*

17

He also noticed that the rhea, a flightless bird of South America, and the emu of Australia look alike but not exactly alike, even though they live in the same type of environment. Darwin had been

Figure 1-5 *Picture of a rhea and an emu.*
Drawing by M. Coley.

taught that all organisms were specially created for specific habitats, so he couldn't understand why species of the same organisms living in different locations would vary, even though they occupied the same types of habitats.

By the time he reached home, Darwin believed that the answer to these differences lay in the theory of evolution. For the next twenty years he worked on his theory. He finally published it in 1859 in a book called *On the Origin of Species by Means of Natural Selection* or the *Preservation of Favored Races in the Struggle for Life*. The book came to be known simply as The *Origin of Species*. In it he pointed out that **traits vary among individuals of the same species**. For example, some lions are swifter and stronger than others are. Some giraffes have longer necks and are able to reach higher tree branches than others. He also stated that **there are limited natural resources to support these individuals**. Therefore, depending on how well they are suited to their environment, they will get more or less of these resources. The stronger, faster lion is more apt to capture food than the weaker, slower one. In a drought the giraffe with the longer neck may survive longer than the

giraffe with the shorter one. In addition, different species often compete for the same food. For example, the lion and the cheetah often eat the same types of animals. He felt that **organisms tend to produce more offspring than can survive**. There simply are not enough resources available to support them all. Therefore, **the environment selects for survival those organisms that are best adapted to it**. The organisms with traits that are well suited to the environment in which they live will survive longer and reproduce more than those that are not well suited. Darwin called this "survival of the fit" **natural selection**. Darwin also pointed out that animals generally have certain traits that help them to survive in a specific environment. For example, an arctic environment would favor animals with thick fur to protect them from the frigid cold. He called these characteristics **adaptations**. Darwin believed these adaptations were developed over long periods of time through the process of evolution.

By explaining the process of natural selection, Darwin had accounted for one part of the evolutionary theory. Nevertheless, he had no clear idea how evolutionary changes could take place. He fell back on Lamarck's **theory of acquired traits** for an explanation. It would take the work of two other individuals to provide another explanation.

Figure 1-6 *An arctic fox—adaptation to climate.* Photo provider: Jupiter Images.

QUESTIONS FOR REVIEW

1. What was Lyell's major contribution to the theory of evolution?
2. Explain Lamarck's Theory of Acquired Traits and Use and Disuse of Organs.
3. Explain natural selection as Darwin pictured it.

SECTION 4: MENDEL'S WORK AND LATER CONTRIBUTIONS

Vocabulary words and concepts to know: dominant, recessive, principle of dominance, and principle of segregation

Gregor Mendel was a Catholic priest who was born in 1822 in a small Austrian village. As a child he was a brilliant student, and he was able to spend two years at the University of Vienna as part of his education. He then entered a monastery to become a high school teacher. While at the university, Mendel had become interested in plant-breeding experiments that were being conducted there. He continued his research when he returned to the monastery, and over a period of several years he discovered the basic principles of heredity. Fortunately, he used logical experimental methods, and he kept meticulous records of all his work.

Photograph courtesy of Mendel University of Agriculture & Forestry.

Mendel decided to use pea plants for his experimental subjects. The peas were readily available and easily cultivated. They also produced many offspring which would provide a great deal of data to analyze. The structure of the flower was also important. The flower contained stamens and pistil, the male and female reproductive structures. The stamen produces pollen containing the male gametes, while the pistil contains the eggs, the female gametes. This made it possible for the pea plant to self-pollinate. Therefore, the offspring would carry the same traits as their parents.

Different varieties of the pea plants displayed several distinctly different characteristics. Mendel chose seven of these characteristics to study. Thus, he could trace how these traits were passed on from generation to generation. At first he allowed the plants to self-pollinate and found they remained the same, generation after generation. Then he cross-bred two different varieties with contrasting traits and studied the results. He began by studying the inheritance of only one trait at a time and eventually worked his way up to three. In each case, he studied and recorded his findings over three generations. He then used these findings to calculate the mathematical ratios in which these traits appeared.

Mendel found that when he crossed two different varieties, he did not get a blending of traits as earlier scientists had assumed. Instead, one trait disappeared in the second (F1) generation. However, in the third (F2) generation the missing trait reappeared in a minority of plants. Mendel determined that the traits that disappeared in the F1 generation had not been lost. Instead, they had somehow been "masked" or prevented from expressing themselves.

After studying for several years, Mendel concluded that a pair of factors controlled each trait. He then developed a law or **principle of dominance**, which states that if the factors for a trait in an organism are different, one factor may prevent the other

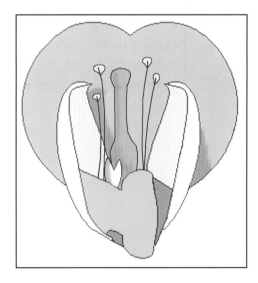

Figure 1-7 *A typical pea plant which Mendel could have used for his experiments. Note: the way the flower is formed tends to trap the pollen, leading to self-pollination unless someone cross-pollinates them. Drawing by A. Margetic.*

factor from being expressed. The factors that are expressed in the organism Mendel called dominant. Those which the organism carries but which are not expressed Mendel called **recessive**. For the recessive trait to show up in the organism, both factors for that trait had to be present. Although one trait might disappear in the F1 generation, Mendel noted that it tended to reappear in the F2 generation in approximately a 3 to 1 ratio. To explain how this occurred, Mendel proposed the law or **principle of segregation**. In it he states that when hybrids are crossed, the recessive factor separates or segregates in some of the offspring. Today we would say that these factors segregate when gametes are formed. We now call Mendel's factors "genes." (We also know that in some cases trait blending does occur due to co-dominance of genes for that trait.) The process which allows for the separation and inheritance of specific genes we call **meiosis**. The work that Mendel did still is accepted today and forms the basis for aspects of modern genetics. It also laid the groundwork for an understanding of meiosis, the mechanism that works with natural selection to cause change in successive generations.

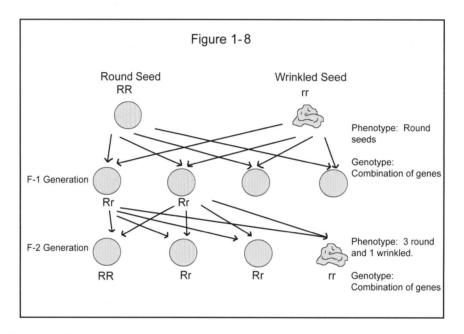

Figure 1-8 *The principle of segregation and the principle of dominance at work is shown in the pea seed shape. Notice F-1, or the hybrid generation shows only the round seed since round is dominant. In the F-2 generation, the wrinkled seed shows up again. Drawing by A. Margetic.*

Meiosis

Vocabulary words to know: meiosis, homologous, crossover, and mutation theory

We now understand that Mendel's results were possible because of a process called **meiosis**. Within a cell are pairs of chromosomes. These chromosomes contain the genes which control the traits Mendel studied. In the sexual reproductive organs, these chromosomes are separated through meiosis. How does this work? Though far from simple, this process now can be explained with relative accuracy.

The human cell contains 23 pairs of chromosomes. Each pair consists of one chromosome from the mother and one from the father. These **homologous** chromosomes have genes for the same trait, **but they are not identical**. For example, a brown haired person might actually be carrying genes for both brown and red hair and thus be **heterozygous** for the trait of hair color. (His actual hair color would be brown.) At the beginning of meiosis, the chromosomes reproduce themselves so that each homologous chromosome now has an **exact duplicate of itself**. These identical pairs remain attached to each other for a while. Homologous chromosomes (those which contain genes from each parent for the same traits) then come together and trade genes during a process called crossover. Whereas each chromosome that began the meiotic process was exclusively from the male or female parent, the chromosomes that result are a mixture of both parents' genes. Through several continuous phases the homologous chromosome pairs are separated, and then the identical pairs which make them up also are divided, forming four cells from the original parent cell. (See Figure 1–9 for a more detailed explanation.) However, unlike the original cell that possessed 23 **pairs** of homologous chromosomes, the daughter cells each have only 23 **single** chromosomes, one half the original number. In addition, the chromosomes of the daughter cells are not identical in makeup to any of the chromosomes in the parent cell, since crossover has mixed up the genes of the parents. Twenty-three chromosomes in the one daughter cell (egg) are then combined with 23 chromosomes in another cell (sperm) during fertilization and form the twenty-three **pairs** of chromosomes of the normal human cell. The following figures show the steps of meiosis. Only two pairs of homologous chromosomes have been used to demonstrate, thus making it easier to understand the process.

   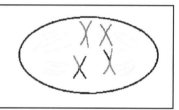

A. Cell Before Meiosis

Chromosomes with same traits—one from both mother and father. These chromosomes are called homologous chromosomes.

B. Prophase I

Each chromosome replicates itself.

C. Prophase I

Crossing over, the homologous chromosomes share genetic information.

D. Metaphase I

Homologous chromosomes line up and become attached to spindle fibers.

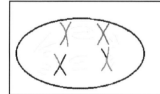 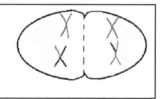 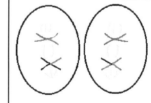 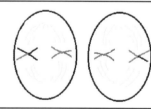

E. Anaphase I

Homologous chromosomes are pulled apart in pairs and move toward opposite ends of the cell.

F. Telophase I

The homologous chromosomes reach opposite ends of the cell and the cell divides in two.

G. Prophase II

A new spindle forms around the chromosome pairs in the new cells.

H. Metaphase II

The chromosomes line up at the equator with spindle fibers attached to their centromeres (where chromosomes are joined).

Figure 1-9 *Meiosis. Drawing by A. Margetic.*

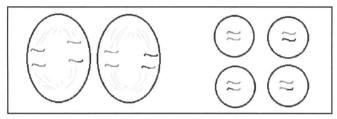

I. Anaphase II

The centromeres duplicate and then separate and move to opposite ends of the cell.

J. Telophase II

A new nuclear membrane forms around each set of chromosomes and the cells divide again, producing four cells from the original one, each cell having one-half the genetic information of the original.

Figure 1-9 Meiosis. Drawing by A. Margetic.

When Mendel crossbred the two varieties of peas, he mixed chromosomes that were not ordinarily together. The dominant genes on these different homologous pairs then determined which traits would show up in each generation. Mendel's "factors" were passed on from generation to generation by meiosis.

Obviously, the process of meiosis provides a tremendous amount of variety in all organisms that reproduce sexually. Natural selection can then act upon this variety to cause small changes and even create new species. However, **meiosis cannot provide the variety necessary to cause the large changes that we generally think of as evolution. These changes require huge additions of information. Meiosis simply "reshuffles" existing information.**

August Weismann and Hugo DeVries

By the turn of the century, scientists realized that natural selection alone could not account for the dramatic changes necessary to develop from molecules to man. A German biologist named August Weismann came to realize that there are two kinds of changes that take place in organisms. These are changes caused by the environment and changes in the organism's heredity. Weismann showed that changes caused by the environment could not be passed on to the organism's offspring. Thus, permanent variation could arise only from within the organism itself. Then in 1901 a Dutch botanist named Hugo DeVries published his **mutation theory**. He felt that it was the random changes in genes and chromosomes that provided the genetic variety on which natural selection could work. Thus, it was DeVries' assertion that genetic mutation and natural selection work together to cause evolution. This belief now has been widely accepted and forms the basis for what is called Darwinian evolution. It was the contributions of each of these individuals that helped to form the most widely accepted theory of evolution which we have today.

QUESTIONS FOR REVIEW

1. Describe Mendel's work with pea plants. What did he discover?
2. Describe the process of meiosis.
3. What contribution did Weisman make?
4. Describe the process which DeVries said caused the changes within organisms.

CHAPTER 2

EVOLUTION—WHAT IS IT?

SECTION 1: THE THEORY AND MECHANISMS OF EVOLUTION

Vocabulary words and concepts to know: evolution, devolution, meiosis, genetic isolation, genetic drift, natural selection, and migration

In Chapter 1 we looked at a brief history of the evolution theory, but to have a real understanding of it, we must study it more thoroughly. First of all, most scientists define **evolution** as change over time. However, is all change truly evolution? This type of change can be divided into two categories—that which occurs primarily through a **loss** of information and that which occurs primarily as a result of a **gain** of information. Change which comes about primarily through a loss of information is called microevolution by many scientists. However, this type of change might be more accurately referred to as **devolution**, since it is caused by a deterioration of existing information. How does this type of change work? One good example is that of the changes in dog species which have occurred over the past few thousand years. All the kinds of dogs we have today likely came from one type of dog (probably a wolf-like creature). However, as members of this original dog "type" interbred, a different combination of genes would be distributed in their offspring (in much the same way that you have a different gene combination than your brothers and sisters). Since different genetic combinations result in the expression of different traits, in a very short period of time there could be a wide variety of characteristics displayed within the dog population. These characteristics result from the "reshuffling" of existing genes that occurs each generation, which is called **meiosis**.

Man has also affected the change in dogs by providing the genetic isolation necessary for it to occur rapidly. **Genetic isolation** is the separation of members of a population into two or more groups so that they no longer can interbreed freely. From time to time, a particular trait that humans consider beneficial might show up in two or more dogs. Humans then breed those dogs primarily to one another in order to increase the chances that that trait will become common among their offspring. For instance, breeders in the nineteenth century decided that a smaller version of the Collie

Collie
Photo courtesy of Tracie Thompson.

would be beneficial. So they took Collies that produced smaller than average offspring and began to breed them together. They then took the smallest of those offspring and interbred them. They also **added** some new genes through breeding the smaller Collies to Spaniels and Pomeranians. Over a period of time, the Collies became progressively smaller, as well as developing some different traits. It is important to note that the smaller Collies could not be permitted to breed with bigger ones, or Collies of many different sizes would be produced. Humans provided the artificial "genetic isolation" necessary for a new breed to emerge, the Shetland Sheep Dog (commonly called the Sheltie).

Genetic drift also is necessary for change to occur. **Genetic drift** is the elimination of genes from a population. Again, when dog breeders wanted to produce a smaller Collie, they created their own "genetic drift." They looked for small Collies to breed to other small Collies. They knew that many of the genes for tallness were missing from these dogs. Each time they bred the offspring of these dogs, they selected only the smaller ones to breed. Thus, by not allowing larger Collies to add their genes for tallness, breeders gradually eliminated these genes, and a population of dogs was produced whose small size was due to a loss of genetic information.

Genetic isolation and genetic drift also occur in nature. **Genetic drift** in nature is the elimination of genes from a population **due to chance**. For example, a particular gene may be present in only a few members of a population. If they die before they have a chance to breed, the genes that only they carry will be completely eliminated from the population just as breeders often eliminate certain genes by selective breeding. Another illustration would be a goose population that has several members with genes for white feathers. That population may somehow be split, with most of the geese with genes for white features in one group. Then if the few possessors of white feathered genes in the other group die without reproducing, that gene will disappear from one population while remaining in the other.

Shetland Sheep Dog and Collie. Photo courtesy of Dana Spears and Tracie Thompson.

Genetic drift can also occur if a small portion of a population unexpectedly survives and the rest die. Finally, genetic drift can be affected by mutation.

Geographic isolation occurs any time a natural barrier such as a river or a mountain range comes between members of the same population of animals and prevents them from freely interbreeding. This, of course, causes **genetic isolation** in much the same way the activity of dog breeders does. Gradually, as different members of the two wild populations die before they produce offspring, genetic drift occurs. As common genes are lost, the populations get progressively less alike. This can lead even to the production of two distinct species. On the north and south rims of the Grand Canyon live two different species of squirrels. Scientists believe that these squirrels were once of the same species. However, the Grand Canyon prevented them from interbreed-

Figure 2-1 *The great depth and width of the Grand Canyon causes geographic isolation which can lead to new species.* Photo provider: Jupiter Images.

ing. Genetic isolation and genetic drift then helped to form two distinct species of squirrels.

It is important to note that devolution does not require the production of new genes, only the reshuffling, isolation, and loss of existing genes. Devolution can cause change up to the genus and species level. (Since our classification system is "man-made," the cutoff level is occasionally between family and order.)

On the other hand, true evolution does require the production of new genes and thus the addition of a great deal of information. **Evolution** requires change that goes beyond the genus and species. For example, for birds to develop from a reptile ancestor would require evolution. Many thousands of genetic changes would have to occur, and many new genes would have to be produced. Evolutionists believe that this production of new genes occurs through genetic mutation. A **genetic mutation** is a spontaneous change in a gene or chromosome. Gene mutations do happen. All of their causes are not known. One agent of mutation is the ultraviolet rays of the sun. Certain chemicals can also produce them. Whatever their origin, they do bring about change, but in the vast majority of cases, these changes are not beneficial; they are harmful. However, evolutionists still believe that over millions of years minute changes caused by countless beneficial genetic mutations, combined with natural selection, have brought about evolution.

Charles Darwin made the term, natural selection, popular in his famous book, *Origin of Species*. **Natural selection** refers to the action of "nature" in deciding which organisms will survive and which will not. **Those organisms best adapted to their environment will survive and reproduce more often than those that are not well adapted**. For example, a swift gazelle is much less apt to be caught and eaten by a predator than a slow one. Its speed makes it better adapted and thus more likely to survive and reproduce. An insect whose coloring matches its environment is difficult to see and is less likely to be eaten. Natural selection helps change populations by selecting against certain organisms and thus against the genes they carry.

There is one last factor that can affect the gene pool of a population and thus influence change within it. This is migration. **Migration** is the movement of organisms into or out of a population. In creating the Shelties, man prevented the smaller Collies from breeding with larger ones, while at the same time permitting them to mix with Spaniels and Pomeranians. This affected the genetic makeup of the Collie population by adding some genes while removing others. Similarly, if an animal leaves its group before it breeds, it may remove any genes only it possesses. Conversely, if an animal enters a new population and interbreeds with its members, it adds its genes to the new population's gene pool.

Both evolutionists and creationists generally believe that meiosis, genetic isolation, natural selection, migration, mutation, and genetic drift work together to cause change. However, only evolutionists believe that mutations add new genetic information to cause evolution. This is where the controversy between evolutionists and creationists exists. For devolution to occur requires meiosis to "reshuffle" existing genes and natural selection to act upon them. In addition, mutations can cause some change, primarily through the loss of genetic information. However, for evolution to happen there must be the creation of tremendous amounts of new genetic information, followed by the action of natural selection. Evolutionists believe change occurs which goes all the way to the kingdom level, primarily through a gain of information through mutation. Creationists believe that change stops basically at the genus level and is due primarily to the loss of genetic information. This loss can be caused by mutation and also by natural selection selecting against organisms and thus eliminating the genes they possess.

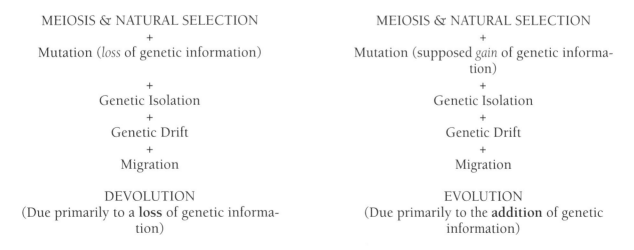

MEIOSIS & NATURAL SELECTION
+
Mutation (*loss* of genetic information)

+
Genetic Isolation
+
Genetic Drift
+
Migration

DEVOLUTION
(Due primarily to a **loss** of genetic information)

MEIOSIS & NATURAL SELECTION
+
Mutation (supposed *gain* of genetic information)

+
Genetic Isolation
+
Genetic Drift
+
Migration

EVOLUTION
(Due primarily to the **addition** of genetic information)

Figure 2-2 *The above table shows the relationship between the different mechanisms of change.*

Evolutionists classify evolution into two main types. They call the process of becoming less alike **divergent evolution**. For example, dogs, wolves, foxes, etc. likely "diverged" from a common canine ancestor. They define the process by which members of a species adapt to different ecological "niches" **adaptive radiation**. However, they also believe that mutation and natural selection can cause widely different organisms to become more alike as a result of adapting to similar environments. They call this **convergent evolution**. For example, the wings of a bird and those of a butterfly both enable the organisms to fly, but they are formed very differently. Evolutionists consider these bird and butterfly wings examples of analogous structures and evidence of convergent evolution.

Figure 2-3 *The different types of bears pictured above illustrate divergence. It is likely they came from a common ancestor.* Photo provided by Jupiter Photos.

QUESTIONS FOR REVIEW

1. Define evolution and devolution.
2. Name the six processes that must interact to cause devolution? What six processes are believed to interact to cause evolution?
3. Since these six processes are the same, why do evolutionists and creationists disagree? In other words, how does evolutionists' view of mutations differ from that of creationists?
4. What is geographic isolation and how does it affect genetic isolation in a population? What does it do to the gene pool of separate populations over time?
5. What is migration and how does it affect the gene pool of a population?
6. Define divergent evolution, convergent evolution, and adaptive radiation.

SECTION 2: EVOLUTION: HOW DO EVOLUTIONISTS BELIEVE IT OPERATES?

Vocabulary words to know: punctuated equilibrium, and stasis

Evolutionists believe that evolution occurs primarily because of the interaction of genetic mutation and natural selection. Perhaps the most common example given today is the case of the peppered moth. In England in the early 1800's these moths were abundant. Most of them were light in color and blended very well with the bark of the trees that was often covered with lichens. However, there was also a much smaller number of dark peppered moths that interbred with the rest of the population. Evolutionists believe that the dark color of these moths occurred as a result of a genetic mutation. At first, the dark colored moths were at a distinct disadvantage. They stood out clearly against the light tree trunks and thus were easily seen and eaten by their predators. Natural selection was selecting against them because they were not well adapted to their environment. However, the industrial revolution struck England, and with it came air pollution. The polluted air killed many of the lichens that grew on the tree trunks. Now the trunks were darker, and the darker moths blended in while the lighter ones did not. No longer were the lighter moths the best adapted to their changed environment. Over the next several years, natural selection selected against the light moths and for the dark moths. As a result, the percentage of light moths in the peppered moth population went down, while the percentage of dark moths went up. Evolutionists point to this event as a prime example of a beneficial genetic mutation and natural selection working together to cause evolution. They feel many more of these beneficial mutations, together with natural selection, will bring about evolution. This particular model of evolution is called Darwinian evolution or gradualism.

Evolutionists also point to the finches of the Galapagos Islands as examples of evolution in action. These finches showed variation in beak size and length after shifts in the environment. For example, following a prolonged drought on the islands, scientists noted that surviving finches had beak sizes that were 6% deeper and 4% longer than the average before the drought. On the other hand, after a period of extreme wet conditions, average beak size was about 1% narrower.

Obviously, since the process of evolution would be very slow, there would have to be literally millions of intermediate or link fossils on the evolutionary path from one group to another. For example, if birds evolved from reptiles, there would have had to be many intermediate organisms that showed some characteristics of both reptile and bird. Darwinian evolution requires the existence of many intermediate species in order to occur. Charles Darwin himself pointed this out. However, in the past few years, a new theory of evolution has been proposed. This is called **punctuated equilibrium**. Proponents of punctuated equilibrium propose that drastic environmental changes can occur which threaten to cause the extinction of entire populations. These catastrophic events would lead to very rapid genetic changes followed by long periods of very little change. (This phenomenon of populations remaining basically the same with little or no change is called **stasis**.) They contend there would thus be very few intermediate species.

QUESTIONS FOR REVIEW

1. Briefly describe the example of the peppered moth.
2. Briefly describe the changes in the Galapagos finches after changes in the weather.
3. Name and describe the new theory of evolution.

SECTION 3: SPONTANEOUS GENERATION OF LIFE

Vocabulary words to know: protocell, anaerobic bacteria, and DNA

As time passed, it became generally accepted that all living things evolved from an original cell. The question then arose as to how this original cell could have developed spontaneously. Alexander Oparin, a Russian scientist, in the early twentieth century developed a hypothesis about how this might have occurred. **Because the basic chemicals of life (carbon, hydrogen, oxygen, and nitrogen) will not come together in the presence of free oxygen**, Oparin proposed the early atmosphere would have to have been much different from what it is today. According to his theory, the early atmosphere probably contained water vapor, methane, hydrogen

and ammonia. It would contain no free oxygen, since the organic components of living things will not combine in the presence of free oxygen. Energy from volcanic heat and lightning or the sun's ultraviolet rays would cause these substances to combine into the organic compounds needed to make living things. However, it was necessary for these carbon compounds to combine further to make even more complex molecules before a cell could develop. Oparin hypothesized that these molecules might accumulate in the ocean and form a type of organic "soup." Over a long period of time, the molecules in this "soup" would gradually combine into types of macromolecules that could reproduce themselves. From these macromolecules the first cell would gradually develop. Oparin guessed that this **protocell** would have had to resemble **anaerobic bacteria**, since no free oxygen would be available.

Gradually the descendants of this protocell would have developed the mechanism of photosynthesis, and free oxygen, a product of their photosynthesis, would thus slowly accumulate in the atmosphere.

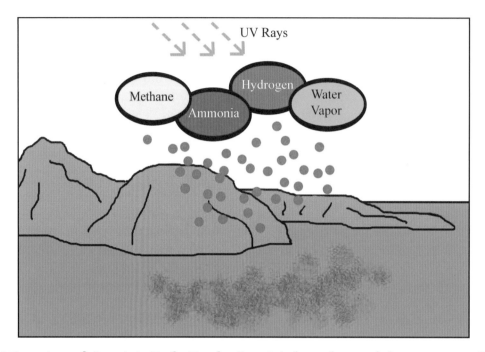

Figure 2-4 Drawing of Oparin's Early Earth. *Oparin's hypothesis of the structure of the early Earth. He believed the atmosphere was composed of methane, ammonia, hydrogen and water vapor. Energy from lightning, or from the sun's ultraviolet rays caused them to come together to form organic molecules and from these organic molecules the first cell arose. Drawing by A. Margetic.*

QUESTIONS FOR REVIEW

1. What element prevents the basic chemicals of life from combining?
2. What elements and compounds did Oparin believe were present in the early atmosphere?
3. What would provide the energy needed for these elements and compounds to combine into organic compounds?
4. What would these organic compounds then do?
5. What do evolutionists believe the first cell (protocell) probably resembled?

SECTION 4: MILLER'S EXPERIMENT

People and facts to know: Stanley Miller, Reactants and Products of Miller's experiment

An American Scientist named Stanley Miller tested Oparin's hypothesis and in 1953 reported his results. Figure 2–5 shows the apparatus he created to perform the experiment.

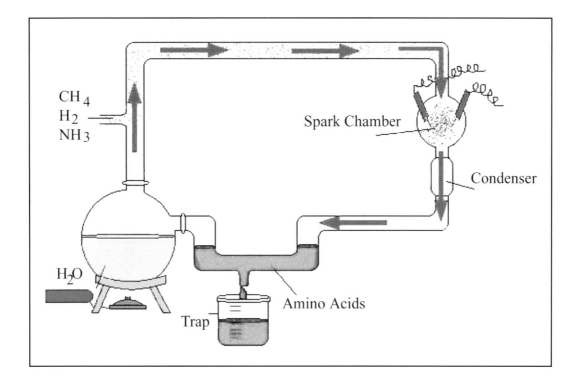

Figure 2-5 *The diagram above shows the experimental apparatus Stanley Miller and his associate used to test Oparin's theory. Drawing by A. Margetic.*

Miller and his associate first filled a flask with water and sealed it, allowing only a small opening in the top for water vapor to escape when the flask was heated. The water vapor (H_2O) was channeled into a long tube. As it moved through the tube, gaseous ammonia (NH_3), methane (CH_4), and hydrogen (H_2) were added to it. Next the mixture was passed through a spark chamber. The electric sparks provided the energy needed for chemical reactions to occur. The new compounds were then passed through a condenser that liquefied them, and the liquefied compounds were collected in a trap. After seven days Miller analyzed the liquid and found some amino acids, the building blocks of proteins. (He also found a great number of other compounds in the liquid. More on this later.) Miller's experiment had shown that given the exact ingredients and circumstances of the laboratory experiment, some amino acids could be formed. Since that time, other scientists, using a different mixture of ingredients, have managed to produce all the essential amino acids in similar experiments. Evolutionists have hailed Miller's experiment as proof that under the right conditions spontaneous generation of the first cell could have occurred. Again, creationists disagree. (More on this later.)

QUESTIONS FOR REVIEW

1. What compounds and elements did Miller use in the experiment?
2. What provided the energy needed for the chemical reactions to occur?
3. What captured the compounds after they were formed?
4. What did Miller find in the liquid that was formed?

Section 5: Evolutionists' Evidence for Evolution

Comparative Embryology

Vocabulary words to know: embryo and comparative embryology

One area that evolutionists say supports the theory of macroevolution is comparative embryology. Comparative embryology is the study of similarities between the embryos of different species such as fish, birds, dogs, and humans. Evolutionists contend that the embryos of such species, in the early stages, show remarkable similarities in their structures. They feel this is evidence of a common ancestor.

The drawings in Figure 2-6 are of fish, chicken, and human embryos. Note the similarities in shape of the head, the pouches in the neck area and the "tails." Evolutionists call the pouches in the neck area "gill slits." More discussion on these drawings later.

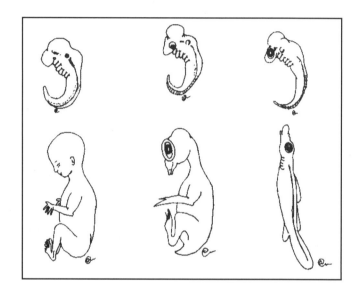

Figure 2-6 *Comparison of Embryos.*
Drawings by A. St. Arno.

Comparative Homology

Vocabulary word to know: homologous structure

Another area which evolutionists believe supports the theory of evolution is that of comparative homology. For example, if one looks at the skeletal structure of a bird, a whale, a dog, and a human, it is immediately apparent that the bones of the bird's wing, the whale's front flippers, the dog's front legs and the human's arm and hands have the same basic pattern. Structures that illustrate this type of similarity are called **homologous**. Evolutionists believe this similar pattern indicates these organisms had a common ancestor in the distant past.

On the other hand, structures that are similar in function but not believed to be alike in recent origin or structure are called **analogous**. For example, the wings of birds and insects would be considered analogous structures. Although they perform the same function, their structure is different and they are not believed to share a close ancestry.

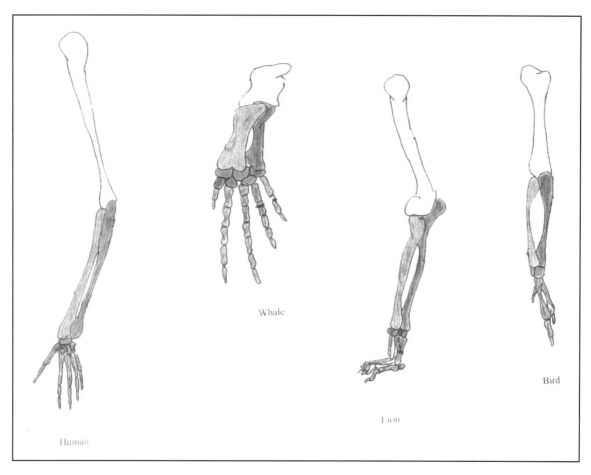

Figure 2-7 *Sketch of a human arm, whale's front flipper, lion's front leg and bird's wing. Drawing by A. Margetic.*

Notice the similarity in the pattern of bones in the four different organisms. Evolutionists believe this occurs because all of these creatures had a common ancestor with this bone pattern in its front limbs. (The homologous bones have been color-coded the same color for quick reference.)

Comparative Biochemistry

Vocabulary word to know: cytochrome c

Scientists have been studying the molecules that make up many living things. They have found that most living things have an enzyme called cytochrome c in their mitochondria. **Cytochrome c** is used in aerobic respiration. It consists of a ring structure with an iron atom in its center. Attached to this ring is a sequence of about 100 amino acids. Researchers have compared the sequences of amino acids in different organisms, and they believe that the more similar those sequences are, the closer the evolutionary relationship. For example, they have found that the cytochrome c of humans and monkeys differed by only one amino acid. In contrast, the cytochrome c of humans and turtles had 14 amino acids that differed. Evolutionists feel that this supports their theory that humans and other primates have a close evolutionary relationship, while humans and turtles do not.

31

The Fossil Record

Vocabulary words to know: fossils, imprints, carbon film fossil, molds, casts, petrified fossils, original remains, archaeopteryx, the whale series, and the horse series

Fossils are the remains of once living organisms. They are usually formed when living things die and are buried quickly by mud or sand. Over time, the mud or sand hardens into sedimentary rock, much like wet concrete solidifies into man-made rock. Parts of the original organisms can be preserved in the rock if they are buried fast enough.

There are several different types of fossils. These include imprints, molds, casts, carbon film fossils, petrified fossils, and original remains. **Imprints** occur when soft body structures, such as leaves or feathers, are pressed into developing rock and leave an impression of their shape. Sometimes a leaf can become buried in sediments, and the weight of the upper sediments causes the leaf to turn to carbon. This forms a **carbon film fossil**. **Molds** are formed when hard body parts or pieces of wood are completely covered by sediments and then decompose, forming a hollow that is shaped like the original organism. **Casts** can then form if other materials later fill in the mold. **Petrified fossils** are created when minerals gradually replace the hard parts of an organism, such as bones. The shape and texture of the bone remain, but the bone is now made of rock. Wood can also be petrified. The Petrified Forest of Arizona has many examples of whole tree trunks now turned into rock.

Sometimes whole organisms can be preserved. For example, many small organisms, such as insects, have been trapped in the sap of trees when they land on tree trunks. The sap then hardens, forming amber, a golden, transparent material that preserves the insects. Larger organisms have been preserved in ice or tar, which prevents their decay. These are all referred to as **original remains**.

Carbon Film Fossil

Trilobite Fossil

Petrified wood

Bug in amber. Photo courtesy of Answers in Genesis

Fossil Cast

Mold Fossil (left) and Cast: Photo courtesy of Joe Taylor.

Figure 2-8 *Pictures of different types of fossils*

Millions of fossils exist all over the world. Scientists dig them up and examine them regularly in an attempt to discover as much as possible about the past. They also search for the fossils of the intermediate species that are so necessary if Darwinian evolution actually happened.

Archaeopteryx

In looking at the fossil record, evolutionists point out some examples which they consider to be link fossils. One of these is Archaeopteryx, a proposed link fossil between reptiles and birds. Archaeopteryx is believed to have lived approximately 140 million years ago. It has the basic structure of a bird, including wings and feathers. However, it also has some features that evolutionists consider to be reptilian. These include claws on the wings, teeth, and a flat breastbone. Because of this "mixing" of bird-like characteristics with features evolutionists consider reptilian, some scientists consider Archaeopteryx to be a link fossil between reptiles and birds.

Proposed Whale Ancestors

It is also believed that the whales evolved from a land mammal. One group in particular has been suggested as possible ancestors of the whales. These are called **Mesonychids**. They are usually described as walking on four legs, and having sharp teeth, fur, and long tails. Some were as large as bears, while others were as small as cats. Some scientists consider **Pakicetus** to be a descendent of the *Mesonychids*. The fossil *Pakicetus* consists of an incomplete skull which was found near a village in eastern Pakistan. Its teeth resemble those of a *mesonychid* called *Condylarthra* and also other fossils classified as ancient whales. Therefore, it is believed to be a link fossil between them. *Pakicetus* is believed to have been a land animal that spent a great deal of time in the water. Another proposed descendent of the mesonychids and ancestor of the modern whale is **Ambulocetus**. *Ambulocetus*, also found in Pakistan, is described as a "walking whale" about 3 meters long, with sharp teeth and short, broad legs. The fossil consists of a partial skeleton with skull, vertebrae, ribs, and partial limbs. The hind limbs have hooves. **Basilosaurus** is yet another proposed link fossil in the ancestry of the whale. *Basilosaurus* had a long, slender body. It also had flippers, small flukes on its tail, tiny hind legs, and a flexible backbone. Although the *Mesonychids* were land mammals, *Basilosaurus* was a

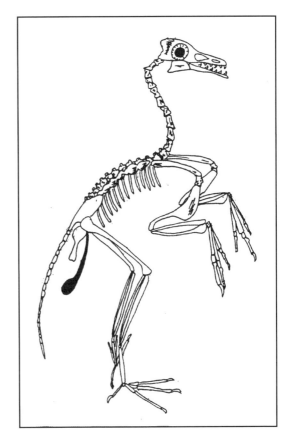

Figure 2-9 *A skeletal outline drawing of an Archaeopteryx. Note the teeth; the claws are not clearly illustrated in the drawing. Drawing by A. Margetic.*

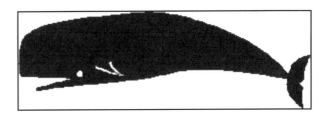

marine creature. Its nostrils are halfway along the snout, whereas mesonychid nostrils are at the end and a whale's are at the top of its head.

The Horse Series

Another fossil series that is commonly mentioned in reference to evolution is the horse series. Scientists have found several fossils that they believe demonstrate the evolution of the horse from a tiny, dog-like creature to the modern horse we have to-day. The first of these, 'Eohippus' (more correctly known as *Hyracotherium*), is believed to have lived approximately 55 million years ago. It was the size of a small dog, with four toes on its front feet and three on the back. *Mesohippus*, the next in the series, is thought to have lived approximately 40 million years ago. It had three toes on both front and back feet. *Merychippus* had three toes on each foot, but the center toe was much more prominent. *Merychippus* is believed to have lived 25 million years ago. By the time of *Pliohippus*, five million years ago, the center toe was the only one left. Finally, *Equus*, our modern horse, is believed to have evolved about two million years ago. It also stands on only the middle toe. These specimens are the ones most commonly mentioned as examples of the fossil ancestors of the horse. Figure 2-10 illustrates this series.

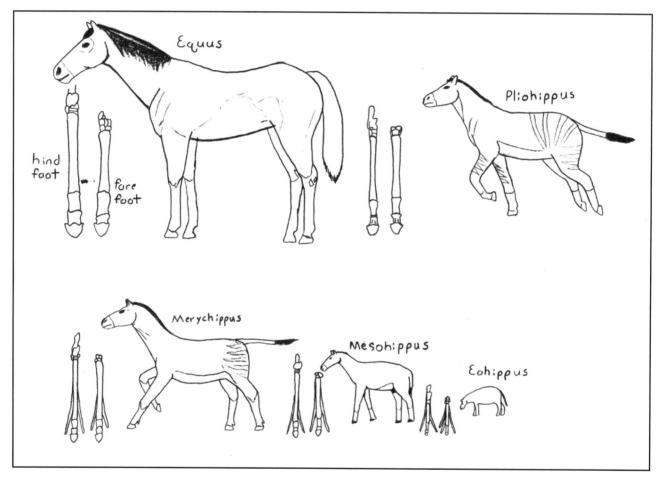

Figure 2-10 *Specimens of the horse series. Note: Not all proposed specimens are illustrated here. However, these are the ones that evolutionists most commonly include. Drawing by K. Bartley.*

QUESTIONS FOR REVIEW

1. How does comparative embryology seem to support evolution?
2. How does comparative homology appear to support evolution?
3. Give one example of how comparative biochemistry seems consistent with evolution.
4. Give an example of a possible link fossil **and** explain why evolutionists consider it to be one.
5. Describe the two fossil series given in the text.

CHAPTER 3
EVOLUTION OF MAN

INTRODUCTION

Vocabulary words to know: primates, link fossils, paleontologists, physical anthropologists, geologists, and bipedalism

Perhaps the most controversial issue in evolution is the development of man. Before discussing human evolution, however, it is important to understand what scientists work in this area. Several different types of scientists look for evidence of evolution. For example, **paleontologists** study fossils of all kinds. **Physical anthropologists** (also known as paleoanthropologists) concentrate on human fossils. **Geologists** use fossils (and other methods) to help determine the history of the Earth.

These scientists particularly are hampered in the field of human evolution by the lack of evidence. First of all, there are only a few hundred fossils and some related information such as the Lake Laetoli footprints of East Africa. Also, only a few pieces of a given fossil are usually found. Thus, evolutionists must work from very limited records and are often changing their interpretations as new evidence is uncovered. The following specimens are by no means all of the ones that have been found. However, they represent what many evolutionists accept as being in the line of man.

Scientists classify humans as **primates**. This means that they, along with approximately 200 other species such as apes, chimpanzees, and orangutans, belong to the same order. They believe that primates began to evolve about 70 million years ago, and as their evolution progressed, led to the ancestors of modern man within the last three to five million years. Initially, evolutionists believed that the human brain was the first characteristic to evolve in the human lineage. However, they later theorized that **bipedalism**, (the ability to walk on two legs) together with changes in the face and teeth came first. Nevertheless, successive hominids discussed in this chapter do show a gradual increase in brain size, with the last, *Homo erectus*, having a brain capacity close to that of modern man.

SECTION 1: A PROPOSED LINK FOSSIL

Since according to Darwinian evolution, humans and the other modern primates came from a common ancestor, there should be a primary link fossil that shows the connection between man and the apes. Several primate fossils have features that have led some scientists to believe that they are possible candidates for this position. However, one of the most commonly mentioned is *Ramapithecus*.

The first fossil classified as *Ramapithecus* was found in India. It is generally described as a small, monkey-like primate dated to be 8 to 17 million years old. A later specimen was found in Africa. Very little of the first specimen was found. However, later, more complete specimens have caused scientists to be in disagreement over whether *Ramapithecus* should be placed in the line of man. Some feel he should be, while others believe him to be an orangutan or, at best, only distantly related to humans.

QUESTIONS FOR REVIEW

1. Where was the first *Ramapithecus* specimen found and what age is he considered to be?
2. What was one problem with the fossil?
3. What do some scientists believe *Ramapithecus* to be?
4. Where do other scientists place him?

SECTION 2: EARLY HOMINIDS

The Australopithecines

Vocabulary words to know and understand: hominid, australopithecines, A. anamensis, A. afarensis, Ardipithecus ramidis, and A. africanus

Australopithecus anamensis

Although some scientists believe *Ramapithecus* to be a primary link fossil between humans and the other primates, for Darwinian evolution to be true, there had to have been many other links in the evolution of man. Evolutionary scientists call these "human like" links **hominids**. In general, hominids are considered bipedal but still retain many ape-like characteristics. Evolutionary scientists generally agree that the earliest known hominids were probably the **australopithecines**. One recent discovery by Meave Leakey, wife of the well-known paleoanthropologist, Richard Leakey, has many scientists debating whether she has found the oldest australopithecine. In 1994 Ms. Leakey and her coworkers found a mandible with an upper jaw nearby in one location. In another location workers found the upper and lower parts of a tibia, the main bone of the lower leg. In the same general vicinity, several other skeletal fragments have been found. Because there are volcanic ash layers in the Turkana Basin where she was working, Ms. Leakey has used radiometric dating to assign a date of 4.1 million years old to her specimen. Meave Leakey states that the tibia fragments prove her specimen walked upright. However, the mandible shows the

Meave Leakey, a zoologist and paleontologist, was born Meave Epps in London in 1942. In 1965 she went to work for British anthropologist Louis Leakey. Under his leadership she studied primates in Kenya. In 1969 she was invited to join a fossil-hunting expedition led by the Leakeys' son Richard. Two years later she and Richard married, and she became part of the famous fossil-hunting family. Photo provider: NewsCom.

creature is "chinless," an apelike characteristic. She also feels the roots of the canine teeth in the upper jaw are more vertical in their placement than they are in chimpanzees – a human characteristic. Ms. Leakey has named her specimen *Australopithecus anamensis*.

Ardipithecus ramidus

At about the same time as Ms. Leakey's discovery, paleoanthropologist Timothy White discovered at a site in Ethiopia the teeth and arm bones of an animal he thinks is bipedal. He dated it at 4.4 million years old. Although he at first thought it to be an australopithecine, he has decided it is more primitive and has created a new genus as well as a new species for it—*Ardipithecus ramidus*. Paleontologists are still discussing whether it belongs in the ancestry of humans or not.

Figure 3-1: *Picture of humans walking, demonstrating bipedalism.* Photo provided by Jupiter Photos.

Australopithecus afarensis

Another specimen that was for many years generally considered to be the oldest known hominid is *Australopithecus afarensis*. Individuals working for an anthropologist named Donald Johanson found *A. afarensis* in 1974. It was discovered in Africa's Great Rift Valley. Johanson dated the fossil, using the geologic time scale and later radiometric dating, and estimated its age to be approximately 3.6 million years old. Later dating efforts have put its age at 3.18 million years old. About 40% of the skeleton was found, including a few parts of a skull. The bones were found with many other fossils representing at least 35 different individuals. The skeleton was believed to be that of a female that had been a little over 3 feet tall and probably weighed less than 50 pounds. Johanson nicknamed the specimen Lucy after a Beatles song that was popular at the time. The arms appear to be long and chimp-like. However, many scientists believe that Lucy's skeleton is hu-

man-like in many respects and that she definitely was bipedal.

Eighteen years later, in 1992, Johanson returned to Africa, hoping to find a complete afarensis skull. He and his associates returned to the general area where Lucy was found and discovered a skull that they believe belongs to the afarensis species. However, it is much larger than Lucy's head would have been and is considered an afarensis male. Johanson has classified *A. afarensis* as an early australopithecine and an early ancestor of humans. However, not all scientists agree. Because no tools were found with Lucy, some scientists believe *A. afarensis* to be the ape's ancestor but not man's. For example, Louis Leakey's wife Mary and their son Richard have also made many discoveries relating to man's ancestry. They feel that *A. afarensis* was simply an australopithecine whose line became extinct.

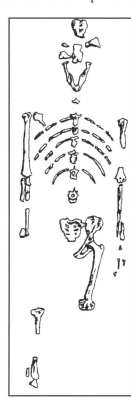

Figure 3-2 *An illustration of the bones of Austalopithecus afarensis (Lucy) that were found in one location. Note: the skull parts are only fragmentary. Drawing by A. Margetic.*

The discoverer of Australopithecus afarensis, Donald Johanson, was born in Chicago, Illinois, in 1943. When his father died two years later, Johanson's mother moved with her son to Hartford, Connecticut, where she worked as a domestic and her son attended school and developed an interest in anthropology. His interest was encouraged by a neighbor who taught anthropology and who became a surrogate father to him. Planning on a career in chemistry, Johanson entered the University of Illinois, but he switched majors and graduated with a degree in anthropology instead.

Johanson later received his master's degree from the University of Chicago and completed work for his doctorate four years later. In 1972 Johanson decided to mount an expedition to the Hadar Valley in northeastern Ethiopia, the home of the Afar people. There two years later in the fall of 1974 members of the expedition discovered Lucy, which became known as Australopithecus afarensis. The term australopithecus means 'southern ape,' while afarensis refers to the Afar region where Lucy was found.

Photo courtesy of Donald Johanson.

Australopithecus africanus

The term, "australopithecus" was coined by Richard Dart, an anthropologist who taught at the University of Witwatersrand, in Johannesburg, South Africa. Because he had so few fossils to use in his anthropology class, Dart had a competition among his students to see who could come up with the most interesting bones for a collection. He even offered small cash prizes as an incentive,

During the competition, one of Dart's students told him that the manager of a local mine often unearthed fossils in the course of his mining operations. Dart made arrangements with the miner to have any fossils he found sent to the university. Later, Dart received two boxes full of fossils. Most of them were unimportant. However, in one box he found a fossilized cast of a brain, along with the front of a skull, including the face, jaw and teeth. Feeling that the skull was more primitive than *Homo erectus*, a fossil receiving a great deal of attention at the time, Dart decided that a new genus and species was necessary to categorize his fossil. He named the fossil *Australopithecus africanus*, which means "southern ape-man of Africa."

Later specimens have also been found and classified as *A. africanus*. There has been some argument as to whether all of them should be classified in this

Figure 3-3 *Great Rift Valley extends through several African countries. This portion is in Kenya. Photo courtesy of Michael Steeves.*

genus and species. Nevertheless, based on a study of all of these fossils, scientists believe that *A. africanus* had a rounded skull, a larger brain capacity than *A. afarensis*, and a broad, flat thumb similar to humans. Some scientists believe it was bipedal. Evidence suggests that an adult male specimen stood about 5 feet tall and weighed between 80 and 100 hundred pounds. However, the teeth of the later *A. africanus* specimens are much like those of modern apes, not humans. *A. africanus* is believed to have used simple tools, lived in groups, and eaten meat. Evolutionists estimate he lived between 2.5 and 3 million years ago.

Because of his family background, Australian-born Raymond A. Dart was an unlikely candidate to become an evolutionist and an anthropologist. Born into a large family of staunch Baptists, Dart's early training included acceptance of the Bible as literally true.

However, Dart's desire to study medicine took him to Sydney University and to the University of Queensland. While at Sydney University he was influenced by two prominent evolutionists of the time and became convinced the Bible was not literally true.

He continued his studies in the U.S. and in England. Then, at the suggestion of Grafton Elliot Smith, a well-known British anatomist and anthropologist, Dart took a post at the University of Witwatersrand in South Africa. It was while teaching there that he discovered Australopithecus africanus.

Mr. Dart was born in 1893. His marriage to Dora Tyree in 1921 ended in divorce in 1934. A few years later he wed Marjorie Gordon Frew, a librarian at the university. They had a son and a daughter. Dart died in 1988 at the age of 95.

Photo courtesy of Professor Tobias, Dept. of Anatomy, University of Witwatersrand, Johannesburg, S. Africa. Photo by Alun Hughes.

QUESTIONS FOR REVIEW

1. When, where, and by whom was *A. anamensis* found?
2. How much of the fossil was found? Was it all in the same place?
3. By what method was it dated and how old is it believed to be?
4. What features does it have which appear to be ape-like, and what features does it have which appear to be human?
5. Why did Timothy White classify his fossil in a new genus and species, instead of classifying it as an australopithecine?
6. When, where, and by whom was *A. afarensis* found?
7. How much of the fossil was found?
8. What features does *A. afarensis* have that evolutionary scientists think are ape-like and what features appear to resemble those of humans?
9. How is *A. africanus* different from *A. afarensis*?
10. What ape-like and human-like characteristics do evolutionists believe *A. africanus* has?
11. The australopithecines are described as bipedal. What does this mean?
12. What appears to be happening to the size of the brain in each of these specimens?

Born near Nairobi, Kenya in 1901, Louis Leakey grew up in a family of British missionaries. Following World War I, Leakey went to school in Great Britian, where he earned a degree in anthropology in 1926. During the next few years he led several expeditions to his native Kenya. An evolutionist, Leakey contended that man had originated on the African continent, rather than in Asia as many other evolutionists believed.

In the late thirties Leakey took time out for some historical work about the Kikuyu tribe of Kenya, and then he served in Kenyan government during World War II. After the war, Leakey and his wife Mary worked for many years excavating at a site at Olduvai Gorge in Tanzania. In 1960 the Leakeys found several fossil fragments. They combined these with some skull parts they found in 1962 and called their new specimen Homo habilis.

Photo provider:
AP Wide World Photos.

SECTION 3: LATER HOMINIDS

Vocabulary words and concepts to know and understand: Homo habilis, Homo erectus, and paleoanthropologists

Homo habilis

In the 1960's Louis and Mary Leakey were excavating at Olduvai Gorge in East Africa. They found a mandible, some skull parts, a foot and some finger bones. John Napier, another scientist working with Louis Leakey, analyzed the finger bones and declared that the creature that once possessed them had had an opposable thumb. This is a definite human characteristic. It is what allows the precise movements that enable humans to make and use tools. The scientists also found some primitive tools nearby. Believing the fossil to have at one time used the tools, they named this new species *Homo habilis*, which means "handy human." They dated this specimen to be 1.5 to 2.2 million years old. However, there continues to be some controversy about this fossil among evolutionists. Some scientists consider *H. habilis* to be simply another species of australopithecine.

Mary Douglas Leakey was born on February 6, 1913, in London, England, the only child of Erskine and Cecilia Nicol. Because her father was a land-scape painter, Mary spent many of her early years traveling throughout Europe with her parents. She shared her father's artistic talent, and he also encouraged her interest in archaeology.

After her father died, Mary and her mother returned to England. In the early thirties she became involved in geological excavations and in draw-ing some of the objects she found. Louis Leakey was looking for an artist to illustrate a book he had written, and Mary was introduced to him as a possible candidate for the job. He hired her. They later married and had three children: Jonathon, Phillip, and Richard.

Mary returned with her husband to Kenya where she became an excellent fossil hunter. They worked together at various fossil sites until Louis Leakey's death in 1972.

Dr. Mary Leakey, right, and her assistant, Dr. Louise Robbins display plaster casts of footprints discov-ered at Lake Laetoli in East Africa. They believe the footprints to be some 3.6 million years old. Photo provider: AP Wide World Photos.

Two years after her husband died, Mary Leakey began excavating at Laetoli, Tanzania, where she found the now famous Laetoli footprints. Mary Leakey died in 1996.

Homo erectus

In the latter part of the nineteenth century, a fossil was found on the island of Java in what is now the country of Indonesia. It was discovered by an expedition working under the leadership of a Dutch medical doctor named Eugene Dubois. This fossil consisted of a skull plate and a femur. It became known as Java man and later *Homo erectus* because it was believed to have walked upright.

Beginning in 1929 another group of scientists under the leadership of Davidson Black, a young Canadian doctor, found several skulls with the faces missing in a cave in China. These skulls came to be known as Peking Man. They were also classified as *Homo erectus*. Unfortunately, the skulls representing Peking Man disappeared during World War II while they were being shipped out of China. Therefore, scientists have not been able to make long term, detailed studies of them.

Since that time, several other fossils have been discovered in other locations and classified as *Homo erectus*. Information recovered at locations where some Homo erectus fossils were found indicates that they were toolmakers. It is likely they were also hunters, since the bones of rhinoceroses, bears, and elephants have been found at their campsites. In addition, their camps have been found in caves with the remains of ancient campfires. Thus, they are believed to have mastered the use of fire. For these reasons, paleoanthropologists consider them much more advanced than any hominid that came before them. *Homo erectus* is believed to have lived less than a million years ago.

Figure 3-4 *The island of Java, a part of Indonesia.* Photo courtesy of U. S. Archives.

QUESTIONS FOR REVIEW

1. When, where and by whom was *Homo habilis* found?
2. What does the name *Homo habilis* mean, and why was the fossil given this name?
3. How old is *Homo habilis* believed to be?
4. Where was the first specimen of *Homo erectus* found, and why was it given this name?
5. What evidence shows some of its behavior to be like humans?

Human skull. Photo provider: Jupiter Images.

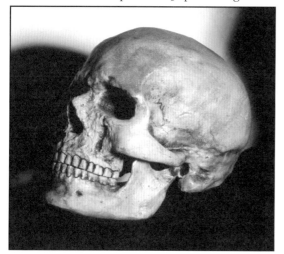

How do scientists tell a human skull from that of an ape? If a complete skull is available, there are several differences which they look for. For example, the ape's skull contains brow ridges that are missing in modern human craniums. Humans also have higher, more vertical foreheads and vertical faces, while apes' foreheads slant back, and their faces slope outward from the skull in the opposite direction from the spine. Finally, the placement of the foramen magnum, and the brain capacity are very important in making the distinction between man and apes. The **foramen magnum** is the opening in the skull through which the spinal cord passes. In humans, the foramen magnum is located at the bottom of the skull, while in apes it is situated near the rear. Last of all, humans have a cranial cavity approximately three times that of the apes. However, the skulls of very young apes are much more human-like than their older relative, which makes it more difficult to tell the difference.

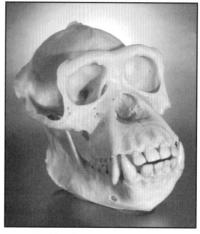

Ape skull. Photo provider: Jupiter Images.

SECTION 4: HUMANS

Vocabulary words and concepts to know and understand: Homo sapiens, Neanderthal, Cro-Magnon, and agricultural revolution

Humans are classified as *Homo sapiens*, which means "wise human beings." In addition to modern man, anthropologists categorize two groups of early humans as *Homo sapiens*. These are the Neanderthals and Cro-Magnon. The first specimen of Neanderthal man was discovered in a cave in the Neanderthal valley of Germany in 1856. In the next half-century several more individuals were found in France and Belgium, as well as in the Middle East. Because the skeletons of the first specimens were bent, many scientists believed they had found a link fossil between the apes and human beings. However, later specimens were shown to have straight skeletons, and

Figure 3-5 *A Neanderthal man in a suit looks quite human, as shown here. Photograph courtesy of the Neanderthal Museum.*

the earlier individuals were then believed to have suffered from some sort of disease such as arthritis, which distorted their bodies. The Neanderthals had thick skulls with heavy brows, slanting foreheads, and protruding jaws. However, their brains were as large and, in some cases, slightly larger than those of modern humans.

The Neanderthals were like modern humans in many ways. They made and used simple tools, wore animal skins as clothing, buried their dead, had rituals and ceremonies, and made war. Neanderthal fossils found in Yugoslavia show evidence of a battle, perhaps between rival tribes. Although a few scientists still categorize Neanderthal as a separate species, most place him with Homo sapiens. Evolutionists believe Neanderthals lived from 130,000 to 35,000 years ago.

Although there may still be some disagreement about Neanderthal, there seems to be none about Cro-Magnon. The first specimens of these people were found in a cave in France in 1868. Five skeletons were found. Since that time, many other camps have been discovered. Physically, the Cro-Magnon people were identical to modern humans. They had rounded skulls, small, even teeth, high foreheads, protruding chins, and large brains like modern people. The Cro-Magnon made and used tools and weapons, utilizing flint in addition to stone. Their cave paintings and engravings show they had a complex culture. They lived and hunted in groups, as well as sharing ceremonies and rituals. Their paintings show them to be efficient, cooperative hunters who worked together to survive. They are believed to have existed on the Earth for the past 40,000–50,000 years. The Cro-Magnon seem to have been a more sophisticated people than the Neanderthals. Perhaps this influenced their survival when the Neanderthals as a group did not survive.

Anthropologists still hotly debate the first appearance of Homo sapiens. Many put their arrival on Earth within the last 200,000 years. The early humans (Neanderthal and Cro-Magnon) were believed to be primarily hunters and gatherers who preyed on animals and foraged for nuts and fruits. However, it is commonly accepted that about 10,000 to 11,000 years ago people stopped hunting and gathering as their primary source of food and began to domesticate animals and plant crops. The earliest known record of farming was found in the Middle East in areas that are now Iraq, Iran, and Turkey. This

agricultural revolution allowed modern humans to have a much more dependable source of food.

Because people did not have to be constantly on the move, they could specialize more. Some could continue to farm, while others might work at different jobs, such as providing tools for the farmers to use. It is believed the steady source of food caused the human population to expand, and it has continued to do so. Today, the population of the Earth numbers in the billions. As a species, *Homo sapiens* has adapted well to this world.

There are several different hypotheses as to how the evolution of man occurred. A common one has *Ramapithecus* as the primary link fossil between man and the apes, with *A. afarensis, A. africanus, H. habilis,* and *H. erectus* as successive links in the evolution of man. This hypothesis was demonstrated in this chapter. Other scientists discount *Ramapithecus* completely and list either *A. afarensis* or *A. africanus* as the primary link. Since *A. anamensis* is fairly new to the scientific community, it will be interesting to see where or if this fossil is placed in the ancestry of man.

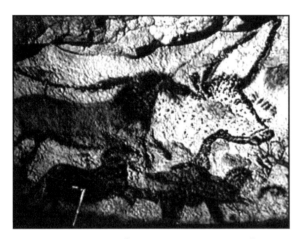

Figure 3-6 *Picture of Cro magnon cave drawings.* Courtesy of Professor David Fein.

QUESTIONS FOR REVIEW

1. Why did scientists at first consider Neanderthal to be a link fossil? What changed their minds?
2. How were the Neanderthals like modern humans, and how long ago were they believed to have lived?
3. Describe the Cro-Magnon.
4. What did the Cro-Magnon do that was typical of humans?
5. What was the agricultural revolution? When do scientists believe it occurred?
6. How did the agricultural revolution help humanity?
7. What has happened to the Earth's population since that time?

CHAPTER 4

SPONTANEOUS GENERATION: WHAT SCIENTISTS PROVED

People and words to know: Francisco Redi, Louis Pasteur, and principle of biogenesis

SECTION 1: FRANCISCO REDI

When A. I. Oparin developed his model on the spontaneous generation of the first cell, he was not the first person to believe that it could occur. In fact, the belief that living things could arise spontaneously from inorganic matter had been around for thousands of years. As early as 300 b.c, Aristotle, the Greek philosopher, suggested that "animals could arise spontaneously from other, unlike organisms or from soil."[1] Since his teachings were widely accepted as accurate, this theory persisted throughout the middle ages into the 17th century. In 1668 an Italian physician named Francisco Redi questioned the belief that flies could arise spontaneously from decaying meat. Instead he proposed that flies came from eggs laid by other flies on the decaying meat. Redi decided to test his hypothesis. He filled two sets of four jars with pieces of eel, veal, fish, and snake. The first set of jars he sealed, while he left the other open to the air.

After observing the jars for several days Redi noted that flies entered the unsealed jars regularly. However, they were prevented from entering the sealed ones. Within a short period of time, maggots developed in the unsealed jars. However, in the sealed jars there were none. Redi concluded that maggots developed from eggs laid on the rotten meat by the flies, which had easy access to the open jars.

Many other scientists of his day did not agree with Redi. They complained that the reason no mag-

gots developed in the sealed jars was that Redi had prevented air from entering them, thus impeding their spontaneous generation.

Redi set out to prove them wrong. He performed a second experiment. In this one he set up two sets of jars as before. However, this time he did not seal the experimental jars. Instead, he covered them with a fine mesh that allowed air to enter but not flies. As before, Redi found that flies entered the open jars. They also attempted to enter the mesh covered ones. After a few days, maggots developed in the open jars but again they did not develop in the covered ones. Redi concluded that the presence or absence of air made no difference. Maggots developed only from the eggs of flies.

In spite of Redi's work, some scientists still believed that spontaneous generation could occur. They stated that though flies might not arise spontaneously, this did not prove that other organisms couldn't. Several other scientists conducted experiments concerning this question with varying results. By the end of the nineteenth century, most scientists agreed that spontaneous generation of more complex organisms could not occur. However, many still believed that the spontaneous generation of microscopic organisms was possible. It took the work of Louis Pasteur finally to settle this debate.

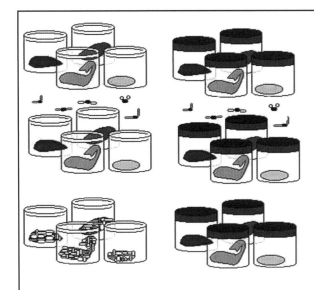

Figure 4-1A *In Redi's first experiment, he put lids on the experimental jars. Some scientist said this stopped air from entering, thus preventing spontaneous generation.*

Figure 4-1B *In Redi's second experiment, he covered the experimental jars with a fine cloth allowing air to enter but not the flies. No maggots formed in the experimental jars.*

SECTION 2: LOUIS PASTEUR

Louis Pasteur was a French scientist. In 1864 he formed the hypothesis that microscopic organisms are carried on dust particles in the air. Pasteur developed an experiment to test his hypothesis. First of all, he took several flasks, filled them with broth, and then boiled the broth for several minutes to kill all the microorganisms. He then took the flasks with him to various locations with different amounts of dust. At each location he opened a different flask and exposed it to the air. After several days Pasteur found that there were microorganisms in each flask. The

flasks exposed to the locations with the most dust had the most microorganisms. Pasteur concluded that the greater amount of dust particles had carried a greater number of microorganisms.

Pasteur then tested his hypothesis in a different way in the laboratory. He took a number of flasks, and filled them with broth. Then he heated the neck of each flask so that he could bend it into an "S" shape. Because of the shape of the neck, the still air of the laboratory could now enter the flask, but dust would be caught in the curve of the "S."

Then Pasteur boiled the broth in the flasks until all the microorganisms in the flasks were dead. As the broth cooled, some air reentered the flasks, but the dust was caught in the curve. After several days, he observed no microorganisms in the broth.

Next Pasteur tipped a flask to allow the dust trapped in the curve to mingle with the broth.

Within a few days there were microorganisms in this flask only. Pasteur concluded that his hypothesis was correct. **Microorganisms are carried on the dust particles in the air, and these contaminated the broth. In light of this, he concluded that spontaneous generation does not occur.**

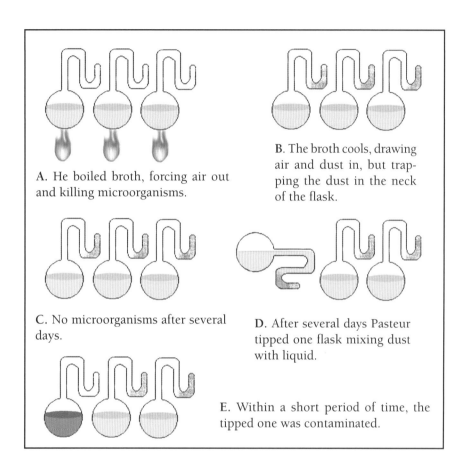

A. He boiled broth, forcing air out and killing microorganisms.

B. The broth cools, drawing air and dust in, but trapping the dust in the neck of the flask.

C. No microorganisms after several days.

D. After several days Pasteur tipped one flask mixing dust with liquid.

E. Within a short period of time, the tipped one was contaminated.

Figure 4-2
Pasteur's experiment. Drawing by A. Margetic.

The work of Redi and Pasteur, along with others, eventually convinced scientists that spontaneous generation does not occur. Instead, a **principle of biogenesis** was developed which states that living things can arise only from other living things. At first, this principle of biogenesis was called the **law of biogenesis**. However, as scientists attempted to explain how the first cell arose through spontaneous generation, the law was changed to a principle, implying that it did not apply in all situations.

QUESTIONS FOR REVIEW

1. Name the first individual to challenge the theory of spontaneous generation **and** describe his second experiment.
2. Who finally settled the question of spontaneous generation once and for all? **Describe his laboratory experiment.**
3. Briefly state the principle that came out of this research.

Section 3: In the Beginning

Vocabulary words to know: amino acids, proteins, organic soup, and enzymes

In the twentieth century the question of spontaneous generation came up again. During the early part of this century, Alexander Oparin developed his famous theory as to how the first cell could have formed. However, creationists point out that while developing his theory, Oparin failed to take into account several things. Some of these were demonstrated when Stanley Miller did his famous experiment. Miller showed what would form, under the conditions that Oparin put forth. However, Miller's experimental apparatus did not exactly duplicate natural conditions. First of all, Miller's experiment had a very important piece of equipment that is not present in nature. This is the trap that collected the "organic soup" after it went through the spark chamber and the condenser. Without this trap, the amino acids, along with the other materials produced,

would have continued back through the cycle. When the amino acids reached the spark chamber, **they would have been broken down into simpler molecules again**. The very energy that formed them would also destroy them 100,000–1,000,000 times faster. Therefore, the trap was absolutely necessary to **protect them**. The problem is that in nature there is no such trap. At first, scientists theorized that the ocean would serve as one. However, the ocean water would actually dilute the molecules so that a soup would be unlikely to form. In addition, amino acids tend to break down if they are dissolved in water. So the ocean would not be a safe "trap" for the organic molecules to collect and become the "organic soup" in which proteins, and eventually the first cell, could form.

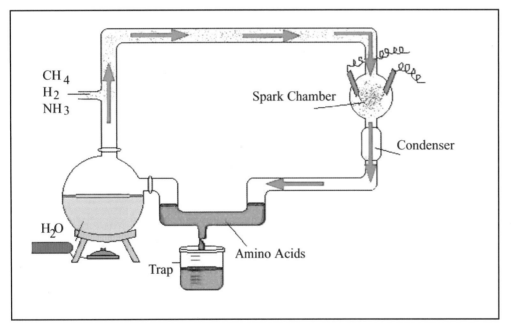

Figure 4-3 *This diagram shows Stanley Miller's famous experiment that produced amino acids. Drawing by A. Margetic.*

Another theory was that the ultraviolet rays present in sunlight might have provided the energy to form amino acids high in the atmosphere. Again there is a problem: how are the amino acids protected once they form, when **those same ultraviolet rays would break them down again?** In fact, even if amino acids had managed to reach the upper ocean and not been dissolved by the water,

they would still have been broken down by the UV rays of the sun shining beneath the surface of the water. Clearly, the lack of a protective trap in nature creates a major problem.

Amino acids are relatively simple in structure in comparison to proteins, the next step in the evolutionary movement toward complexity. **For spontaneous generation to occur as Oparin assumed,**

proteins would have to be able to arise spontaneously from these amino acids. The problem is that Miller's experiment created many substances besides some of the amino acids that occur in proteins. For example, the experiment produced non-biological (right-handed) amino acids, (see Figure 4–6) along with formic, acetic, succinic, and lactic acids and urea.[2]

This creates a major difficulty for the formation of proteins because, as demonstrated by Miller's experiment, the amino acids in the "organic soup" **would be more likely to combine with the other products than with each other**. Hence, proteins would not form. The cross-reactions between the amino acids and the other products of the organic soup create yet another roadblock in the spontaneous formation of life.

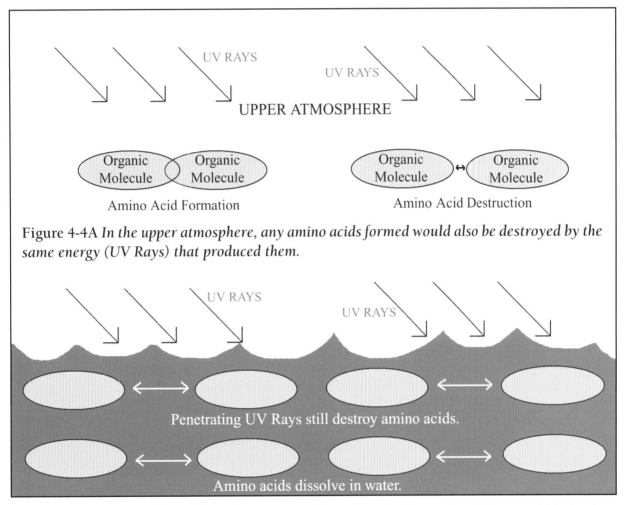

Figure 4-4A *In the upper atmosphere, any amino acids formed would also be destroyed by the same energy (UV Rays) that produced them.*

Figure 4-4B *Amino acids reaching the ocean would not be safe there either. They would be broken apart by the penetrating UV Rays or dissolved in the water. The above illustrates the difficulties in maintaining amino acids in the environment. Drawing by A. Margetic.*

In addition, even if the amino acids were somehow isolated from the other products of the "organic soup," proteins still would not form. In order to produce proteins, a great deal of energy is necessary. However, if left unprotected, amino acids tend to break down into their component parts when exposed to energy. **Thus, Miller's trap was necessary to prevent the energy from breaking down the amino acids, but at the same time it protected the amino acids from the energy they needed to advance to the next stage—proteins. So how can** proteins be produced? The answer is that in living things they are synthesized under the control of enzymes, which are themselves proteins. Chemical energy in the form of the activated nucleotide GTP is supplied at every stage of production.[3] In addition, other proteins called initiation factors and release factors are needed for the production of proteins. Without all these elements and several others working together, proteins do not form. It is difficult to see how life could have arisen spontaneously. Percival Davis and Dean H. Kenyon, in their book, *Of Pandas and People*, point out that while some compounds form relatively easily, others do not. "The simple building blocks of life [amino acids] form relatively easily but the chemical reactions required to form proteins and DNA do not occur readily. In fact, these products haven't appeared in any simulation experiment to date."[4]

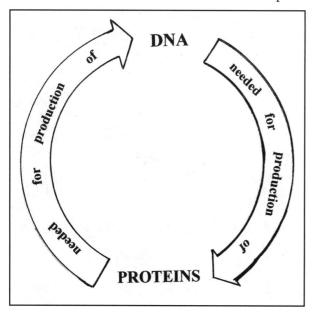

Figure 4-5 *DNA Production is dependent on pre-existing protein and vice versa. Drawing by A. Margetic.*

QUESTIONS FOR REVIEW

1. Why does the absence of a trap in nature cause problems?
2. Why does the presence of other products in the experiment create problems?
3. If amino acids could somehow be isolated from the other experimental products, why couldn't they spontaneously form proteins?

SECTION 4: ADDITIONAL PROBLEMS

Vocabulary words to know: organelle, mitochondria, left and right handed amino acids, left and right handed sugars

Another problem with Oparin's theory is related to the interdependence of DNA and protein. In order to be called a true cell, the first cell would have had to contain DNA, as well as most of the organelles that enable it to do its work. Before DNA can be formed, however, **there must be pre-existing protein which is necessary in its production.** Likewise, in order for protein to be produced, **there must be DNA present to guide its formation.**[5] So how could each evolve independently of the other? In much the same way, the **cell's individual organelles are dependent upon each other.** For example, without the mitochondria, the eukaryotic cell has no source of energy to perform its other functions. Without the cell membrane to protect them, the organelles could not even stay together, let alone form a harmonious functioning unit. These facts place some serious doubt on Oparin's theory.

There is also the difficulty with what Kenyon and Davis call "uniform orientation." They point out that amino acids, as well as sugars, proteins, and even DNA, have "very specific three dimensional structures." Amino acids come in two forms that are identical except that they are "mirror images of each other." Because their shapes are identical but **mirror images** of each other, they are often called "left-handed" and "right-handed" amino acids. (This phenomenon is common in nature and is called chirality.) Miller's experiment produced both left—and right-handed amino acids in roughly a fifty-fifty ratio. Nature produces both kinds also. The problem is that only left-handed amino acids are used in protein production. "**If just one right-handed amino acid finds its way into a protein, the protein's ability to function is reduced, often completely.**"[6] On the other hand, only right handed sugars are used in DNA and RNA. The problem is **who did the sorting in nature?** Kenyon and Davis point out, "Researchers have found no way to produce only correct three-dimensional structures in simulation experiments."[7] The interdependence of DNA and protein, as well as of the cell's organelles, together with the exclusive selection of left-handed amino acids and right-handed sugars, point to intelligent design in nature rather than to random action.

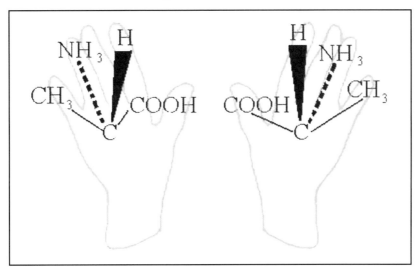

Figure 4-6 *Left and right handed amino acids. NOTE: The complex molecules don't necessarily resemble human hands. However, since they are mirror images of each other in the same way that your left and right hands are mirror images of each other, it is a common way to distinguish between them. Drawing by A. Margetic.*

Figure 4–6 illustrates what is meant by left—and right-handed amino acids. They are mirror images of each other as our hands are. Just as you could not make a left-handed glove fit on a right hand, you also cannot make an organic molecule "fit properly on" a right-handed amino acid.

QUESTIONS FOR REVIEW

1. Why would it be difficult for DNA and protein to evolve separately and independently?
2. Why would there be problems with the different organelles of the first cell evolving independently?
3. Why does the spontaneous production of both right—and left-handed amino acids create a problem for the production of proteins?
4. What does the exclusive use of left-handed amino acids and right-handed sugars in living things indicate?

Section 5: Photosynthesis and a Reducing Atmosphere

Vocabulary words to know: chloroplasts, grana, electron transport chain, ATP molecules, hydrogen acceptor, light phase, dark phase, and reducing atmosphere

Creationists also note that one of the most serious problems with Oparin's theory is that he provides no explanation for how the process of photosynthesis could have evolved. Yet, if his theory of spontaneous generation were true, this would have to have occurred. Otherwise, the evolution from bacteria to man would be impossible. Yet, photosynthesis is extremely complex, involving two complicated cycles called the light phase and the dark phase, and requiring the action of several very specific enzymes for these processes to proceed.

The first phase, called the light phase, begins within the chloroplasts, structures within the leaves and sometimes the stems of green plants. The green pigment chlorophyll within the grana of the chloroplasts absorbs photons of light. This light energy boosts electrons in the chlorophyll molecules to a higher energy level. The "supercharged" electrons then move from one chlorophyll molecule to another in what is called an **electron transport chain**. As each transfer is made, some energy is released. This energy is used to form **ATP** molecules from ADP. (ATP, adenosine triphosphate, is an energy carrier in many living cells.)

The electrons lost from the chlorophyll molecules are replaced by splitting water molecules into oxygen and hydrogen and taking the electrons from the hydrogen. A great deal of light energy is used to split the water molecule. The hydrogen ions that are left then combine with a **hydrogen acceptor**, while the oxygen is released into the atmosphere. It is interesting to note that **when chemists try to produce artificial photosynthesis, the energy that is needed to break the water molecule destroys the artificial photosynthetic molecule.**

The second, or dark phase, of photosynthesis is so named because it can take place in the dark. (Actually, it can also proceed in the light. However, light is not needed.) In this phase, carbon dioxide from the atmosphere combines with a sugar called **RDP** (ribulose diphosphate) to form **PGA**. This reaction uses energy from the ATP formed during the light reaction. The PGA then combines with the hydrogen ions from the hydrogen acceptors to form **PGAL**. In a normal cycle, twelve molecules of PGAL are formed. Two PGAL molecules combine to produce glucose, while the other ten go back to make more RDP and begin the cycle once more.

The dark phase requires several enzymes in order to occur. By lowering the amount of activation energy required to start them, enzymes permit reactions that otherwise would take place too slowly in a cell. (In fact, it is because of enzymes that the activities within living things can proceed. Enzymes solve the problem of molecules being destroyed by the energy needed to combine them.) Enzymes are very complex proteins that perform highly specific jobs. How did these enzymes evolve? What would their purpose be outside the chloroplast? What about the two phases of photosynthesis? Since one phase has no function without the other, both had to be present and functioning in the first photosynthetic cell. So how did their evolution occur? The tremendous difficulty of explaining how photosynthesis evolved has never been overcome.

Figure 4–7 illustrates the light and dark phases of photosynthesis.

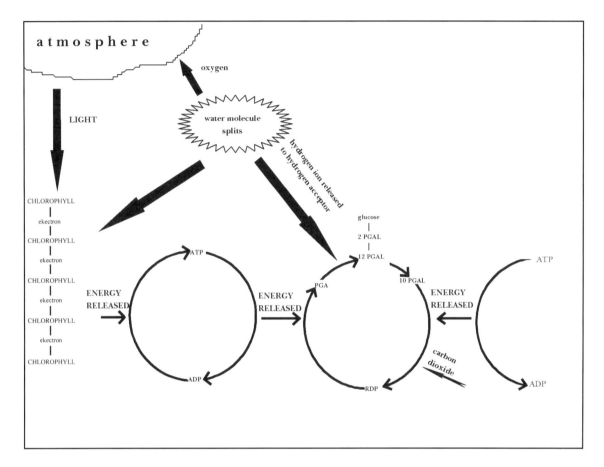

Figure 4-7A *Light phase of photosynthesis. Light causes electrons to move from one chlorophyll molecule to another. Energy is released and stored in ATP molecules. Water molecules split, releasing oxygen to atmosphere, electrons to the chlorophyll and hydrogen to acceptor.*

Figure 4-7B *Dark phase of photosynthesis. RDP combines with CO_2 and energy from light phase to form PGA. PGA combines with hydrogen ion to form 12 PGAL. 2 PGAL make one glucose. 10 PGAL use more energy to make more RDP and start the process again.*

Finally, Oparin believed the early Earth had a **reducing atmosphere**. This means that it contained little or no free oxygen. A reducing atmosphere was vital to his theory because organic molecules will not react with each other to form the components of living things if they are exposed to free oxygen. Instead, they combine with the free oxygen to form other compounds. Therefore, an atmosphere like we have today would make it impossible for Oparin's method of spontaneous generation to work. However, there is an abundance of evidence that the early Earth's atmosphere did contain free oxygen. In fact, such information has been common knowledge in the field of geology for several years. For example, as early as 1982, Harry Clemmey and Nick Badham pointed out that because of the presence of ferric iron in rocks which are considered very old, "it is suggested that from the time of the earliest dated rocks at 3.7 billion years ago, Earth had an oxygenic atmosphere."[8] Iron oxide indicates the presence of free oxygen at the time when the iron was being deposited. Other scientists have discovered sulfate deposits in Precambrian formations, also indicating the presence of free oxygen. This evidence would indicate that the early Earth's atmosphere did contain free oxygen, making it impossible for life to have arisen spontaneously. Clemmey and Badham take this one step further when they point out that "Earth's aerobic and anaerobic environments are mutually sustaining; failure to acquire one would have resulted in failure of the other."[9] **In other words, you can't have one without the other!**

When Oparin developed his hypothesis, he failed to take into consideration the many scientific reasons why spontaneous generation could not occur. (These also create problems for other models of spontaneous generation.) Miller's attempt to test Oparin's hypothesis served only to demonstrate its problems rather than to prove its validity. Redi and Pasteur both showed that spontaneous generation does not occur on the modern Earth. There is no valid reason to believe that it occurred in the past.

QUESTIONS FOR REVIEW

1. Briefly describe the light phase of photosynthesis.
2. Briefly describe the dark phase of photosynthesis.
3. What is the role of enzymes in the dark phase?
4. What is a reducing atmosphere and why was it necessary in order for spontaneous generation to occur?
5. What have geologists found that indicates the early atmosphere did contain free oxygen?

COMPARISON OF EVOLUTIONIST AND CREATIONIST POSITIONS

EVOLUTIONISTS

Evolutionists theorize that spontaneous generation must have occurred on the early Earth.

Alexander Oparin theorized about how the first cell could have spontaneously generated on an early Earth that had little or no free oxygen.

Oparin believed that elements such as hydrogen, ammonia, methane, and water, together with energy from the sun's UV rays, could have united to form amino acids.

Stanley Miller performed an experiment in which he produced amino acids using the compounds Oparin mentioned.

For spontaneous generation to occur as Oparin assumed, proteins would have to be able to arise spontaneously from amino acids.

Miller's experiment produced an "organic soup" similar to what Oparin suggested. The soup contained several other compounds besides amino acids.

Miller's experiment produced both left—and right-handed amino acids in a roughly fifty-fifty ratio.

Oparin theorized that the first cells were anaerobic bacteria and that the photosynthetic process somehow evolved in some of them.

CREATIONISTS

Creationists point out that both Francisco Redi and Louis Pasteur have already proven that spontaneous generation does not occur.

Scientists have found oxidized iron in ancient rocks, indicating that free oxygen was present on the early Earth.

The ultraviolet rays of the sun would have broken the amino acids down again. If they reached the oceans, the water would have dissolved them, and the UV rays would have continued to break them down.

Miller's experimental apparatus had a trap to protect the amino acids once they formed. Without a trap, the energy that formed the amino acids would also destroy them. Yet without additional energy, the amino acids cannot combine into proteins. Nature has no such trap.

Modern cells use enzymes as catalysts, as well as several other factors, to make proteins. Enzymes are proteins. DNA also requires enzymes to form. Even the organelles of the cell are mutually dependent on one another.

The amino acids in this "soup" would be much more likely to combine with the other products than with each other.

Nature uses exclusively left-handed amino acids. Who did the sorting in nature? Nature also uses exclusively right-handed sugars, another indication of "sorting."

Photosynthesis is a very complex process, consisting of two very complicated, mutually dependent phases. This process also requires several enzymes. There is no proof or explanation as to how such evolution could have occurred.

CHAPTER 5

THE SCIENTIFIC FACTS ABOUT GENETICS AND COMPARATIVE EMBRYOLOGY, HOMOLOGY AND BIOCHEMISTRY

Vocabulary words to know: cytochrome c, homology, homologous structures, pentadactyl pattern, yolk sac, gill slits, gene frequency, genetic stability, pleiotrophy, start and stop codons, adenine, guanine, thymine, and cytosine

Genetics, comparative embryology, comparative homology, and comparative biochemistry are often mentioned as offering a great deal of proof for evolution. However, is this truly the case? Creationists state that recent scientific discoveries have helped to illustrate that this evidence is not as supportive as some scientists once thought it to be.

SECTION 1: GENETICS

All living things develop as they do because of the genetic information that resides in the nuclei of their cells. As early as 1910 scientists discovered that heredity was controlled by genes carried on chromosomes. During the next forty years biochemists began to analyze the chemical compounds which make up the chromosomes. They discovered that chromosomes are composed of two substances—**proteins and deoxyribonucleic acid (DNA)**. It wasn't until the late 1940's and early 1950's that scientists came to understand that it was the DNA that contained the genetic information. In 1953 one of the most important discoveries of microbiology occurred when two scientists—James Watson and Francis Crick—reported the structure of DNA according to the now-famous double helix model which is shown in Figure 5-1.

DNA contains four nitrogen-carrying bases. These bases are called **adenine, guanine, thymine, and cytosine**. So how does the DNA work? The most logical comparison is to call it a "code" or "language" which is composed of four "letters." The letters are called nucleotides. Each nucleotide consists of one of the bases mentioned above combined with a sugar molecule and a phosphate group. Three of these nucleotides together make a codon, the "words" of DNA. The genetic code even has a sort of "punctuation," in the form of **start and stop codons**. Strings of codons make up genes, the "sentences" of DNA. Codons are used for the production of amino acids, which in turn are attached together to form proteins. (Therefore, a specific gene is responsible for the production of a particular protein.) Some codons code for the production of the same amino acid, so there are even "synonyms" in the DNA code. Furthermore, DNA replication employs "editors"—enzymes that correct mistakes. How could these enzymes and DNA have evolved separately? They must both be in place and functioning together.

The type of organism created depends on the "words" and "sentences" formed by the DNA "letters." "If the amount of information contained in one cell of your body were written out on a typewriter, it would fill as many books as are contained in a large library."[1] The first question that comes to mind is how could a perfectly logical, sensible language arise spontaneously? Humans use language as a means of communicating information to each other. The DNA code communicates the information necessary to construct all the living organisms on the Earth. This is the heart of the problem for many scientists who are not creationists but who recognize that **information is always a result of intelligent action**. It does not arise randomly or spontaneously.

Much has also been made of the fact that the DNA of humans and that of the apes vary by only 5%. Yet, does this indicate extreme closeness between our two species? If DNA is a language, then perhaps an illustration from our own language might help to clarify the situation. Consider the two sentences written below.

1. Timothy billed Jonathon during the night at the exclusive Hiltonhead Hotel.
2. Timothy killed Jonathon during the night at the exclusive Hiltonhead Hotel.

Note that only one letter has been changed, a difference of only 1 1/2 percent of the sentence! Yet that slight change makes a tremendous difference. In the construction of a single protein chain of 500 amino acids, if even one amino acid is incorrect, the protein is likely not to work. Evidently, nature

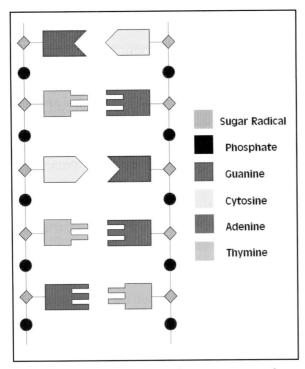

Sugar Radical

Phosphate

Guanine

Cytosine

Adenine

Thymine

Figure 5-1 *A DNA strand. NOTE: It is the sequence of the base pairs, Adenine-Thymine and Guanine-Cytosine, that "spell out" the letters and words of the DNA sentences. Drawing by A. Margetic.*

requires a remarkable degree of exactness, **and a little difference means a lot!**

The effect of genes on the development of structures that are not under their *primary* control is also quite amazing. Ordinarily, it would be logical to assume that a specific gene or set of genes is totally responsible for the expression of a particular structure in a species. Until recently, this was thought to be the only way that genes influence phenotypes. In some cases, the phenotype was believed to be controlled by only one parent's dominant genes. In other situations, the phenotype was believed to be a result of the blending of both parents' genes. However, it is really much more complicated than that. As scientists continued to study the effects of individual genes, they discovered that **genes affected more than one structure**. This phenomenon is known as **pleiotrophy**. As Ernst Mayr states in *Population, Species, and Evolution,* "Every gene that has been studied intensively has been found to be pleiotropic to a greater or lesser extent. It is obviously naïve to regard a gene as a mold into which a character is poured."[2] For example, in the ordinary house mouse the gene for coat color generally has some effect on the body size. In the fruit fly, inducing mutations in the eye color will also generally cause a change in the shape of the sex organs.[3] This phenomenon is "species specific." For example, the gene for hair color in a house mouse also influences its body size, but in another species, the gene for hair color might influence something totally different. Obviously, the operation of DNA is far more complicated than it was at first thought to be. Both DNA and RNA contain massive amounts of information. How to get this information by chance is a huge problem. The staggering complexity of DNA and of the structures it produces makes it very difficult to believe they were not the result of intelligent design.

Figure 5–2 shows the multiple effects of one particular pleiotrophic gene in the domestic chicken. When the gene was mutated, the effect on the chicken's development was remarkable. The wings developed only partially or not at all. The digits on the legs were malformed. The lungs and air sacs, as well as the ureter, fail to develop at all.

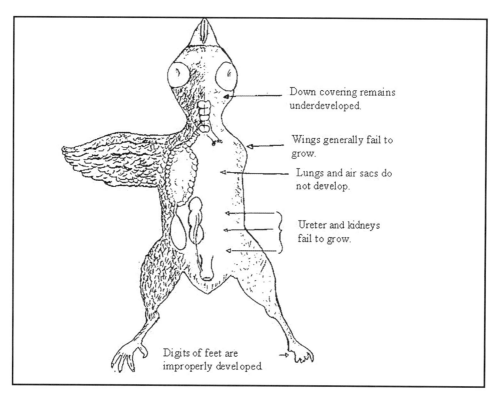

Down covering remains underdeveloped.

Wings generally fail to grow.

Lungs and air sacs do not develop.

Ureter and kidneys fail to grow.

Digits of feet are improperly developed

Figure 5-2 *Effects of the mutation of one pleiotrophic gene on the development of the domestic chicken. The right side of the drawing shows the effects of a mutation on one pleiotrophic gene. For comparison, the left side of the drawing shows normal development. Note: the consequences to the chicken's development were remarkable. This drawing modified from Ernst Hadorn, Developmental Genetics & Lethal Factors, Fig. 7, p. 191. Drawing by A. St. Arno.*

James Dewey Watson was born in Chicago, Illinois in 1928. He was a brilliant student who entered the University of Chicago when he was only fifteen. He graduated with a bachelor's degree in 1947 and by 1950 had already completed his doctoral research work. While doing postdoctoral research at Cavendish Laboratory in Cambridge, England, Watson met Francis Crick. Since both were interested in the nature of DNA, Watson and Crick decided to work together to determine its structure. In 1953 they proposed the double helix model of the DNA molecule. As a result, they shared the 1962 Nobel Prize in physiology or medicine. Watson returned to the United States where he served on the faculties of California Institute of Technology and Harvard University. He gave up his position at Harvard to work on various other genetic projects, including a two-year term as director of the Human Genome Project sponsored by the National Institute of Health. Watson has continued his research as well as facilitating and encouraging the research of other scientists. He is married and has two children.

Photo courtesy of Cold Spring Harbor Laboratory Archives.

Creationists contend that genetic stability also poses a problem for evolutionists because evolution requires change on a grand scale. After Gregor Mendel's discovery of dominant and recessive genes, many scientists thought that traits controlled by dominant genes would gradually become more common while those controlled by recessive genes would become rarer. Thus, there would be a mechanism for evolutionary change in species. An Englishman and a German decided to study this problem inde-

pendently. The Englishman's name was Godfrey Hardy; the German's name was Wilhelm Weinberg. Out of their studies came the famous **Hardy-Weinberg principle** which bears their names. Although a population's gene frequencies can be affected by outside influences such as genetic drift or natural selection, the main conclusion of their work was that **gene frequencies tend to remain stable over long periods of time.**[4] In other words, the proportion of various genes within a population tends to remain the same over long periods of time. There is not much change. Change does occur as a result of the outside agents of genetic drift, natural selection, isolation, migration and mutation working on different meiotic combinations. However, it has definite limits. **Devolution is achieved largely through the loss of genetic information**. Organisms get less alike because they lose genes they once had in common. However, in order to bring about the kind of change needed for evolution, there must be another agent actually changing existing genes and **creating new genes**. Evolutionists believe this agent to be mutation. What is mutation? If DNA is a language "written" in our cells, then mutations could best be called "typing errors," mistakes in the genetic code. Is mutation capable of producing the millions of genes necessary to control all the organisms on the Earth? It is not likely. First of all, mutations generally cause the **loss** of genetic information. Yet it is assumed mutations also produce **new** genes. For the sake of argument, let us accept this assumption as correct and that mutations do produce **new** genes. Does this account for all the genetic information necessary to go from single cells to man? Not really. First of all, only one in 1000 mutations is not harmful.[5] The vast majority of these harmless mutations are simply neutral in their effect. It is also estimated that it would take five of these mutations to cause one change, according to E.J. Ambrose.

> It is most unlikely that fewer than five genes could ever be involved in the formation of even the simplest new structure, previously unknown in the organism. The probability now becomes one in one thousand million million. [1000x1 000x1000x1000x1000]. We already know that mutations in living cells appear once in ten million to once in one hundred thousand million. It is evident that the probability of five favorable mutations occurring within a single life cycle of an organism is effectively zero.[6] (Emphasis added by author.)

But what if the mutations occur in different organisms and survive because they are neutral? Couldn't they come together in later generations to form a beneficial change? Dr. Ambrose points out, "the probability of the five genes coming together simultaneously within a single organism will be extremely small."[7] Obviously, mutation does not appear to be the source of new genes for evolution. According to Dr. Jonathon Sarfati, in *Refuting Evolution* II, (pp. 102–105) mutations generally result in the loss of information. They can sometimes be neutral or give occasional selective advantage. They can also result in genes "switching on" in the wrong places or even the duplication of some genes. However, they do not add information. They merely alter existing information. **Because mutations generally result in the loss and not the gain of genetic information**, they clearly illustrate the second law of thermodynamics, which states that systems, if left to themselves, tend to go from an organized to a disorganized state. It appears that mutations do not improve the organism or make it more complex; instead, they tend to "erode" its DNA.

QUESTIONS FOR REVIEW

1. What has DNA been compared to? Why is this important?
2. What is pleiotrophy? Give an example.
3. What did Hardy and Weinberg's research prove?
4. How many genetic mutations are believed not to be harmful? Are all of these beneficial?
5. It has been estimated that five beneficial genes would have to occur at the same time to cause a change in an organism. Why do some scientists think this makes it impossible for mutations to be the source of new genes for evolution?
6. To what does mutation generally lead—the gain or the loss of genetic information?

Almost twelve years older than James Watson, Francis Crick got a late start in biology. Dr. Crick studied physics and mathematics and received his bachelor's degree in 1937. However, World War II interrupted his work on an advanced degree. When the war ended, Crick switched to a career in biology. His studies eventually brought him to the Medical Research Council Unit for Molecular Biology at Cavendish Laboratory. There he met James Watson who shared his interest in DNA. The two men began to collaborate together on genetic research while Crick continued his work on his doctorate. By 1953 they had developed their now-famous double helix model of the DNA molecule. For this discovery, they received the Nobel Prize in 1962.

James Watson and Francis Crick.
Photo courtesy of Cold Spring Harbor Laboratory Archives.

SECTION 2: COMPARATIVE EMBRYOLOGY

Evolutionists also cite comparative embryology as evidence for evolution. Biology textbooks usually have pictures of the embryos of different species supposedly drawn at the same stage of development. Because these embryos look very much alike, evolutionists point to their similar appearance as evidence for evolution. However, creationists point out that **the drawings are inaccurate**. Over one hundred years ago, a man named Ernst Haeckel published a series of drawings of the embryos of several species. The embryos looked similar. Haeckel used the drawings as proof that evolution had, in fact, occurred. However, other members of the scientific community soon realized that Haeckel's work was fraudulent. He had altered the drawings to make them more alike. When Haeckel was confronted, he blamed an assistant for careless work. He never apologized for his error or attempted to rectify it. The drawings disappeared for over twenty years. Then, near the turn of the century, similar drawings appeared in a comparative anatomy book. Since

that time, these incorrect pictures have continued to show up in books teaching evolution.

Michael Richardson, an embryologist and senior lecturer at St. George's Medical School in London, England, could find no evidence that anyone had actually compared the embryos of different species. He assembled a panel of scientists to photograph the same embryos "roughly matched by species and age to those Haeckel drew."[8] (He also photographed many embryos that Haeckel had not drawn.) The findings are shown in Figure 5–3. On top are the drawings of Ernst Haeckel while on the bottom are pictures of the embryos as they really look. Not only do the embryonic parts generally look different, but also they vary widely in size. Even the pharyngeal pouches are not alike, and there are also other major differences.[9] Compare these pictures to the ones you find demonstrated in chapter two of this book. Unfortunately, many current high school biology books and other textbooks continue to use Haeckel's drawings to support comparative embryology.

The photographs show that the embryos do not look alike. However, do the same parts of the embryos develop into similar organs and body parts? Again, the answer is often "no." For example, because of Haeckel's deception, the pharyngeal pouches (neck portion) of the human embryo are still called "gill slits." However, gill slits are not normally present in the human embryo. Although

this area in the fish embryo does develop into the respiratory system, **in the human embryo it develops into the palatine tonsils, the middle ear canals, the thymus and parathyroid glands.**[10] The parathyroid glands assist in calcium balance in the blood. The palatine tonsils and thymus play a part in the immune system.

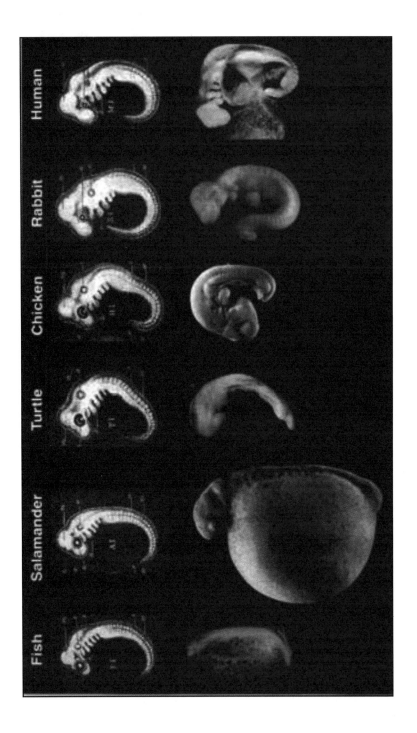

Figure 5-3 A comparison between the drawings of Ernst Haeckel and pictures of the actual embryos. On the top row are Haeckel's fraudulent drawings of several different embryos at the 'tailbud' stage. On the bottom row are Michael Richardson's and other scientists' photographs showing how the same embryos actually look at the same stage. The embryos are not the same size either. According to Mr. Richardson there is "a greater than 10-fold variation in greatest length at the tailbud stage." (Michael Richardson, et. Al., "There Is No Highly Conserved Embryonic Stage in the Vertebrates," Anatomy & Embryology 196 (2) 1997, p. 91). Photos courtesy of Springer-Verlag Publishers and Michael Richardson.

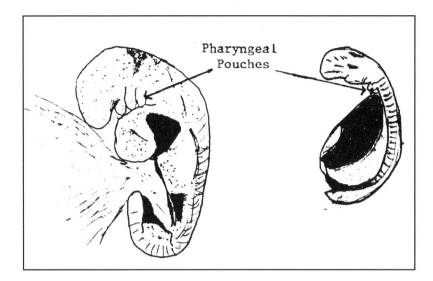

Figure 5-4. *Pharyngeal pouches in the human embryo (left) become palatine tonsils, middle ear canals, thymus and parathyroid glands. In fish they become the gills (respiratory system).*

Other parts of the human embryo often have been cited as being vestigial organs that were needed in our evolutionary ancestors but are no longer needed by us. For example, the **yolk sac**, which is attached to the early embryo, has been cited as being there because our common ancestor with the birds needed this organ to supply food. It is true that this is its purpose in birds. However, this organ has a definite and different function in the human embryo. Since the human heart starts to beat in the fourth week of the embryo's existence, it begins to pump blood throughout the circulatory system long before there is bone marrow to produce red blood cells! So where do they come from? **The red blood cells are produced by the yolk sac until the bone marrow is able to take over this function.**[11] When the bone marrow begins to produce blood cells, the yolk sac stops its work and is slowly absorbed by the body.

Evolutionists have also pointed to the "tail" of the human embryo as vestigial and thus evidence of our evolutionary relationship to other mammals. However, **this so-called embryonic tail is nothing more than the end of the spine before the legs begin to grow.** It becomes the tailbone, which is "an important point of muscle attachment required for our distinctive upright posture."[12] For these reasons, creationists feel comparative embryology does little to support evolution.

QUESTIONS FOR REVIEW

1. What did Ernst Haeckel do to create support for evolution?
2. What happened to his drawings?
3. Who discovered that there was something wrong with the drawings in current comparative anatomy books? How did he prove it?
4. Name two parts of the human embryo which evolutionists once thought were vestigial structures and describe their actual uses.

Section 3: Comparative Homology

You may remember from Chapter two that homologous structures are body parts that have the same basic structure as those in another species. However, creationists assert that the term, "homology," may be used selectively by evolutionists. A good example of the selective use of homology is the pentadactyl pattern that exists on the limbs of many organisms. The arms and legs of man have the same basic pattern. There is one large bone in the upper arm (the humerus), two smaller bones in the lower arm (the radius and ulna), the carpals and metacarpals in the wrist and upper hand, and finally the fingers (phalanges). In the leg there is also a large upper bone (the femur), two smaller bones in the lower leg (the tibia and fibula), the tarsals and metatarsals in the ankle and upper foot, and finally the toes (also called phalanges). The pattern is very similar. (See Figure 5–5.) This same situation exists in any number of vertebrates, where the front and hind legs follow exactly the same pattern. However, evolutionists believe that the front legs of land vertebrates (or the arms of man) evolved from the pectoral fins of fish, while the hind legs (or man's legs) evolved from the pelvic fins of fish. So, why are they so much alike? **If evolution occurs, they had to have evolved independently and by chance from two different types of fins to form two structures with identical types of bones.** This poses a difficult problem. Therefore, only the front legs of different animals and the arms of man are generally compared.

It has been shown that seemingly homologous parts of embryos often do not develop into the same types of structures in the fully developed organism. The reverse is also true. **Structures that are considered homologous in adults of various species often develop from different parts of their embryos.** For example, the arms of man and the forelimbs of a newt and a lizard are considered homologous. Yet the forelimbs of the newt develop from trunk segments 2–5 of its embryo, while they develop from segments 6–9 of the lizard's embryo. In man, they develop from segments 13–18.[13] This also applies to other organs. Michael Denton, in *Evolution: a Theory*

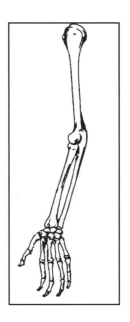

Figure 5-5 *Skeleton of man's arm showing the pentadactyl pattern. Note the pattern of the bones. There is a single upper bone connected to two lower arm bones. These two lower bones are then connected to five digits—thus the term, pentadactyl pattern.*

in Crisis, states, "The development of the vertebrate kidney appears to provide another challenge to the assumption that homologous organs are generated from homologous embryonic tissues."[14] He adds that the kidney in fish and amphibians develop from totally different embryonic tissue than the kidneys of reptiles and mammals. This phenomenon is also common in insects where there are many examples of homologous organs and structures that are developed in radically different ways.[15]

Equally amazing is the fact that homologous structures often are not controlled by **homologous genes in different species.** As Sir Gavin de Beer points out in "Homology: An Unresolved Problem," "Characters controlled by identical genes are not necessarily homologous. The converse is no less instructive . . . . Homologous structures need not be controlled by identical genes."[16] What this means is that chromosomes are organized differently in different organisms. Therefore, **the genes that control presumed homologous structures are frequently found in different locations and on different chromosomes in various species.** Creationists feel pleiotropy is also a strong argument against homology, since non-homologous genes are involved in the expression of so-called homologous structures. Thus, the gene for coat color in one species may affect body size, while in another species body size may be influenced by a totally different pleiotropic gene.

In the glossary of *Origin of Species*, homology is defined as "the relationship between parts which results from their development from corresponding embryonic parts."[17] If this definition is correct, there appear to be very few truly homologous structures.

QUESTIONS FOR REVIEW

1. What problem does the pentadactyl pattern in all four limbs of land vertebrates pose for evolutionists?
2. What problem do evolutionists have with supposed homologous structures in embryos and in adults of the same species?
3. Give one example of this (See question 2).
4. What problem do evolutionists have with homologous structures and the genes that control them?
5. Why is pleiotrophy a strong argument against homology?

SECTION 4: COMPARATIVE BIOCHEMISTRY

Finally, comparative biochemistry often is mentioned as supporting evolution. Particularly, cytochrome C in different organisms is compared. You may remember that cytochrome C is a respiratory enzyme that occurs in a wide variety of organisms—including bacteria, birds, fish, and humans. It has the structure of a central ring with an iron atom, which is attached to a sequence of about 100 amino acids. Evolutionists believe the more similar the amino acid sequences of cytochrome C, the closer the evolutionary relationship of different organisms. However, extensive studies have been made of the cytochrome C in many organisms. This research revealed that when the different species were classified using cytochrome C, they fell into the same distinct groupings as they did when they were classified using more traditional methods, such as that proposed by Linnaeus. "**All sequences of each subclass are equally isolated from the members of another group. Traditional or intermediate classes are completely absent.**"[18] Creationists feel the missing links are still missing—even in comparative biochemistry.

For example, evolutionists consider insects to have evolved fairly early and to be some of the more primitive organisms on the evolutionary scale. Fish are considered to have evolved later and to be somewhat more advanced. Reptiles, birds and finally mammals are considered to have evolved later and in that order. Therefore, there should be less difference between the cytochrome C of bacteria and that of insects than between the cytochrome C of bacteria and that of reptiles or mammals. The gap should widen as one goes higher on the evolutionary scale because more changes would have occurred. A sample chart has been produced below, showing the **hypothetical** difference between the cytochrome C of bacteria and that of other organisms. **Note: this is a *hypothetical* chart, since it is impossible to determine with any accuracy the exact percentage of difference there should be between the cytochrome C of different organisms. However, if evolution were true, a pattern similar to this *should* exist.**

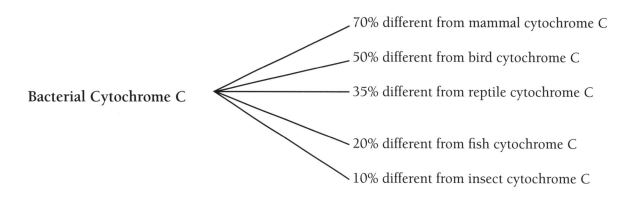

Above is a hypothetical (**imaginary**) chart of differences which *should* exist if evolution is true.

It **is important to know that this kind of pattern does not exist.** As Davis and Kenyon point out in *Of Pandas and People*, "bacterial cytochrome C is almost exactly as far removed from the cytochrome C of a human as it is from a pigeon, a rattlesnake, a bullfrog, a carp, a lamphrey, a fruit fly, a sunflower or a yeast. **In other words, no species is intermediate to any other.**"[19] (Emphasis added by author.) Figure 5-6 illustrates the **actual** difference.

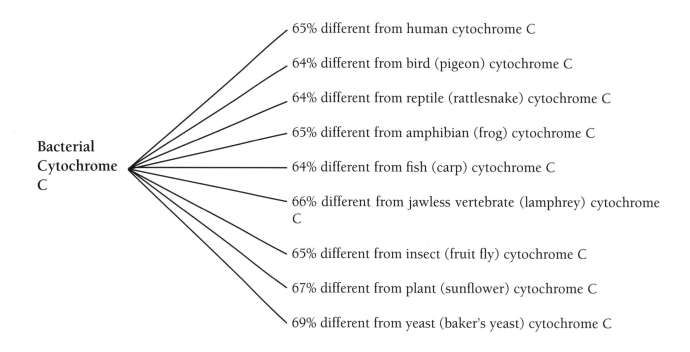

Figure 5-6 *The above chart shows the actual percentage of divergence between bacterial cytochrome c and that of various categories of organisms. Note the degree of difference is almost identical. Information gleaned from* Of Pandas and People, *p. 37.*

QUESTION FOR REVIEW

1. What problem does comparative biochemistry create for evolutionists?

What does all this mean?

Genetics is often cited as giving supporting evidence for evolution. However, creationists contend the evidence simply is not there. A study of genetics shows that DNA is a language complete with "synonyms" and "punctuation." Pleiotropy further complicates matters, since it allows non-homologous genes to exercise partial control over homologous structures. Mutation does not seem to be useful as a mechanism for evolution. Finally, genetic stability is a huge problem for evolutionists because evolution requires massive amounts of genetic change and new genetic information.

Creationists feel comparative embryology, comparative homology and comparative biochemistry also pose problems for evolutionists. First of all, the embryos of different species generally do not look alike. In addition, homologous parts of the embryos often do not develop into homologous parts of the adults of different species. Conversely, nonhomologous parts of embryos often grow into so-called homologous structures in the adults. Also, homologous structures are often controlled by non-homologous genes. Finally, comparative biochemistry shows no species is intermediate to any other. **None of these sciences shows a pattern of control and development that should be there if evolution is true**. It is clear, then, that none of these sciences offers any substantial support for evolution. Instead, they provide evidence for genetic stability and for clear and separate groups with variation **within** those groups only.

Some examples of evolution in action which scientists have postulated appear to be flawed also. The studies done on the peppered moth are one example the creationists cite. First of all, the moths fly mainly at night. Secondly, there is no evidence that moths land on tree trunks. Scientists glued dark and light moths to the tree trunks and took photographs of them for textbooks![21] For these and other good reasons, the peppered moth generally has been discarded as an example of evolution in action. However, even if the research work had not been flawed, **the change within the peppered moth population would not be evolution in action, but simply minor variations caused by natural selection acting on the moth population's existing gene pool.**

The same is true for the changes within the beak size of the Galapagos Islands finches. During drought conditions, birds with larger beaks would be better adapted because of their ability to eat tougher food. Therefore, they would be more likely to survive the drought. As soon as the drought was over, the birds with smaller beaks became more common because they could also survive in the easier conditions. The finches' beaks remained beaks. They did not change into a different structure. There was only temporary modification of an existing structure.

QUESTION FOR REVIEW

1. What do the examples of the peppered moth and the Galapagos finches actually demonstrate?

BACTERIAL EVOLUTION

Evolutionists often cite the phenomenon of bacterial resistance to antibiotics as evidence of evolution. However, there are at least three reasons why a strain of antibiotic resistant bacteria can develop, and none of these require the addition of new information, which is absolutely necessary for evolution.

First of all, some bacteria have a natural resistance to antibiotics. If a population of bacteria is subjected to an antibiotic, some of the bacteria may have a resistance to it. All those without the resistance will be eliminated by the antibiotic, leaving only the resistant ones to reproduce. Thus, a strain of bacteria immune to that particular antibiotic is produced.

The second reason that resistant bacteria can arise is a process called a plasmid transfer. In this process, a bacterium inserts a "tube" into another bacterium and gives it a part of its DNA. If the genes that are transferred contain information about resistance to an antibiotic, the second bacterium will also be unaffected by that drug. **However, this is merely an exchange of existing information, not the creation of new information.**

A third reason that resistant bacteria can develop is through mutation. However, these mutations appear to be the result of a **loss, not an addition of information.**
Dr. Carl Wieland describes this process clearly.

> There are sophisticated chemical pumps in bacteria which can actively pump nutrients from the outside through the cell wall into the germ's interior. Those germs which do this efficiently, when in the presence of one of these antibiotics, will therefore efficiently pump into themselves their own executioner. However, what if one of these bacteria inherits a defective gene, by way of a DNA copying mistake (mutation), which will interfere with the efficiency of this chemical pumping mechanism? Although this bacterium will not be as good at surviving in normal circumstances, this defect actually gives it a survival advantage in the presence of the man-made poison.*

Thus, although the resistance was achieved through a mutation, it did not come about as a result of the addition of information. Germs that appear to be extremely powerful because of their resistance to several antibiotics are often quite weak when they are forced to compete with average bacteria.+ They generally survive only in "artificial" environments such as hospitals, where antibiotics and disinfectants destroy most of the regular bacteria.

- *Carl Wieland, "Superbugs: Not Super After All," *Creation Ex Nihilo, Volume 20, December 1997–February 1998, p. 12.*
- +Roland F. Hirsch, *Impact of Forty Years of Advances in Chemistry on Evolutionary Theory,* Lecture given at American Chemical Society's national meeting Sept. 8, 2003, New York City

COMPARISON OF
EVOLUTIONIST AND CREATIONIST POSITIONS

EVOLUTIONISTS

Evolutionary textbooks have drawings of the embryos of various species which look very much alike. They point to this as proof of a common ancestor.

Evolutionists point out that certain body parts, such as the front legs of various vertebrates and the arms of man, have the same pattern of bones. They call these homologous structures and say this similarity is proof of evolution.

Evolutionists point to cytochrome C, a protein involved in the production of energy in both plant and animal cells. They say that because the cytochrome C of humans and monkeys is closer than that of humans and turtles, this indicates a closer evolutionary relationship between humans and monkeys.

CREATIONISTS

A. In actuality, the embryos of various species do not look alike. The drawings were originally made by Ernst Haeckel and were falsified to provide proof for evolution. Later textbook writers simply copied these drawings without checking their authenticity.

B. Corresponding parts of the embryos of different organisms often develop into different parts of their adults.

A. Creationists point out that the arms and legs of man, as well as the front and back legs of these vertebrates, have the same basic patterns. Yet the front legs (or man's arms) and the hind legs are supposed to have evolved from the pectoral and pelvic fins of fish. How could two different types of fins evolve by chance into structures with the same pattern of bones?

B. Creationists also point out that structures which are considered homologous in adults of various species often develop from different parts of their embryos.

C. Creationists add that homologous structures are often not controlled by homologous genes. Pleiotrophy is also a strong argument against homology, since non-homologous genes are involved in the expression of homologous structures.

A. Creationists point out that a comparison of cytochrome C shows that the species fall into the same groupings as they do when using Linnaeus' methods.

B. Creationists also point out that if all organisms evolved from a first cell, then the percentage of difference in the cytochrome C of bacteria and that of more "primitive" organisms should be smaller than that of more "advanced" species. Yet the percentage of difference is almost the same between bacteria and yeast as it is between bacteria and humans.

C. Creationists add that DNA is a code or language. Language is a result of intelligent action. Genetic stability is also a problem for evolutionists, since evolution requires genetic change on a grand scale.

69

CHAPTER 6

WHAT DOES THE FOSSIL RECORD REALLY SAY?

INTRODUCTION

It is obvious the possibility of the spontaneous generation of the first cell is extremely remote. However, is it possible that all the organisms we have today still evolved from a created cell? In other words, could both evolution and devolution still have occurred? Evolutionists believe that both did happen. However, creationists assert that while devolution does occur, evolution does not. They further contend that devolution is not true evolution, since it simply involves the reshuffling of existing genes and the **loss of genetic information** through genetic drift. In trying to prove that both devolution and evolution do occur, evolutionists often refer to both the geologic time scale and the fossil record. They use the geologic time scale as proof that the Earth is old enough for evolution to have occurred, and they state that the fossil record provides proof that evolution did occur. These are points that creationists debate.

SECTION 1: THE CREATION AND STRUCTURE OF THE GEOLOGIC TIME SCALE

Vocabulary words to know: correlating rocks, and principle of uniformity

As was mentioned in Chapter 1, the geologic column or geologic time scale was first created in the late eighteenth and nineteenth centuries by several geologists. But how does it work, and how is it used for dating? The easiest and clearest way to explain this is to give an example. (Refer to Figure 6-1 as you read this explanation.) Suppose a geologist sees a hill that has several layers of rock exposed. He might see a layer of light beige sandstone at the top. Beneath the sandstone might be a layer of shale, followed by layers of conglomerate and then limestone. On the bottom could be a layer of dolomite. In another area, on a hillside which has been cut away for construction, he might find most of these same layers in the same order. However, there could be other strata either on top or beneath these layers. In yet a third area, another hill or canyon might have some of the same layers with the same fossils and still other rock strata above or beneath them. By examining the types of rocks and the fossils within them in these locations, scientists can determine with relative accuracy which rocks were laid down at the same time and the order in which they were laid down.

71

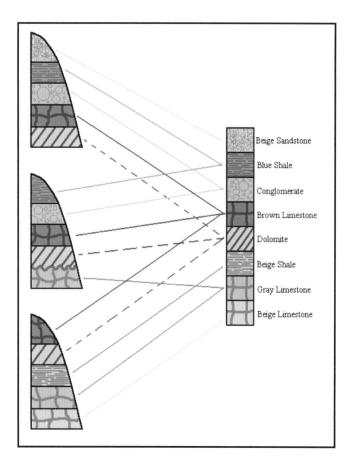

Beige Sandstone

Blue Shale

Conglomerate

Brown Limestone

Dolomite

Beige Shale

Gray Limestone

Beige Limestone

Figure 6-1 *To create a geologic column for an area, a geologist examines exposed sedimentary rock layers in various locations. By noting the sequence of the layers he can make a good estimation of the order in which they were deposited. Geologists also use core samples to determine the nature and sequence of unexposed sedimentary rock formations. Drawing by A. Margetic.*

When scientists examine rock strata in different locations and determine through the character of the rocks and the fossils that they hold that they are of the same age, this is referred to as **correlating the rocks**. During the past century, geologists, particularly Charles Lyell, have taken local geologic columns from around the world and correlated them to form one large column. The **principle of superposition** states that in an undisturbed rock layer, the oldest rocks will be on the bottom and the youngest rocks will be on the top. Therefore, it is generally easy to tell which rock layers are older and which are younger in a given formation. The problem comes when scientists attempt to give a more **exact age** of a particular rock layer or fossil. In order to do this, there has to be some way to determine accurately the age of either the rock or the age of the fossils within the rock. For example, if the age of a rock can be accurately assessed, then it is logical to assume that the fossils within the rock are of the same age.

Many scientists believe they have determined the ages of much sedimentary rock to be very old, using the **principle of uniformity**. This principle states that "the present is the key to the past." In other words, the processes that are at work today are also the processes that were at work in the past and **they work at the same rate of speed**. Therefore, if it would take several thousand or even a million years to lay down rock strata at the slow rate it takes under *normal conditions* today, it would also have taken that amount of time in the past. However, this principle fails to take into account the rapid sedimentation rate that occurs during catastrophic events. For example, during the 1993 floods in the Midwest, deposits as thick as 4 meters were observed on the floodplain downstream from Hermann, Mississippi. These deposits were made in **three months**[1] during a local flood. Without knowledge of how this sediment was laid down, a geologist in the future, when looking at the sedimentary rock that could be produced by this flood, might assume it took thousands of years of time to be laid down. Similarly, when Mt. St. Helen erupted in 1980, geologists studying the event witnessed several mudflows. These mudflows deposited 150 feet of sediment in some areas in a matter of days. Therefore, creationists point out it is unreasonable to assume that it always took long periods of time to produce thick deposits in the past, when this is not the case today.

However, once the principle of uniformity had been used to establish an old age for sedimentary rock formations, scientists began to look at the fossils within the rocks. If a particular rock layer, because of its depth within a formation, was believed to be perhaps 100 million years old, then the fossils within that formation were considered to be 100 million years old also. Gradually, some fossils came to be connected with rocks of a certain age and thus became known as **index fossils**. In order to be classified as an index fossil, a particular fossil

Figure 6-2 *The Mississippi Valley flood of 1993.* Photo courtesy of U.S. Geological Survey.

species must be found in rock strata in a number of areas. It is particularly helpful if it is found on several continents. However, these fossils must also be distributed only in a few rock layers. To the evolutionary geologist, this means that the species existed during a geologically short period of time. (This "short" period of time might be a few million years.) Therefore, the rocks containing these fossils are believed to have been laid down during that "short" period, and a date is thus assigned to them based on the presence of these fossils. For example, certain trilobites are considered index fossils for Cambrian rock. When these trilobites are found, scientists generally classify the rock layer in which they are discovered as Cambrian rock. **Thus, scientists use the rocks to date the fossils, and they use the fossils to date the rocks!** Creationists point out that this is **circular reasoning** and it is very unreliable. In view of the fact that they don't know the age of either the rocks or the fossils to begin with, it seems

highly unlikely that they know the ages of **any** rocks or of the fossils they connect with them.

What is more, creation scientists have managed to show that rock strata such as coal, because of its organic origins, can be dated using Carbon 14 dating and shown to be much younger than the age given to it by the geologic time scale. For example, in the Newvale No. 2 Coal Mine, north of Sydney, Australia, workers found a partially fossilized tree stump sitting directly on top of a coal seam. Both the coal seam and the mudstone in which the fossil was found had previously been dated, using the geologic time scale, to be Upper Permian strata, about 250 million years old. Samples were sent to an internationally recognized laboratory with the most sophisticated equipment. Particular care was taken to insure that no contamination occurred. Although there should have been no carbon 14 left in such an old tree stump, the laboratory results showed that there indeed was carbon 14 remaining in the stump. **It was dated to be approximately 33,700+/-400 years old!**[2] This date was well within the acceptable dating limits for Carbon 14 dating.

This discrepancy between the results of carbon 14 and geologic column dating is not uncommon. Coal and natural gas have both been dated, using carbon 14, to be thousands rather than millions of years old.[3] Thus, creationists point out that one of the evolutionists' own methods disproves the other.

It is also a fact that the geologic column is not found in its fullest expression anywhere in the world. If it were, the layers would be impossibly thick. Rather, the column is put together piecemeal from locations all over the globe. This makes it difficult to determine with certainty the exact order of the rocks. In spite of these problems, geologic column dating is still commonly used by the world's major museums of natural history.

QUESTIONS FOR REVIEW

1. How is a geologic column for an area put together?
2. What method did scientists use for determining an age for most sedimentary rock strata?
3. What is wrong with using the principle of uniformity to determine the ages of rocks?
4. What is wrong with the method of reasoning described in the text?
5. Describe one discrepancy creation scientists have discovered?

Like Raymond Dart, Dr. Henry M. Morris was raised in a Christian home. He became a theistic evolutionist when he studied evolution at college. He received his bachelor's degree "with distinction" from Rice University in 1939 and went on to receive his Master's degree from the University of Minnesota in 1948. Two years later he received a doctorate with a major in hydraulics and minors in geology and mathematics. However, after college, Dr. Morris became involved in a strong church and began studying the Bible more carefully. He went back to teach at Rice University, still undecided about evolution. In order to solve this problem once and for all, Dr. Morris decided to make an intensive study of both the Bible and evolution. He came to realize two important facts. First of all, the theory of evolution and the Bible could not be reconciled. Equally important, Dr. Morris discovered that evolution had virtually no scientific proof for its support.

Since that time Dr. Morris has served as instructor, professor, or department head at several universities, including Southern Illinois University and the Virginia Polytechnic Institute. He has also served as college president of Christian Heritage College from 1978–1980. It spite of this busy schedule, Dr. Morris has continued his studies into the scientific facts about origins. He included his first defense of creationism in a book he wrote during World War II. He was one of the founders of the Institute for Creation Research and served as its president from 1970 to 1995. He is married and has six children, as well as several grandchildren.

SECTION 2: THE FOSSIL RECORD

Vocabulary words to know: link fossil, transitional form

When looking at a typical geologic column in a museum or in a textbook, it appears that there is a gradual progression of organisms from simple to complex, as one moves from bottom to top. If evolution is true, then this kind of gradual progression would be very reasonable and is to be expected. After all, the bottom layers are logically the oldest, and the rock should be progressively younger as one moves to the top. However, creationists point out this is **not the true structure of the fossil** record. What does the fossil record really demonstrate?

1. **The Cambrian Explosion**: Instead of beginning with a few simple creatures and gradually progressing to more complex organisms, there is a sudden "explosion" of fossils in rocks dated to be very old. **In fact, representatives of 95% of all the phyla found in the fossil record show up suddenly in this Cambrian rock**, while the Precambrian rock immediately beneath is virtually empty of all evidence of multicellular life. This is a fact that has not been widely published

until recently, when *Time Magazine* in its December 4, 1995 issue devoted a long article to the problem.[4] The few fossils found in Precambrian rock have been easily assigned either to existing phyla or to phyla completely different from any present ones. As James Valentine, of the University of California, states, none of them "can yet be considered as ancestral to any specific living phylum."[5]

2. **Stasis**: After over one hundred and fifty years of collection and study of fossils, scientists admit **that the species we find in the fossil record are essentially the same as today's living representatives.** Clams are clams, fish are fish, and deciduous trees are deciduous trees. This state of equilibrium with very little change is called **stasis**. However, there is one important difference. With the exception of clams and snails, there is a much greater variety of invertebrates in the fossil record than are alive today, and many of these extinct creatures are much more complex in structure.[6] Also, many of the animals still in

existence today, such as beavers and wolves, are represented by larger, more robust varieties in the fossil record. **More than anything else, the fossil record demonstrates a sudden "explosion" of highly complex forms (many of which have become extinct) followed by stasis.**

3. **Missing Links:** If Darwinian evolution is true, there should be millions of link fossils, which represent the intermediate stages between the species we have today. If, indeed, amphibians evolved from fish and birds evolved from reptiles, there should be thousands of transition fossils that demonstrate the stages of evolution between the fish and the amphibian or the reptile and the bird. This should also be true for all the other species on planet Earth. Charles Darwin realized this when he wrote his book, *Origin of Species*. He knew if his theory were true, "the number of intermediate varieties which have formerly existed [on the Earth] must be truly enormous."[7] He recognized that the absence of link fossils in the fossil record was "the most obvious and serious objection" to his theory.[8] Darwin had not seen many fossils that he considered transitional. He assumed

this was because most of them had been destroyed and because the geologic record had not yet been searched extensively. After all, his book was written in the mid-nineteenth century when the world had not yet been thoroughly explored. Today, this is no longer the case. After extensive exploration and study of the fossil record, **scientists have found very few fossils that they consider intermediate, and none of these are uncontested.**

The problem of the "missing links" has become so acute that paleontologists Stephen J. Gould and Niles Eldredge were forced to postulate an alternative theory called "punctuated equilibrium." It is Dr. Gould and Dr. Eldredge's theory that species remain in stasis for long periods of time until some event triggers rapid evolution, perhaps in small populations. This rapid evolution does not allow for intermediate species to be trapped and preserved in the fossil record.[9] However, there is little or no evidence to support this theory. It is simply a way to explain the absence of transitional forms in the fossil record. Thus, creationists feel that to one who knows the facts, the fossil record provides evidence for intelligent design.

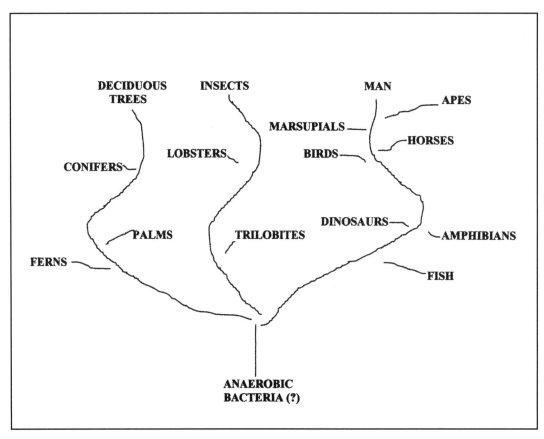

Figure 6-3 *A sample evolutionary "tree" demonstrating descent from a common ancestor. This is meant to be an example only and is by no means a definitive explanation of the evolution of all life as evolutionists believe it to have occurred. NOTE: There are gaps where the "branches" do not meet the "limbs." This is because link fossils are missing.*

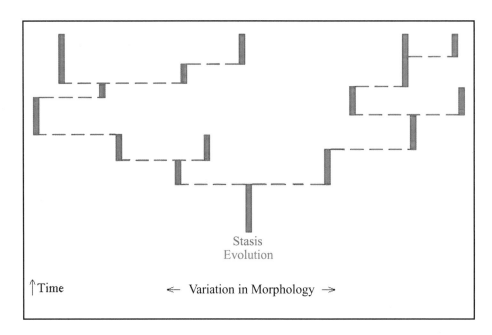

Figure 6-4 *Evolutionary tree illustration according to theory of Punctuated Equilibrium, which states that organisms go through long periods of stasis followed by rapid periods of evolution. Drawing by A. Margetic.*

QUESTIONS FOR REVIEW:

1. Describe the three main characteristics of the fossil record. Give details.
2. Describe punctuated equilibrium. Why is it a poor substitute for Darwinian evolution?

SECTION 3: A MISTAKEN LINK

Vocabulary words to know: extinct, archaeopteryx, and coelacanth

It has already been mentioned that evolutionists can find very few fossils that they classify as link fossils, but what about those that they do consider to be transitional forms? Why are they contested? One reason is that often fossils that are at first thought to be transitional are later found to be something else entirely. One good example of this is the **coelacanth**. The coelacanth was believed to be a transitional form between the fish and the amphibians because of a bone structure that was slightly different from present-day fish. Since scientists had no soft parts to study, it was hard to determine the nature of the fossil, but they still categorized it as a transitional form and believed it to be **extinct**. (That is, they believed there were no longer any living examples of the species, since no coelacanth fossils were found in rocks "dated" under seventy million years old.) However, in 1938 a fisherman caught two living coelacanths off the eastern coast of South Africa and brought them to a scientist to examine. Because the scientist had the soft parts, it was easy to determine that the coelacanth was merely a fish and not a transitional form at all. As Michael Denton states so clearly in his book, *Evolution: a Theory in Crisis,* "If the case of the coelacanth illustrates anything, it shows how difficult it is to draw conclusions about the overall biology of organisms from their skeletal remains alone. Because the soft biology of extinct groups can never be known with any certainty, then obviously the status of even the most convincing intermediates is bound to be insecure."[10]

In spite of the danger of making too many assumptions based on bones only, the practice of assigning "link fossil status" to various fossil bones continues today. In fact, these assumptions often are based on two or three bones rather than a complete skeleton. For example, one of the supposed ancestors of the whale, *Pakicetus,* is based on only a few jaw and skull fragments. Creationists assert it takes a large leap of the imagination to produce a whale's ancestor from this small amount of information. This practice is especially common in the study of ancient man, where most of the specimens are based on skull and teeth fragments only.

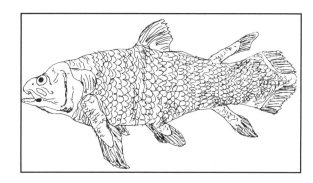

Figure 6-5 *The coelacanth was thought to have been extinct for almost one hundred million years. Then a fisherman caught two living coelacanths off the coast of Madagascar. Their soft anatomy revealed them to be fish rather than ancestors of the Amphibia. Drawing by A. Margetic.*

SECTION 4: SOME CURRENTLY CONTESTED LINK FOSSILS

Archaeopteryx

In discussions of link fossils, **Archaeopteryx** often is mentioned. *Archaeopteryx* is believed by some scientists to be a transitional form between reptiles and birds. There are at least five specimens that are considered to be *Archaeopteryx* fossils. The specimen in the Berlin Museum is fairly complete with a well-preserved head, and many plaster casts of this fossil have been made and are present in several museums around the world. But is it truly a transitional form? This is open to debate. It is true that the specimen possesses some characteristics that may be considered reptilian. For example, it has claws on its wings. However, so do modern baby ostriches and a bird called a hoatzin, which lives in northern South America.

Archaeopteryx also has a flat breastbone, but many birds also possess this trait. Finally, it has teeth. Chickens also possess the gene for teeth. Although it is suppressed in modern chickens, if it were "turned on," it would allow them to develop teeth. Some extinct birds also had teeth. Creationists contend that some modern birds possess each of these traits, **and they are still birds**. This holds true for other birds found in the fossil record which have teeth and yet are still considered birds.[11] These differences can be considered as simply an example of variety within the **class** (used here as a taxonomic term). As Davis and Kenyon point out in their book, *Of Pandas and People,* "The fact that it [*Archaeopteryx*] possessed reptilian features not found in most other birds does not require a relationship between birds

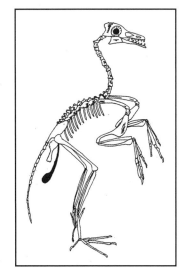

and reptiles, anymore than the duck-billed platypus, a mammal, must be related to a duck."[12]

There are other important reasons why creationists and some evolutionists consider *Archaeopteryx* to

Figure 6-6A *A skeletal outline of **archaeopteryx**. Some evolutionists believe it lived approximately 140 million years ago. It has the basic structure of a bird, including wings and features. However, it also has some features which can be considered reptilian. These include claws on the wings, teeth, and a flat breastbone. Because of this "mixture" of characteristics, some scientists consider archaeopteryx to be a link fossil between reptiles and birds. However, there is also another explanation. Drawing by A. Margetic.*

be simply a bird. First of all, scientists have made a cast of the skull cavity which reveals the basic shape and outline of the brain. Based on evidence from a study of this cast, its brain appears to be essentially that of a bird.[13] Secondly, the structure of the feathers and the wing are basically modern in nature and indicate that *Archaeopteryx* was capable of powered flight.[14] Finally, in 1986 well-known paleontologist, Sankar Chatterjee, found what he believes to be the skeleton of a modern bird. He discovered it **in a rock layer that appears to be older than the layer in which *Archaeopteryx* was found**. [15] Naturally, there arose a great debate over the authenticity of this bird, *Protoavis*, because it challenged the well-accepted theory of bird evolution. The problem is that as in the case of *Archaeopteryx*, without the soft parts, it is very difficult to determine the exact nature of the organism being studied. In any case, for many reasons, *Archaeopteryx* does not stand unquestioned as a link fossil between reptiles and birds.

Figure 6-6B *An artist's depiction of Archae-opteryx, based on its skeletal structure. Drawing by A. St. Arno, based on art of Steve Cardno, Answers In Genesis.*

Figure 6-7 *Hoatzin (South American Bird)*
Photo provider: Jupiter Images.

QUESTIONS FOR REVIEW

1. What did some scientists believe the coelacanth to be? What happened to change their minds?
2. What do some scientists consider *archaeopteryx* to be?
3. Why is *archaeopteryx* considered a link fossil?
4. Why is *archaeopteryx* not considered to be a link fossil by others?

The Horse Series

The horse series also presents some problems to creationists and to some evolutionists. Again, there are no soft parts to compare, and based on bone structure alone, the fossil of the earliest ancestor, *Hyracotherium* ('Eohippus') looks suspiciously like a hyrax, a small, rabbit-like mammal that lives in Africa today. (See Fig. 2-10, P. 34.) Then, too, members of this fossil series have never been found together in one rock formation anywhere in the world. In fact, the specimens have actually been found **out of the proper order**.[16] Another problem is the fact that many of the animals were constructed from fossil skeletons which were very incomplete. Obviously, there are many inconsistencies. However, if *Hyracotherium* ('Eohippus') were not included, many

scientists wonder if the "evolution" of the horse is nothing more than variety within kind, with changes due to a loss of genetic information.[17] After all, there is a wide variety of types among living horses. The ribs of different breeds vary from 17 to 19. Their sizes range from sixteen inches high (the Fallabella) to eighty inches (the English Shire horse). Then, too, genes can be turned "on" or "off" by other, regulatory genes. Dr. Jonathon Sarfati explains that these genes "control whether or not the information in a gene will be decoded, so the trait will be expressed in the creature."[18] Thus, traits such as extra toes could be controlled by such genes and "switched off" in modern horses. Whatever the position taken on the horse series, it is difficult to think of it as an example of evolution.

Figure 6-8 *Horses come in all sizes.* Photo courtesy of Answers in Genesis.

Whale Evolution

Whale evolution also demonstrates some problems for creationists. Evolutionists believe that whales evolved from an ancient land mammal. However, because of the enormous difference between the anatomies of whales and those of terrestrial mammals, there would have had to have been innumerable transitional species. There should be ample evidence of their existence in the fossil record, yet this is not the case. Creationists point out that even the few that have been suggested as link fossils show very little evidence to support such a claim. For example, many evolutionists believe that the whales evolved from a group of ancient meat eaters called *Mesonychids*. The *Mesonychids* are believed to have returned to the water because of a greater supply of food and because of protection from predators. Gradually they evolved and adapted into the "monsters" of the deep we recognize as whales today.

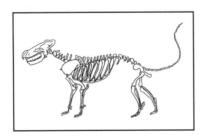

Figure 6-9A *A skeletal outline of a mesonychid. Sizes of these creatures varied. Drawing by A. Margetic.*

Figure 6-9B *An artist's depiction of a mesonychid, based on its skeletal structure. Drawing by A. St. Arno.*

Scientists who accept this theory often cite *Pakicetus* as a transitional form. *Pakicetus* is a fossil that was found in Pakistan in the late 1980's. It is believed to be the remains of a "walking whale." In fact, in *The Journal of Geological Education* (Volume 31, 1983), a representative drawing is given of *Pakicetus*, which is supposed to be correct according to the fossil bones. It shows an animal with feet, swimming after fish in the water. Yet **this theory and drawing were based solely on a few jaw and skull fragments!** The University of Michigan's Museum of Natural History has a drawing of a *Pakicetus* skull that looks remarkably like that of a modern whale. The display includes drawings of the few small bones that were found of *Pakicetus*. However, the rest of the picture is made up of the drawings of whalebones. Is it any wonder that the head looks like a whale's skull?

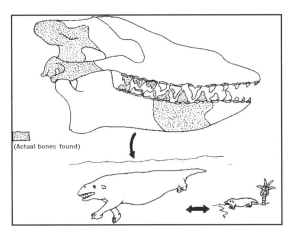

Figure 6-10 *The upper drawing is of the skull of Pakicetus. NOTE: The shaded parts are the only ones actually found. Based on these parts, an evolutionist's drawing similar to the lower one was created and published. Drawing by A. Margetic.*

Ambulocetus is also described as a "walking whale." One writer states that *Ambulocetus'* relationship to other whales is "uncertain," but reaffirms that the specimen is a whale "using a definition based on ancestry."[19] In other words, *Ambulocetus* is assumed to have an ancestor in common with the whales, and based on this assumption, it is defined as a whale. Figure 6-11A shows the fragmentary nature of the fossil. The "evidence" for *Basilosaurus*

is equally meager. The specimen does appear to have hind limbs, but these are very tiny. What is more, there is no connection between these hind limbs and the rest of the skeleton. There is no spot for these bones to attach, so they could not be used for walking. Most evolutionists feel they were probably used for grasping during reproduction.

In order for a marine creature to develop from a land mammal, hundreds of thousands of changes would have had to be made. For a *Mesonychid* or any land carnivore to evolve into a whale, it would have had to lose its fur, its flexible backbone, and its tail. Its nostrils would have had to move to the top of the head from the end of its snout. Its front legs would have had to change into flippers, and its back legs would have had to disappear. The carnivore's external ears would have had to become internal for the shape to become streamlined.[20] And that's only the beginning. Think about the breathing, skin and hearing changes, as well as the birthing and feeding of babies underwater. Think about the development of echolocation, that special "sonar" which whales use to find things underwater! None of these theorists discuss or appear to take into account these changes that would have to be made in transforming four-legged, carnivorous, wolf-like mammals into marine creatures. Nor do they discuss the absence of the **thousands** of link fossils which should document this transition in the fossil record.

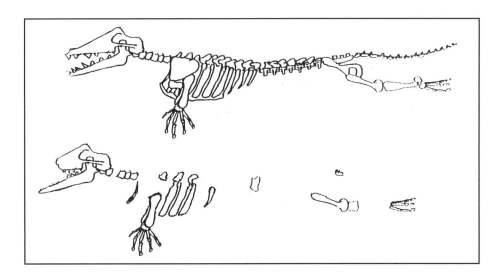

Figure 6-11A: *Ambulocetus. The upper figure is generally what is found in books. The lower figure shows the actual bones which were found. Drawing by A. Margetic.*

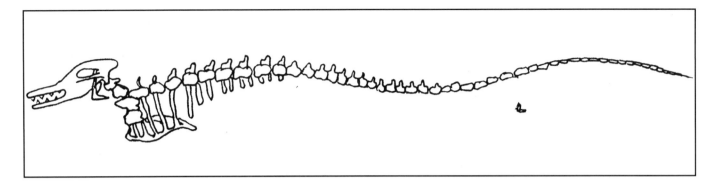

Figure 6-11B *Basilosaurus—not drawn to scale. Basilosaurus is much larger than ambulocetus. NOTE: There are no bones connecting the hind limbs to the body. Drawing by A. Margetic.*

QUESTIONS FOR REVIEW

1. In the horse series, what does "Eohippus" resemble?
2. What is one problem with the position of the horse fossils in the fossil record?
3. If eohippus is excluded from the series, what do some scientists believe the horse series to be?
4. Briefly describe the *Mesonychids, Pakicetus, Basilosaurus* and *Ambulocetus* and tell why they are questionable as an ancestor of the whales.

SECTION 5: WHAT DOES ALL THIS MEAN?

The geologic time scale is a useful way of studying and correlating rock strata. The fossils which these rock layers contain provide fascinating information about the past. Yet, do they really demonstrate irrefutable evidence for an ancient Earth and evolution? Creationists assert that without the use of the principle of uniformity, it is impossible to attempt to assign ages to the various strata. It is also obvious that the principle of uniformity does not take into account that rock strata can be laid down relatively rapidly. Therefore, its validity as a means of determining age is questionable.

Taken at face value, the fossil record is a marvelous storehouse of circumstantial evidence concerning the past. It contains the remains of thousands of other organisms that are extinct. On the other hand, because of a **preconceived belief system**, it is possible to **read too much into** the fossil record. Just as we would find it difficult to convict a man of murder solely on the basis of his owning a gun, it is equally difficult to believe that a fossil is a transition form, when the "evidence" consists of only a few fragments. As Colin Patterson, director of the British Museum, once stated, "Fossils may tell us many things, but one thing they can never disclose is whether they were the ancestors of anything else."[21]

In addition, there is a sudden appearance of highly complex organisms in the strata of the geologic column, and these organisms **remain basically the same** throughout geologic history to the present day. There is a notable absence of the millions of link fossils, which should be present in the fossil record, if evolution were true. **These are scientific facts**. They are facts which give the creationist good reason for questioning whether evolution has occurred. Darwin understood this problem over one hundred years ago. He pointed out that geologic research, "does not yield the infinitely many fine gradations between past and present species required on the theory; and this is the most obvious of many objections which may be urged against it."[22] After a hundred and fifty years, this still appears to be the case.

QUESTIONS FOR REVIEW

1. What does the fossil record really show? Describe **three** things.
2. What is the main problem with geologic time scale dating?

A COMPARISON OF EVOLUTIONIST AND CREATIONIST VIEWS

EVOLUTIONISTS

Evolutionists originally used the principle of uniformity to determine an old age for the geologic column.

Evolutionists then determined the age of certain fossils, called index fossils, by the age they had given the rocks in which they were found. They now use index fossils as the primary means of dating rocks and other fossils.

Evolutionists believe that all life evolved gradually from a protocell over millions of years of time. The typical geologic column shows simple species at the bottom and species getting more advanced as one moves from the bottom to the top.

Darwinism requires that there be millions of intermediate forms between the various species.

Stephen J. Gould and Niles Eldredge formulated a different theory of evolution called punctuated equilibrium. This states that species remain in a state of stasis for long periods of time, only to evolve rapidly, then settle back into another long period of stasis.

For many years evolutionists believed the coelacanth to be extinct and also to be a link fossil between fish and amphibians.

CREATIONISTS

Creationists point out that the principle of uniformity is fallible because it fails to take into account catastrophic processes which cause rapid deposition of sediments.

A. Creationists point out that using the rocks to date the fossils and then using the fossils to date the rocks is an example of circular reasoning. It is necessary to have an exact age for either the rocks or the fossils before one can determine the other.

B. They add that a partially fossilized tree trunk found in a coal bed dated by the geologic time scale to be 250 million years old was tested using radiocarbon dating and found to have Carbon-14. In fact, it was dated at approximately 33,700 years old.

Creationists point out that the fossil record actually shows a sudden explosion of complex forms in very old rock. This is followed by stasis, which is the opposite of evolution.

Creationists point out that scientists have found very few fossils which they consider intermediate, and none of these are uncontested. In other words, the missing links are still missing.

Creationists point out that there is absolutely no proof that this actually occurred. They feel it is simply a way to explain the lack of link fossils.

Creationists point out that when two coelacanths were found alive, it was discovered merely to be a fish.

Evolutionists often cite Archaeopteryx as a link fossil between reptiles and birds. They point to its claws, teeth, and flat breastbone as reptilian features, while the creature also has feathers and other bird features.

Creationists point out that baby ostriches have claws on their wings. Chickens have teeth genes; fossil birds have teeth. Also, many modern birds have flat breastbones.

Evolutionists often point to the horse series as an example of evolution.

Creationists counter that nowhere do we find the members of this "fossil series" together in the proper order. In fact different specimens have been found in the wrong order. They also point out that if Hyracotherium (which looks suspiciously like a hyrax) is left out, the others might be a good example of devolution only.

Evolutionists cite a number of fossils as links in the evolution of the whale. These are the Mesonychids, Pakicetus, Ambulocetus, and Basilosaurus.

A. Creationists point to the lack of soft parts as a continuing problem.
B. Creationists point out that literally thousands of changes would have to occur to transform a meat-eating terrestrial animal into an aquatic mammal.
C. The fossil Pakicetus consists of a few head and jaw fragments. Creationists doubt this is enough information to consider it a "walking whale."
D. Ambulocetus is also known as a "walking whale." Although there is more of this skeleton, there is very little evidence to support this description.
E. Basilosaurus has hind legs that are attached to its skeleton by muscles only. They appear to be used for grasping during reproduction. This creature did not use its hind legs to walk.

CHAPTER 7
RADIOMETRIC DATING

Vocabulary words to know: intrusion, half-life, stable element, unstable element, isotope, radioactive, parent element, daughter element, assumption, and leaching

SECTION 1: HOW DOES RADIOMETRIC DATING WORK?

Lord Ernest Rutherford, a British physicist, attempted the first long-range method called uranium-helium dating in 1904. However, it soon became apparent that this method was inaccurate. Then, in 1905, a young chemist named Boltwood developed a method of dating using radium-lead ratios. At first radiometric dating was largely ignored by many geologists. However, a scientist named Arthur Holmes became convinced it had promise. He continued to work on the dating method. As the twentieth century progressed and a greater understanding of radioactivity was developed, radiometric dating gradually became acceptable.

Today, although evolutionary scientists use the geologic column to date rocks and fossils, they also employ radiometric dating as a means of verification. Scientists are at a disadvantage in doing this for several reasons. First of all, fossils are found primarily in sedimentary rock, while radiometric dating is performed primarily on igneous rock. Therefore, it is impossible to date a fossil radiometrically unless there is an igneous rock intrusion or a volcanic ash layer within the sedimentary rock layers. An **intrusion** occurs when magma forces its way up through a crack in sedimentary rock and then hardens. If such an intrusion exists in sedimentary rock, scientists attempt to date the intrusion radiometrically. Once they have the age of the intrusion, they assume the sedimentary rock which contains it to be older. Figure 7-1 illustrates an igneous rock intrusion.

If radiometric dating can be used to verify the ages developed through geologic column dating, then why is there a problem? The problem lies with

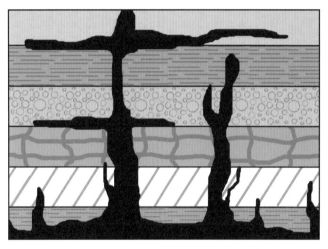

Figure 7-1 *This diagram shows several black igneous rock intrusions extending upward through sedimentary rock layers. Drawing by A. Margetic.*

radiometric dating methods themselves. However, before the difficulties can be discussed, it is necessary to explain how radiometric dating works.

There are over one hundred known elements. Most of these elements are **stable**. That is, they remain the same element throughout their existence. They do not spontaneously decay into other elements. Generally, elements that have low atomic numbers and about the same number of protons and neutrons are stable. However, there are also several elements that are **unstable** and do decay into other elements. Elements are usually unstable for one of three reasons:

- They have more neutrons than protons. (This is most common.)
- Their nuclei are too large for stability.

87

- They have an excess of protons.

Whatever the cause of the instability, unstable atoms eventually break down into other, more stable elements. Elements that undergo this change are called **radioactive**. These elements may change into several different isotopes during their transformation. In a decay series, the radioactive element is often called the **parent element** while the stable element into which it decays is referred to as the **daughter or decay element**. Figure 7-2 demonstrates the decay of uranium-238 into lead-206. In addition, relatively stable elements can have at least one **isotope*** that is radioactive. For example, hydrogen has a radioactive isotope called tritium.

---

*Isotopes are elements that have the same number of protons but different numbers of neutrons.

Scientists have been studying radioactive materials since the end of the last century. They have discovered that during this time each radioactive element has broken down to its daughter product at a fixed rate. This rate is known as its **half-life**. The half-life of an isotope is the time it takes for one half of its atoms to break down into its daughter element. For example, the half-life of barium-131 is 12 days. After 12 days one half of the barium in a given sample will have decayed into a more stable isotope. You might expect that in another 12 days the rest of the barium will break down also, but this is not the case. Instead, **one half** of **what is left** will break down. At the end of the third twelve-day period, another one half of the radioactive material *that is left* will have decayed. Figure 7-3 demonstrates how this occurs.

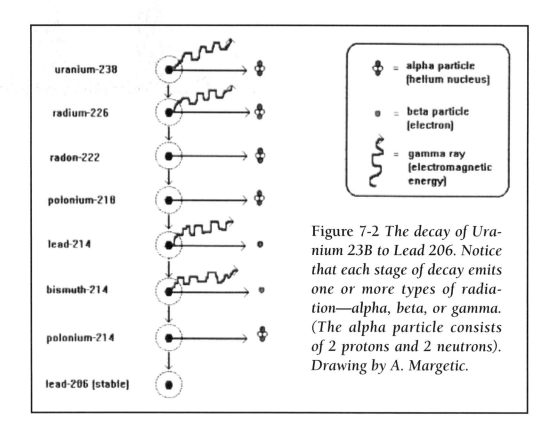

Figure 7-2 *The decay of Uranium 23B to Lead 206. Notice that each stage of decay emits one or more types of radiation—alpha, beta, or gamma. (The alpha particle consists of 2 protons and 2 neutrons). Drawing by A. Margetic.*

If at the beginning of the test there are one billion atoms of barium-131:

In **12** days there will be	50% of the barium-131 left
In **24** days there will be	25% of the barium-131 left
In **36** days there will be	12.5% of the barium-131 left
In **48** days there will be	6.25% of the barium-131 left

Figure 7-3 *The decay of barium-131. Note: during each half-life only one half of the remaining radioactive material decays into daughter element. This decay rate continues until only a few atoms of the radioactive element remain, and then they too change into the daughter element.*

Scientists look on radioactive decay as a clock that has kept track of the time that has passed since the radioactive rock was formed. As time passes, more and more of the parent material decays into the daughter material. Therefore, if a scientist knows the rate of decay, and he measures the ratio of radioactive element to decay element in a rock, he should be able to tell how old the rock is. For example, if a scientist finds a rock that is one half uranium-238 and one half lead-206, and he knows it takes 4.5 billion years for one half-life of uranium, he might assume the rock is 4.5 billion years old.[*]

How is a sample tested? Well, first of all, after a rock sample is selected, perhaps from an igneous rock intrusion, the scientist requesting the test must give his own estimate of its age. This is because the half lives of the various isotopes differ, and radiometric dating specialists state that using a method with the wrong half-life would give erroneous dates. For example, to get his own estimate of the sample's age, a geologist might first estimate the age of the sedimentary rock through which it intrudes, using geologic time scale dating. After using this method to develop an age for the sedimentary rock and knowing that the intrusion must be younger, he would then estimate an age for the igneous rock sample. Next, he sends the sample, along with his estimate to the radiometric dating lab for its opinion. The lab uses his figure to determine which dating method should be most accurate. If, after testing the sample, the lab comes up with a date which is close to the estimate of the scientist, it assigns this date to the sample. If the error margin is too great, the lab says there has been contamination which makes it impossible to date the rock correctly. Labs always state the margin of error for the results of a particular sample. This is called an **error bar**. At first glance, radiometric dating may appear to be foolproof, but it is not. There are several reasons why this is true.

---

[*] This is an oversimplification, since there would be several other isotopes within the rock in addition to the uranium-238 and lead-206.

QUESTION FOR REVIEW

1. Why do unstable elements break down into stable ones?
2. What is an element's half-life?
3. Element X has a half-life of 10 minutes. What percentage of the element will remain after one half hour?
4. Explain how a sample is tested radiometrically.

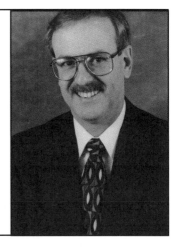

Dr. John Morris, son of Dr. Henry Morris, received his bachelor's degree in civil engineering at Virginia Tech in 1969. He then received his master's degree in geology and his doctorate in geological engineering at the University of Oklahoma. Dr. Morris was on the faculty at the University of Oklahoma before he joined the staff of the Institute for Creation Research in 1984. He now serves as the Institute's president. Dr. Morris has written several books and papers defending and explaining creationism. He is married and has three children.

SECTION 2: THREE ASSUMPTIONS OF RADIOMETRIC DATING

The main reason why radiometric dating has problems is that it rests on three premises or assumptions. Assumptions are ideas that are accepted without proof. The three main assumptions of radiometric dating are:

1. The rate of decay has always been constant.
2. There is no other way that either parent or daughter material has gotten out of the rock.
3. The original composition of the rock is known.

Of the three assumptions, the one which is most reasonable is the first. Scientists have been checking the decay rate for the past few decades and have found it to be stable during that time and, for the most part, difficult to change by experimentation.[1] However, some scientists feel that assuming this rate has been constant and unaffected by any external factors for the past 4.5 billion years (the assumed age of the Earth) is stretching scientific reasoning. We simply don't know.

The second assumption is totally unfounded. It has been proven repeatedly that both parent and daughter elements can be removed from the rock.

For example, ground water can wash or leach parent and/or daughter material out of rock formations. In some cases, daughter material can be added. Naturally, removing some of the radioactive element or adding some of the daughter element will make the rock appear to be older than it actually is. Although scientists attempt to determine whether leaching has occurred in a rock they test, it is virtually impossible to tell for sure if it has happened.

The last assumption is equally flawed. There is no way to know the exact composition of the rock when it was first formed. There was no one there to test and record its content. Also, there is no reason to assume that the rock had no daughter element to begin with. Radioactive rocks are generally mixtures of several elements and compounds, often including both parent and daughter elements. If scientists assume this to be true, they must first determine the amount of daughter element which was present at the beginning, and this is virtually impossible to do. Without first-hand knowledge of the initial composition of the rock, it is impossible to "set the clock" and determine how much time has passed. For these reasons radiometric dating appears to be as unreliable a method of determining the ages of rocks and fossils as geologic column dating is.

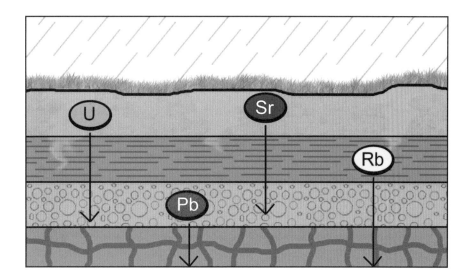

Figure 7-4 *Ground water can leach uranium, lead, rubidium, and strontium out of rock. Drawing by A. Margetic.*

Figure 7-5 *A major problem for scientists is how to set the "radiometric clock." Remember: no one was there when the rock was formed, so how do we know how much of the rock was radioactive in the beginning? Drawing by A. Margetic.*

QUESTION FOR REVIEW

1. State the three assumptions upon which radiometric dating is based, and explain what is wrong with them.

SECTION 3: LONG RANGE DATING METHODS

Uranium—Lead Dating

Vocabulary words to know: uranium-lead dating, potassium-argon dating, rubidium-strontium dating, leaching, isochron dating

In spite of these problems, could there be a radiometric dating method in use that is somewhat more accurate and thus able to give an approximate date? To answer this, it is necessary to explain the basic methods in use today and to give illustrations of their accuracy. One method of radiometric dating is uranium-lead. As a rock ages, increasing amounts of uranium-238 decay into lead-206. At the present rate of decay, scientists have calculated a half-life for ^{238}U of 4.5 billion years. Thus, they realize that they cannot use it on any rock samples which are younger than 10 million years old.[2] The amount of change from uranium to lead in shorter periods of time would be negligible. Obviously, the more lead and the less uranium a rock contains, the older it would appear to be. However, this assumes that there was no lead-206 in the rock to begin with, an assumption for which there is no proof. In addition, it has been repeatedly proven that uranium can be leached out of rock material by ground water. Lead and the intermediate elements can also be removed naturally. *Encyclopedia Americana* states this in explaining the testing of samples of uranium-bearing rock. "The decay of Uranium and thorium to lead yields three dates for each sample. In many cases these dates do not agree because of the varying losses of lead or intermediate daughters from minerals."[3] So, which date is right? If both parent and daughter elements can be removed naturally from the rock, how can a reliable date be found? Although scientists attempt to get test specimens that have not been contaminated, it is virtually impossible to know for sure whether they have or not.

Potassium—Argon Dating

In recent years, other radiometric dating methods have been developed. One of these is potas-sium—argon dating. Scientists using this method check the ratio of potassium-40 to argon-40. First, volcanic ash and rock are collected from the sites to be dated. Scientists attempt to collect rocks that have not been contaminated by lava from earlier or later eruptions. They then take the specimens to a laboratory where they crush the rock sample into mineral powder. The radioactive potassium in the sample is measured, and then the sample is put into an airtight container and heated until it melts, releasing the argon gas it contains. Using a mass spectrometer, the scientists determine the amount of argon in the sample. Then they compare the amount of radioactive potassium to the amount of argon and give the sample a date based on this ratio.[4] Obviously, the more argon and the less potassium the sample contains, the older the rock is believed to be. Potassium-40 has a half-life of 1.25 billion years and is used to date rocks older than 100,000 years.[5] Many authorities believe it cannot be used effectively for ages less than 200,000 to 400,000 years.

Is this method more accurate than uranium-lead dating? Probably not. For example, scientists believe that any original argon gas trapped in the lava is lost as the rock cools down. However, recently a dacite lava dome at Mt. St. Helens was tested. Using the potassium-argon method, the dome was dated to be 350,000 to 500,000 years old even though scientists know it was formed in 1986! Evidently, excess argon from the magma was trapped in the rock.[6] Another problem is that argon in the atmosphere is absorbed by rocks. If daughter material (in this case argon) is added, this also makes the rock appear older. Also, pressure from the upper part of a rock can force argon from its lower sections to rise. Thus, the amount of argon tends to be greater in the surface layers than in lower ones Again, the more argon, the older the rock is believed to be. For these reasons, potassium-argon dating tends to give widely different dates when samples are taken from different parts of the same rock. So, which one, if any, is right? **Scientists tested lava rocks that were formed in 1800 and 1801 in Hualalai, Hawaii. However, the rocks showed an age of 160 million years to three billion years, using the potassium-argon method.**[7] This type of result has occurred in other tests. Obviously, potassium-argon dating is also inaccurate.

Rubidium—Strontium Dating

A third method used today is rubidium-strontium dating. Rubidium, a trace element similar to potassium, is naturally radioactive. Twenty-eight percent of rubidium atoms are the isotope ^{87}Rb which decays into ^{87}Sr, a common, stable isotope of strontium. Rubidium has a half-life of approximately 47 billion years, so it is used to date rocks believed to be older than 10 million years.[8] However, the same problems occur with this method as with the others. Both rubidium and strontium can be leached out of rock by ground water.[9] This obviously will alter the rock's apparent age. Scientists took samples from two basalt rock strata in the Grand Canyon. One was from the deeply buried Cardenas Basalt, and the other was from the Western Grand Canyon lava flows. The Cardenas Basalt is considered to be Precambrian and thus billions of years old. On the other hand, the Western Grand Canyon lava flows lie

Figure 7-6 *Fluid basalt lava flow, Hawaii.*
Photo provider: Jupiter Images.

on top and are considered to be some of the youngest in the Canyon. An independent analytical laboratory tested the samples. **The Cardenas Basalt was given an age of 1.07 billion years (plus or minus .07 billion years). However, the Western Grand Canyon flows were assigned an age of 1.34 billion years (plus or minus .04 billion years). Thus, the obviously younger rock was tested to be 270 million years older, using this method!**[10] It is interesting to note that dates on the younger rock formations were also obtained using both the potassium-argon and the lead-lead dating methods. The potassium-argon method gave dates ranging from 10,000 years to 117 million years ($\pm$ 3 million), while the lead-lead method (an isochron dating method) yielded an age of 2.6 billion years ($\pm$ .21 billion).[11] Obviously, all these dates can't be right, so which one is?

Isochron Dating

Because of the serious problems with these methods, scientists have developed another system of dating called isochron dating. Actually, isochron dating is simply a variation of Rubidium-Strontium or Uranium-Lead dating. However, instead of measuring the ratio of only the initial radioactive and the final, stable elements, scientists also check the amount of intermediate isotopes that are present. For example, Figure 7-2 shows the decay of Uranium-238 into Lead-206. You will see there are several isotopes in between the ^{238}U and the ^{206}Pb. Scientists attempt to measure the ratio of the intermediate isotopes in the samples, as well as the amount of Uranium-238 and Lead-206. Scientists can project the amount of different isotopes that should be present in a sample if all the original material were radioactive and it has been breaking down at a constant rate. If they feel the different isotopes are in the proper ratio, then the scientists consider the data to be valid and assign an age based on them. If the isotopes are not in the proper ratio, scientists assume that contamination has occurred and do not attempt to date the sample. At first glance, this method appears to be much more accurate. Scientists attempt to determine the initial ratio of parent to daughter elements by comparing non-radiogenic isotopes. However, contradictory results are often obtained from the same rock, and scientists tend to choose the one consistent with their preconceptions as valid. The same problems that plague the other radiometric dating methods also influence this one. **For example, it is impossible to determine how much of the different isotopes were already present when the rock was formed. Also, different isotopes of rubidium, strontium, uranium, and lead can be leached out of the rock, affecting the apparent age.**[12] It is difficult to see how isochron dating is an improvement over the original methods.

Radiometric dating specialists deny there is any serious problem with radiometric dating. They state that if the correct method, with the proper half-life, is used, the dates will be reliable. They provide an **error bar** for each test and insist that if the proper method is used, the percentage of error will be small, but if the wrong method is used, the error bar will show a much larger percentage of error. Therefore, the tester will know that something is wrong. However, as mentioned in Chapter Six, when wood from a coal deposit which was dated by geologic time scale dating to be 250 million years old was tested using carbon 14, the lab reported an age of 33,700+/-400 years, well within the acceptable range. In fact, if the wood were older than 80,000 years, there should have been absolutely no ^{14}C present.

Figure 7-7A *Cardenas Lavas in Lava Canyon. Photos courtesy of Dr. John Morris.*

Figure 7-7B *Plateau Basalts at Lava Falls, west end of Grand Canyon.*

QUESTIONS FOR REVIEW

1. Is it possible to determine how much uranium there was in a sample to begin with? **Why or why not?**
2. Is there any other problem that might make uranium-lead dating unreliable? Explain.
3. What **two** problems concerning argon gas in rocks make potassium-argon dating unreliable?
4. What can happen to both rubidium and strontium in a rock which can alter the apparent age?
5. Describe isochron dating.
6. What problems arise with this method?
7. What can happen when different dating methods are used on the same rock formation? Give an example.

SECTION 4: THE MOST COMMON SHORT-RANGE METHOD

Radiocarbon Dating

All of the methods that were discussed above are considered long-range dating methods, generally giving dates in the millions of years, and all are used on rocks. However, radiocarbon dating is used on relatively young artifacts and is useful only up to approximately 50,000 years. Its use is also restricted to once-living things. Radiocarbon dating involves measuring the ratio of carbon-14 to carbon-12 in an organic sample. For many years scientists have recognized that there are two isotopes of carbon present in the atmosphere. ^{12}C is the stable and most common form of carbon. However, high in the Earth's atmosphere cosmic rays bombard nitrogen atoms and change one of their seven protons into a neutron. The resulting element is carbon-14 with six protons and eight neutrons. Since it has an excess of neutrons, ^{14}C is unstable and over time will break down into nitrogen once again. Once carbon-14 is formed in the upper atmosphere, it circulates into the lower atmosphere where it is taken in by plants in the same way that carbon-12 is. Animals and humans then eat the plants, and thus ^{14}C becomes a part of all living things. As long as organisms are alive, they continue to take in carbon-14, and its amount is believed to remain fairly constant in their bodies. However, when living things die, they no longer are taking in carbon-14, and the ^{14}C that is present in their bodies begins to break down. As time passes, the amount of carbon-14 slowly declines. Since its half-life is only 5730 years, very little should remain after about 50,000 years. Thus, it cannot be used for dating older artifacts. (See Figure 7-8.)

In the late 1940's Dr. Willard F. Libby, professor of chemistry at Chicago University, recognized the possibility of using the decay of carbon-14 as a means of dating ancient artifacts. He created a formula which he felt could be used to determine the ages of once living things with a fair degree of accuracy. So unfossilized trees, bones, clothing—in short, any organic sample – could be tested and dated. However, Libby made some serious mistakes. He

assumed the carbon-14 in the atmosphere was built up to a steady state. This means that the amount being created in the upper atmosphere equaled the amount being absorbed by plants. If this was the case, then the amount of carbon-14 available for plants to absorb had been constantly the same for the past 50,000 years. This was very important, for if ^{14}C had been building up in the atmosphere during this period of time, there would have been less in the past for plants to absorb. Thus, radiocarbon dating would give inaccurate results: the test samples would appear to be older than they really were. In actuality, ^{14}C levels have not been constant. Over the past several years carbon-14 has been building up in the atmosphere. Some scientists attribute this buildup to the burning of fossil fuels and nuclear testing and assume it has thus been occurring only in the past one hundred years. However, there is no way to prove this is true. In fact, most scientists also recognize that carbon-14 levels have fluctuated in the past. For example, Dr. Alexander Wilson at the University of Arizona points out, "One of the mysteries during the ice ages is that the carbon dioxide level was a lot lower then than in the interglacials [periods between the ice ages] like now. So carbon must have gone somewhere during the ice age."[13] If carbon dioxide levels were lower, both the ^{12}C and the ^{14}C which made it up would be lower too. If the amount of carbon-14 has not been constant in the past, radiocarbon dating results are not going to be reliable.

Scientists are now trying to correlate radiocarbon testing results with other dating methods such as tree-ring chronology in order to get a greater degree of accuracy, but this method also has its problems. In short, radiocarbon dating results must be taken as very tentative. Many scientists, both creationists and evolutionists, question their validity. As R. E. Lee states in the Anthropological Journal of Canada, "No matter how 'useful' it is, the radiocarbon method is still not capable of yielding accurate and reliable results. There are gross discrepancies, the chronol-

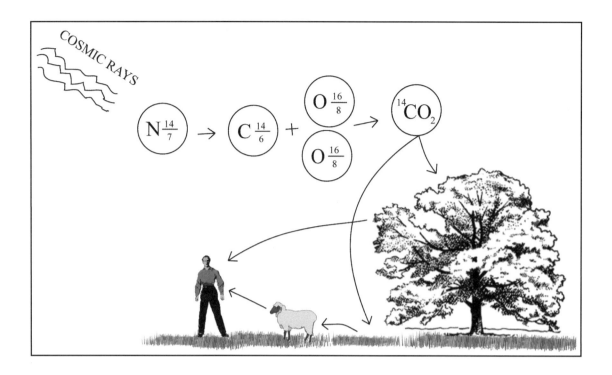

Figure 7-8 *The formation and distribution of Carbon-14. Cosmic rays bombard Nitrogen atoms (N $^{14/7}$) high in the atmosphere, turning a nitrogen proton into a neutron and thus forming carbon-14 ($C^{14/6}$, commonly written as ^{14}C). ^{14}C then combines with 2 atoms of Oxygen ($O^{16/8}$) to form radioactive carbon dioxide ($^{14}CO_2$). The radioactive carbon dioxide is then absorbed by plants on the Earth's surface. The plants are eaten by animals and man. Thus, carbon-14 becomes a part of all living things. Gradually, over time, the carbon-14 will turn back into nitrogen. The half-life for this process is 5,730 years. Drawing composed by Brian Schick.*

ogy is uneven and relative, and the accepted dates are actually selected dates."[14] He also points out, "Despite 35 years of technological refinement and better understanding, the underlying assumptions have been strongly challenged, and warnings are out that radiocarbon [dating] may soon find itself in a crisis situation."[15] Although this statement was made twenty years ago, the problems remain. Carbon-14 dating does not give reliable results.* However, there is one way that carbon-14 dating can be used with a fair amount of reliability. The half-life of carbon-14 is approximately 5730 years. Even if Carbon-14 is still building up in the atmosphere, if the decay rate has remained constant, virtually all the ^{14}C in organic material should have decayed back into nitrogen in about 50,000 years. Both evolutionists and creationists agree that any organic material older than 50,000 years should have no remaining testable ^{14}C. Thus, test results could show if an organic sample is older or younger than 50,000 years. Determining how much younger or older is a far greater problem.

---

*Two other assumptions affect results also:

1) ^{14}C is distributed evenly throughout the atmosphere.
2) Cosmic ray flux has been constant over long periods.

Method	Measures	Problems
Uranium-lead dating	ratio of uranium to lead in rock	Uranium and lead leach out of rock.
Potassium-argon dating	ratio of potassium to argon in rock	1. Argon gets trapped in rock. 2. Rocks absorb argon from air. 3. Much argon comes to the top of rock
Rubidium-strontium dating	ratio of rubidium to strontium in rock	Both rubidium & strontium can be leached from magma & rock.
Isochron dating	ratio of various isotopes in rock	Leaching of isotopes also occurs.
Carbon-14 dating	ratio of carbon-14 to carbon-12 in artifact	1. Amounts of ^{14}C have varied in the past 2. ^{14}C still building up today.

Figure 7-9 *Some of the major forms of radiometric dating, together with the problems associated with them.*

QUESTIONS FOR REVIEW

1. What does radiocarbon dating measure?
2. How is carbon-14 formed?
3. What kinds of materials are tested by radiocarbon dating?
4. What is the half-life of carbon-14 and what is its testing range?
5. What is one problem with ^{14}C dating?
6. Is there any way that radiocarbon dating can be used with a degree of accuracy? Explain.

Section 5: Other Short-range Methods

Vocabulary words to know: dendrochronology, and thermoluminescence

There are several other dating methods which scientists are attempting to use. **Dendrochronology** or tree ring dating, is utilized for dating trees which have lived in the past 10,000 years. Scientists collect samples using an increment borer, which is a metal tube that can be driven into a tree to collect core samples. Then they split the core in the laboratory and count the rings. They attempt to correlate the ring sequences of many trees (especially those with overlapping ages) to get a picture of climate conditions in the past. However, differing weather patterns and variable accessibility to water and nutrients all influence the growth of tree rings. Trees living today don't always show the same tree ring patterns. Therefore, this method is not totally reliable.

Thermoluminescence is a method used to date archaeological materials such as flint or pottery. This method relies on the fact that minerals and other crystalline materials, if they are exposed to radiation, will release electrons which can then be trapped in crystal defects. "Heating the substances at temperatures of about 450° C and higher enables the trapped electrons to return to their normal positions."[16] As the electrons do this, energy is released in the form of light. Generally, the longer the substances have been exposed to radiation, the greater the amount of displacement, and thus the greater the amount of light released. However, scientists must first estimate the annual dose of radiation that the substance received, and this creates problems with the method's accuracy. There are several other dating methods, including fission track dating, obsidian dating, and varve chronology. However, most are not widely accepted as giving accurate, dependable results.

Questions for Review

1. What is dendrochronology? What problems occur with this method?
2. How does thermoluminescence work? Are there any problems?

Section 6: Young Earth Indicators

Much is said about uranium-lead, potassium-argon, rubidium-strontium, and radiocarbon dating and how they indicate an old Earth. However, if we apply the same uniformitarian principle so popular today to other processes and assume constant rates of accumulation or decay, there are over eighty indicators of a much younger Earth. These have been virtually ignored in most scientific literature. However, the fact that they exist bears mentioning. Examples of five of these are printed below.

Salt in the Ocean

Each day rivers bring billions of gallons of water to the oceans of the world. Dissolved in this water are tons of various salts that have been eroded from the land. Volcanic and atmospheric dust also adds salts. Waves and tides pounding the shores add more. Once the water reaches the ocean, much of it evaporates, forms clouds and returns to the land as rain, completing the water cycle. However, in spite of some loss through various processes, most of the salt remains in the oceans, so the oceans are gradually getting saltier. At the present rate of accumulation, "the ocean's present salt content would accumulate within 32 million years."[17] (Note: this figure is an upper limit – the maximum amount of time it would take.) This is a far shorter time than what is required for evolution to have occurred on the Earth.

Decay of the Earth's Magnetic Field

Scientists believe every heavenly body has or has had a magnetic field. The Earth is no exception. However, both the strength and the intensity of the Earth's magnetic field have been decaying at a steady rate since they were first measured in 1835. (The present half-life of the magnetic field's strength is about 1400 years.) Yet if this is true and the Earth is billions of years old, it should no longer have a magnetic field. Scientists who believe in an old Earth have attempted to explain this by stating that the Earth's interior has a "self-exciting dynamo" in its core which produces electricity and adds to the Earth's magnetic field from time to time. However, this theory simply does not fit the scientific facts.

A good theory should enable a scientist to make accurate predictions that are substantiated by the data he collects. There is another theory, called the Rapid Decay Theory, which does this. The Rapid Decay Theory makes much more accurate predictions than the Dynamo Theory. For example, scientists using the Rapid Decay Theory have correctly predicted the magnetic field of every planet that has one, while those using Dynamo Theory have often been wrong. The Dynamo Theory predicted no magnetic field on Mercury, while the Rapid Decay Theory said there was one. **Mercury has a magnetic field.** The Dynamo Theory also predicted a magnetic field on Mars; the Rapid Decay Theory said there wasn't one. **The data indicate Mars has no magnetic field.** Evolutionary scientists reject the Rapid Decay Theory, even though it makes accurate predictions, because it indicates the Earth is young. **However, using this theory, at the present rate of decay, if we project backward in time, the Earth's magnetic field would have been comparable to the field of a neutron star just 100,000 years ago.**[18] Just **twenty thousand years ago, the electric current producing it would have been so strong that the heat it generated would have made life on Earth impossible.**[19]

Short Period Comets

Comets are masses of rock and dirt held together by ice; they travel through space on regular orbits. Many of the ones that visit our solar system are short period comets, those that have an orbital period of 200 years or less. These are comets whose orbits bring them close to the sun quite often. Each time they circle the sun, some of the ice that holds them together is vaporized. When all of the ice is melted, the comet breaks up into meteoroids, rocks that circle the sun in the same path as the original comet. (Evolutionists believe that a cloud of comets called the Kuiper Belt exists within Pluto's orbit and supplies new short period comets. However, no reproducible evidence currently exists to support this hypothesis.) Thus, if the solar system were older than 10,000 years and no source of new comets exists, there should be no short period comets left. **However, there are about one hundred still in existence, indicating the solar system is younger than 10,000 years.**[20]

Figure 7-10 *Comet in the night sky. Photo courtesy of Answers in Genesis.*

Supernova Remnants

Massive stars are believed to end their lives in a violent explosion called a supernova. It is one of the most spectacular of stellar events. A galaxy such as the Milky Way should produce a supernova about every 25 years .[21] A supernova creates a huge expanding cloud of dust called a Supernova Remnant (SNR). Using computers and applying physical laws, scientists have been able to explain what will happen to this Supernova Remnant. First of all, the cloud of dust will continue to expand until it reaches a diameter of approximately seven light years. This takes about 300 years and is called the first stage. At the end of the first stage a blast wave occurs and the second stage begins. This stage produces very powerful radio waves and should continue to expand to a diameter of 350 light years in the next 120,000 years. As Dr. Jonathan Sarfati, research scientist and author, points out, "the number of observed SNR's of a particular size is an excellent test of whether the galaxy is old or young."[22]

Both the evolutionist uniformitarian model and the young Earth creation model predict that there should be approximately two observable SNR's in the first stage. However, the evolutionist model predicts 2260 second-stage SNR's should be observable if our universe is at least 120,000 years old. On the other hand, if the universe is 7,000 years old, the model predicts only about 125 second stage supernova remnants would be observable. In reality, there are 200 observable second stage SNR's. Of course, if the universe is less than 120,000 years old, there should be no third stage SNR's in our galaxy, and there are none. **These figures are consistent with a young universe.**[23] **The chart below should make this clearer.**

Supernova Remnant Stage	Number of observable SNR's predicted if galaxy is at least 120,000 yrs old.	Number of observable SNR's predicted if galaxy is only 7,000 yrs. old	Number of SNR's actually observed
First	2	2	5
Second	2,260	125	200

Helium in the Atmosphere:

Helium is produced in radioactive rocks by the process of radioactive decay. One of the products of radioactive decay, the alpha particle, is simply a helium nucleus. Since helium is so light, it is able to move up through the liquid in the pores of rocks and escape into the atmosphere, but it is too heavy for much to escape the Earth's gravity. How fast this occurs depends on the type of rock, but eventually all rock is believed to give up its helium to the atmosphere. Studies have shown that helium is accumulating in the atmosphere at the rate of thirteen million helium atoms, per square inch, per second.

Since the estimated loss of helium to outer space is only 300,000 helium atoms per square inch per second, helium is building up in the atmosphere at a very fast rate. Even if we make the generous assumption that the atmosphere had no helium to begin with, **dividing the present amount of helium in the atmosphere by the known accumulation rate shows that all the helium we have today could have accumulated in just two million years.**[24] This is much too little time for evolution to occur.

It is important to note that these figures do not indicate that the Earth must be that old. These figures are simply upper limits for the age of the Earth.

They demonstrate that taking the same uniformitarian principle used with radiometric dating and sedimentation rates and applying it to other rates results in much younger ages for the Earth. **There is no infallible, scientific method of dating the age of the Earth.** For all, it is really a matter of faith.

Method of Determining Age	Age Projected
Salt in the Ocean	32 million years
Decay of the Earth's Magnetic Field	25,000–100,000 years
Short Period Comets	10,000 years
Helium in the Atmosphere	2 million years
Erosion of the continents	14 million years
Super Nova Remnants	about 7,000 years

Figure 7-11 *Young Earth Indicators—each indicate an Earth too young for evolution to occur.*

QUESTIONS FOR REVIEW

1. How does the amount of salt in the ocean indicate a younger Earth?
2. How does the decay of the Earth's magnetic field indicate a young Earth?
3. How does the presence of short period comets in our solar system indicate a young solar system?
4. Explain how the build up of helium in the atmosphere indicates a much younger Earth than assumed by old Earth enthusiasts.
5. How does the present erosion rate of the continents indicate a younger Earth?
6. Explain how Super Nova Remnants indicate a young universe.
7. Is there any totally reliable scientific method of dating the Earth's age?

A COMPARISON OF EVOLUTIONIST AND CREATIONIST VIEWS

EVOLUTIONISTS

Evolutionists rely on radiometric dating methods to support dates determined by the geologic time scale.

Evolutionists assume that the rate of radioactive decay has always been constant.

Evolutionists assume that there is no other way that either parent or daughter material has gotten out of the rock.

Evolutionists assume that they know the original composition of the rock.

Evolutionists use Uranium-Lead, Potassium-Argon, Rubidium-Strontium, Isochron, and Carbon-14 dating to assign ages to rocks and artifacts.

Evolutionists largely ignore the indicators of a young Earth

CREATIONISTS

Creationists point out that radiometric dating is unreliable for several reasons.

Creationists feel this assumption has the most Scientific support. However, they point out that scientists have been monitoring the decay rate for only about a century, and it is stretching scientific reasoning to assume this rate has been constant for the past 4.5 billion years.

Creationists point out that ground water can leach both parent and daughter elements out of rock formations, and it is extremely difficult to tell if this has occurred or not.

Creationists counter that there is no way to know the exact composition of a rock unless there is someone there to test the rock at its formation.

Creationists point out that there are serious flaws with each of these methods as detailed in this chapter.

Creationists point out that there are many of these indicators which point to an Earth too young for evolution to have occurred.

Chapter 8
Evolution of Man?

Vocabulary words to know: hominids, articulated, extinct, sexual dimorphism, brontosaurus, and bipedal

Section 1: Paleontologists' Research Methods

Perhaps no other area of evolution has been so widely debated as the evolution of man. Since Neanderthal, Java Man, Peking Man and other "early men" were discovered, there has been continuing controversy over their validity, not only between creationists and evolutionists but also among evolutionists themselves. There are many good reasons for this debate. However, perhaps the greatest problem is the methods that scientists use in determining hominid status for the bones they find. Paleontologists and anthropologists often employ methods that would be unacceptable in any other branch of science. Following are a few of their procedures that cast doubts on their results.

1. Paleontologists and anthropologists often gather bones from different locations and put them together to form one fossil. Often these locations are a mile or more apart.
2. Often these fossils are found in different rock strata dated by their own methods to be thousands of years apart in age.
3. Scientists often "adjust" radiometric dates to fit the age they have already determined using the geologic time scale.
4. Scientists assign hominid status to fossil parts that are much too few and too small. (For example, a tooth or a few teeth and jaw fragments)

An especially serious problem for paleontologists is the lack of **articulated skeletons**. It is very rare to find a fossil with clearly distinguishable parts and joints connecting them. The lack of complete skeletons, the use of bones from several different places to form one fossil, and the use of dating methods that can be unreliable make the results of studies of early man highly questionable. How can we know for sure that these bones are even of the same species, let alone of the same individual, if they are not found all together in the same place? This was illustrated some time ago when scientists using the same methods with dinosaur bones actually created a dinosaur which never existed. Until recently we saw pictures of "Brontosaurus" in every book on dinosaurs. However, a few years ago, it was discovered that "**Brontosaurus**" did not exist. Scientists putting together dinosaur skeletons mistakenly put the wrong head on the body of an *Apatosaurus*. This occurred because they used body parts from different locations. Another problem is that scientists putting together bones from creatures with which they are unfamiliar can often put them together incorrectly. For example, if the bones of the foot are not properly aligned, the foot can be made to look as if the creature is bipedal, when, in fact, it may not be. It is obvious the study of early man has many difficulties.

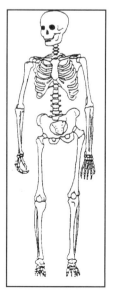

Figure 8-1 *Articulated human skeleton—all parts are present and connected in the proper order.*

Figure 8-2 *Drawings of Apatosaurus and Brachiosaurus by Mercedes Coley.*

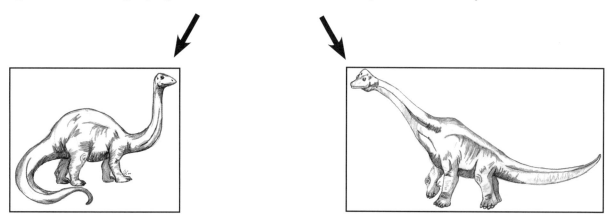

QUESTIONS FOR REVIEW

1. List the problems concerning research on early man that are often cited.
2. What effect does this have on the reliability of the research findings?
3. Explain the meaning of "articulated."

SECTION 2: SOME "EARLY MEN" DISPROVED BY EVOLUTIONISTS

Nebraska Man

In 1917 a rancher and geologist named Harold Cook found a human-looking tooth in sediments in Nebraska. Five years later he gave the specimen to Henry F. Osborn, a paleontologist and president of the American Museum of Natural History. Osborn became convinced that he had discovered the tooth of a hominid. He sent casts of the tooth to several scientists in Europe and the United States. Although some evolutionists disagreed, one of them, British anatomist Grafton Smith, was in complete agreement with Osborn's assessment. He even wrote an article in the *Illustrated London News* about this fossil. The article had accompanying pictures of ape-men together with other mammals. The artist's entire illustration of the ape-men, of course, was based on the fossil evidence of **one tooth**. About four years later the tooth was discovered to be that of an extinct peccary. In their desire to find evidence to support their belief, some evolutionists had made a serious mistake. It is a lesson both creationists and evolutionists should heed.

Piltdown Man

Another creature considered to be a hominid was Piltdown Man. This fossil consisted of skull parts and a jaw fragment with some teeth. It was found in an archaeological dig in Piltdown, England, in 1912. Some evolutionists immediately cited its human-like skull piece and ape-like jaw as evidence of its being a link fossil between the apes and man. However, others were not so quick to accept its authenticity.

At first, Piltdown Man attracted controversy, with many prominent scientists insisting that the apelike jaw did not belong with a skull so human. Some believed that the remains of an ape and a human had been accidentally buried together. They thought that Piltdown Man had been created through human error and never really existed.[1] Still, the discoverer, Charles Dawson, an amateur geologist, and Arthur Smith Woodward, a paleontologist and his colleague, insisted that the odds against ape and human remains being buried accidentally together were enormous. Therefore, the fossil should be accepted as a true link.

Figure 8-3 *A modern day peccary which is similar to the peccary from which the tooth known as Nebraska Man came.* Photo courtesy of America Zoo.

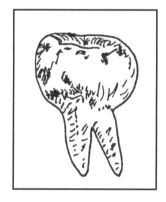

Nebraska Man. Drawing by A. Margetic.

A few years later, Dawson found two skull fragments in a different place. He never disclosed the exact location. These fragments, later known as Piltdown Two, helped to quiet the controversy about the original find. For almost forty years, Piltdown Man was generally accepted as a link between man and the apes, with pictures and discussions of it included in most evolutionary textbooks.

However, shortly after World War II, Joseph Weiner, a professor of anthropology at Oxford University, developed nagging doubts about its authenticity. These doubts grew four years later, when he learned that no one knew the exact location where Piltdown II had been found. Eventually Weiner began to suspect fraud. He carefully inspected the fossil, paying particular attention to the teeth, which he studied with a magnifying glass. He came to the conclusion that the teeth had been filed down and the fossil had been given the appearance of age with chemicals.[2]

Weiner tested his hypothesis by taking a modern ape's molar, filing down the surface, and staining it with permanganate. He managed to produce a tooth surprisingly like Piltdown Man's. Though it would take the work of several other scientists to substantiate his theory, eventually the scientific community came to accept that Piltdown Man was an "elaborate hoax" made up of the skull parts of a human and the jaw and teeth of an orangutan.[3] This textbook example of human evolution was a deliberate fraud.

Since then several people have been suspected of perpetrating the hoax, including Piltdown's discoverer, Charles Dawson, who seemed a possible candidate. Another possible perpetrator of the hoax was a man named Martin Hinton, a former curator of zoology at London's Natural History Museum. According to Professor Brian Gardiner of King's College, London, a trunk with Hinton's initials on it was found in the museum's attic. The trunk contained fossil hippopotamus and elephant teeth and other bones which "were stained with iron and manganese in the same proportions as the Piltdown Man specimens."[4] The haste of some evolutionists to assign link fossil status to fossil fragments has led to some embarrassing situations in the past.

Nebraska Man and his "wife" as shown in *Illustrated London News* 1922

Figure 8-4 *An artist's conception of the "society" which was supposed to be Nebraska Man.* Drawing in public domain.

QUESTIONS FOR REVIEW

1. How much of Nebraska Man was found, and what convinced scientists he was not our ancestor?
2. How much of Piltdown Man was found?
3. What did scientists later find out about Piltdown man? How did they know?

SECTION 3: CURRENTLY CONTESTED LINK FOSSILS

Ramapithecus

There continues to be a great deal of controversy over which fossils belong in the line of man. The ones mentioned in Chapter 3 are perhaps the most widely accepted. However, their position as man's ancestors is somewhat tenuous when all of the evidence is considered. For example, *Ramapithecus* was mentioned in Chapter 3 as a possible link fossil between man and the ape family. This claim was based on a fossil found in India. It consisted of a few jaw fragments and teeth. Later, an entire skull with the same type of teeth was found. When scientists put all the pieces together, they discovered they had the head of an orangutan, a member of the ape family. For this reason, many scientists, evolutionists and creationists alike, no longer consider *Ramapithecus* to be a link fossil. However, some evolutionists still place him in man's line, citing the fact that some specimens were found on the continent where they believe man began, and *Ramapithecus* has the correct apparent age (8–17 million years old) to be a link fossil.

Figure 8-5 *Photo of an orangutan.* Photo provider: Jupiter Images.

Hominids:
Australopithecus anamensis

The oldest fossil currently accepted by many prominent evolutionists is actually one of the last to be discovered. In 1994 Meave Leakey, wife of the prominent anthropologist, Richard Leakey, and a well known anthropologist in her own right, discovered the upper and lower sections of a tibia (lower leg bone) in sediments at Kanapoi in Kenya, East Africa. Because of the structure of the ends of the bone, she believes them to be the fossil of a hominid (a human-like creature). In another location a member of the Leakey expedition found an almost complete set of lower teeth and a skull fragment. In still another spot, half of an upper jaw was found. The rock layer where the teeth were found was dated to be 4 million years old while the layer holding the tibia was "older than 3.5 million," a difference of possibly 500,000 years. Because of this there is some question among evolutionists as to whether they belong to the same species.[5] The most that has been found in one place is a complete lower jaw and a piece of the ear region of a skull.[6]

The tibia is very human in its character. In fact, if it had been found in a younger rock formation, it would probably have been classified as human. However, because it was found in older rock strata, it was assumed it had to be a hominid bone, since according to evolutionary theory, man was not on the Earth that early.

In contrast, the tooth and jaw fragments are very apelike. Ms. Leakey herself states that the lower jaw "proved more 'chinless' and thus more apelike"[7] than *A. afarensis.* However, she goes on to say that "the vertically placed root of the heavily worn canine in the upper jaw is clearly more humanlike than the angled root in chimps."[8] However, the vertical placement of the canine is also found in fossil apes.[9]

Based on these fragments, found in three different locations and at least two different rock levels, Ms. Leakey believes she has found a new species that she has named *A. Anamensis.* Again, the fragmentary nature of the fossil and the fact that the parts were found in different locations greatly diminishes the value of the "evidence." Ms. Leakey cites the

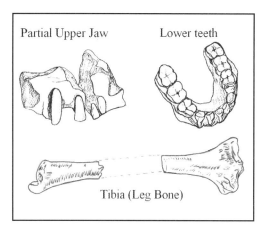

Figure 8-6 *These are drawings of the bones that make up A. anamensis. The central portion of the tibia is missing. Drawings by A. J. Tersigni.*

structure of the ends of the tibia as evidence that the creature walked upright. If, in fact, this is a human bone, it would be reasonable to assume that it did. However, suppose it is a fossil hominid bone. Although the Leakey article mentions that "bipedalism is the primary factor separating apes from hominids,"[10] this is a poor basis for a separation. Members of the ape family such as the pygmy chimpanzee often walk on two legs, yet are obviously not hominids. More evidence is definitely needed before this fossil is classified as a hominid.

Timothy White's recent discovery, which he named *Ardipithecus ramidus,* is also based on teeth and arm bones discovered in one place and pelvic and tibia bones in another. The same methods of research as those of *Australopithecus anamensis* are used here with the same questionable results.

Australopithecus afarensis

In Hadar, Ethiopia, in 1974, a paleoanthropologist named Donald Johanson discovered one of the most complete fossil skeletons classified as a **hominid**. He gave it the scientific name of *Australopithecus afarensis.* However, members of the expedition nicknamed the specimen "Lucy" for a Beatles song popular at the time. About 40% of the skeleton was recovered. However, only a few fragments of the skull were found. Based on the structure of the leg and pelvic bones, Johanson believed that the creature had walked upright. However, it also had long, apelike arms which dangled by its body.[11] Johanson and his colleagues believed they had found "the common ancestor of all later hominids, including our own genus *Homo*."[12] There was a great deal of disagreement over this idea, even among evolutionists. For example, Johanson failed to allow any other anthropologists or paleontologists besides members of his own expedition to examine the fossil until several years after the find. He stated he needed to keep it for further study. When he finally allowed others to examine the specimen, some specialists in anatomy disagreed as to whether it was bipedal or not. However, as has been mentioned before, some members of the modern ape family also may be considered bipedal, but they are definitely still apes.

In addition to Lucy, Johanson and his workers found bones from at least thirteen other individuals nearby. They varied greatly in size, and the skeletons were largely fragmentary. Other paleoanthropologists believed Johanson had found two distinct species. However, Johanson considered them all to be *A. afarensis*. He felt that the size difference occurred because of **sexual dimorphism**.[13] This refers to the

male members of a species being much larger than the females – a phenomenon that occurs among the gorillas. The male gorilla is much taller and much heavier than the female. Thus, Johanson was convinced that all the bones came from the same species.

The lack of a skull continued to plague Johanson. The Ethiopian government imposed a moratorium on fieldwork in the country in the 1980's, and Johanson's group was not allowed to work in the country. During this time two of Johanson's colleagues pieced together a partial male skull from fragments of several different individuals found at Hadar. However, Johanson admitted there were too many pieces missing and there was no way to know that they had all the details of a distinctive *afarensis* skull.[14] (Besides, the skull which was pieced together was decidedly apelike.) When the Ethiopian government allowed work to resume, Johanson returned with his expedition workers to Hadar to search for a skull. They began to explore a **different site** than the earlier one where they had found Lucy. At the new site they found most of the bones of a skull. They did not find these skull bones along with skeletal bones that could be compared to their earlier specimens. However, they assumed these skull fragments were of *A. afarensis*. They returned to the

Photo provider: Jupiter Photos.

Figure 8-7 *Photo of a male gorilla (picture on the left) and female gorilla (pictured below).*

Photograph courtesy of Allen Easler.

United States where they reconstructed a skull, using these fragments. Because the skull was of a much larger individual, Johanson assumed they had found a male of the species. Over the span of three more years they collected additional facial fragments from another site. These they assembled into another composite skull that they believe to be female. Johanson now feels confident that he has a nearly complete picture of *A. afarensis*.

One important find which is rarely mentioned in discussions of *A. afarensis* is the **Kanapoi hominid**, also known as KP 271.[15] This is the fossil of a human upper arm bone found in rock strata dated to be older than all the australopithecines! It thus seems difficult to believe that Lucy is our evolutionary ancestor. Again, this information is ignored because **it does not fit with the preconceived beliefs about early man that are popular at this time.** The methods of finding and compiling data, coupled with this fact, make the evidence that *A. afarensis* is our ancestor debatable.

Australopithecus africanus

In 1924 Professor Raymond Dart was working as an anatomist at the University of Witwatersrand in Johannesburg, South Africa. The skull of a primate child was brought to him; it had come from a lime works at a place called Taung. Professor Dart recognized that the skull was different from anything he had seen before. He cleaned it up and after studying it briefly, he announced in an article in *Nature*, a British scientific journal, that he had found an ancestor of man. He gave the Taung skull the scientific name of *Australopithecus africanus*.[16] The scientific community in London did not accept Dart's opinion of the fossil. Members noted that the skulls of young apes look much more like humans than do those of adult apes. Most refused to accept that *A. africanus* was a link fossil between apes and man. Dart took the fossil to London in 1930 to prove its authenticity. However, Davidson Black was also in London at that time with Peking Man fossils. Dart and his Taung skull were ignored. He returned to South Africa, a discouraged and defeated man. Dart suffered a nervous breakdown and gave up his fossil work for an extended time. **For years the Taung skull was not intensively studied.** Instead, the fossil sat like a collector's item on the desk of a colleague.[17] However, others, most notably Robert Broom, a medical doctor and amateur anthropologist, continued looking. Broom

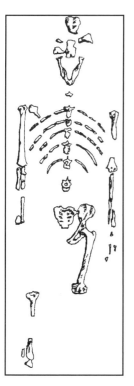

Figure 8-8A *An illustration of the bones of Austalopitethecus afarensis (Lucy) that were found in one location. Note: the skull parts are only fragmentary. When Johanson's assistants attempted to put the skull fragments together, the result was too apelike. Thus, Johanson traveled to Africa later to find an afarensis skull. Drawing by A. Margetic.*

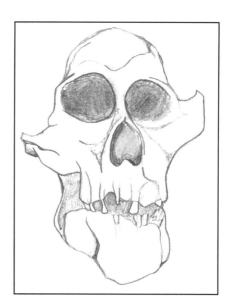

Figure 8-8B *The A. Afarensis skull found by Donald Johanson. Drawing by A. J. Tersigni.*

later found several specimens in a different location and labeled some of these *A. africanus*.

Time passed and other human "ancestors" such as Nebraska Man and Piltdown Man were proven to be false. The need for more link fossils was great. By the middle of the twentieth century, *A. africanus* had become widely accepted. By 1970, the Tuang skull was generally regarded as the skull of an ancestor of man.

The age of *A. africanus* was believed to be approximately 2.5 to 3 million years old. This, of course, was an appropriate age because it would supposedly take over a million years for such a primitive human ancestor to evolve into *Homo sapiens*. **Then, in 1973, a geologist named T.C. Partridge, after studying the area, stated that the age of the cave in which the Tuang skull was found was "somewhat less than 0.87 million years old!"**[18] Once again, the evolutionists' own dating system had disproved a hominid fossil. Obviously, this amount of time was not enough for this hominid to have evolved into *Homo sapiens*. Since 1973, the evolutionary scientific community has been divided on the issue. At first, the Tuang skull was removed from man's ancestral line; it was suggested instead that he was a late example of *Australopithecus robustus*. Then other scientists proposed that the skull might be an example of *Homo habilis*. Lately, Mr. Partridge's dating methods have come under fire, and the Tuang skull (*A. africanus*) has regained some "respectability" as a human ancestor.

However, in the past few years, the Taung skull itself has finally been carefully studied, but this has not quieted the controversy. **Many scientists now believe that the dental development of *A. africanus* shows it is not an ancestor of man.** [19]

The son of well-known anthropologists, Louis and Mary Leakey, Richard Leakey very early became involved in anthropology. Born in Nairobi, Kenya in 1944, Leakey never attained a college degree, preferring instead to study with his parents in the field. In the course of his work, he has discovered several fossils including the well-known Skull 1470. In 1984 a member of Leakey's expedition found this almost complete human skull dated at about 2.8 m.y., using the Geologic Time Scale. Mr. Leakey later left full-time fossil hunting to work for the Kenya government. He married anthropologist Meave Epps in 1971.

Photo provider: AP Wide World Photos.

Homo habilis

In 1964 Lewis and Mary Leakey, two paleoanthropologists, announced the discovery of a hominid that they named *Homo habilis*. Earlier, the Leakeys, along with members of their family, had recovered several fossil specimens. The fossils consisted of hand bones, foot bones, and cranial fragments belonging to both juveniles and adults. The pieces of skull **were not found in the same location as the skeletal bones.** Immediately, some people questioned the authenticity of the new species because of this. The skull capacity was also very small. In addition, the juvenile bones are much more difficult to evaluate.[20] Nevertheless, Mr. Leakey continued to argue for *Homo habilis* being man's true ancestor, evolving from *A. africanus* and into modern man, because the type of skull of these three species was similar. *Homo habilis* specimens were dated at 1.8 million years old, using the Geologic Time Scale.

Then, in 1972 the Leakeys' son Richard found a skull that he labeled KMN-ER 1470. This skull became known simply as Skull 1470. Although there were other specimens found, the skull was of particular interest because it was obviously **so human in nature and was found in rock strata which Richard Leakey dated to be at least 2.8 million years old!**[21] The skull had a cranial size within the human range, and its shape and wall thickness were also distinctly human. In addition, it showed evidence inside the skull of a **Broca's area**, the part of the brain that controls muscles for speech in hu-

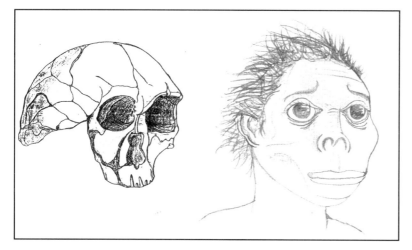

Figure 8-9 *The skull known as 1470 Man, along with an artist's conception of the appearance of the original individual. Drawing by A. J. Tersigni.*

mans.[22] Leakey himself was aware of the importance of this find. He pointed out that the skull was very much like modern man.[23] He even went so far as to state that "either we toss out this skull or we toss out our theories of early man. It simply fits no previous models of human beginnings."[24]

If, in fact, human remains were found in older rock strata than *Homo habilis*, how could he be our ancestor? This Richard Leakey understood. However, other evolutionists did not agree. Instead of tossing out *Homo habilis* as a human ancestor, **they simply classified skull 1470 as another Homo habilis specimen!** In fact, the addition of this skull to the *Homo habilis* specimens made *Homo habilis* more acceptable as an ancestor of modern man to many scientists. Yet the original specimens have very little in common with this later skull, since they are much smaller in size, with a brain capacity much below that of both skull 1470 and modern man.[25]

In 1986 Timothy White, while working in East Africa with Donald Johanson, discovered a partial adult skeleton which he named Olduvai Hominid 62. The skull and teeth of this specimen are very similar to the early, small *Homo habilis* specimens and thus OH 62 is classified as *Homo habilis*. However, the partial skeleton reveals that this *Homo habilis* adult was smaller than Donald Johanson's Lucy, (otherwise known as *A. afarensis*), instead of resembling the larger, human-like skull 1470.[26] *Homo habilis* seems to be two types of individuals and only the larger of them appears to be human. The smaller specimens are definitely ape-like.

QUESTIONS FOR REVIEW

1. For what reason do some scientists believe *Ramapithecus* to be a link fossil?
2. Why do many scientists now believe he is not a human ancestor?
3. Under what circumstances were the different parts of the *A. anamensis* specimen found?
4. For what reasons do some scientists question its authenticity?
5. Under what circumstances was *A. afarensis* found, and what important skeleton part was missing?
6. How did Johanson get a skull for *A. afarensis*? Were there any skeletal bones with the skull? What problem does this pose?
7. What is the Kanapoi hominid, and how does it affect the fossil status *of A. afarensis*?
8. What are two major problems with the *Australopithecus africanus* specimens?
9. Under what circumstances were the first *Homo habilis* specimens found?
10. What is important about Richard Leakey's discovery of skull 1470?
11. How did the evolutionists "solve" the problem of modern man being in older rock strata than *Homo habilis*?
12. What did Timothy White's find reveal about the size of the smaller *Homo habilis*?

Unlike many creationists, Dr. Duane Gish never went through a period of time when he believed evolution to be true. He early accepted the Biblical account of creation and never changed his opinion. In fact, his research as a biochemist at the University of California, Berkeley strengthened his faith. As he studied bacteria, he became convinced that their complexity required a creator. He later worked at the Virus Laboratory of U.C.L.A. and during that time was given a pamphlet which summarized the known creation research. This stimulated his own research into origins. He began to speak on the subject. Later, while living in Michigan and working for the Upjohn Company, he met other creation scientists and formed the Creation Research Society. Dr. Henry Morris, also on the executive board of C. R. S., resigned in 1970 and started the Institute for Creation Research in California. Dr. Gish joined him on staff in 1971 at I.C.R., where he continues to serve. He lives in the San Diego area with his wife Lolly and has four grown children.

SECTION 4: HOMO ERECTUS

The first specimen of *Homo erectus* was found in Java in 1891. A Dutch doctor and anatomist named Eugene Dubois went to the island of Java, in what was then the Dutch East Indies, specifically to find the "missing link" between apes and humans. He supported himself in Java as an army doctor, and once he was there, he received permission to dig for fossils. However, his work for the army prevented him from doing the digging himself. Instead, he assigned two army corporals and fifty forced laborers to dig in an area which looked as if it contained fossils. Dubois himself was restricted to making periodic visits on horseback to the site. Neither he nor his engineers had any real knowledge of geology.[27]

Although he claimed to have dated the fossil by the other fossils found in the area, it is a fact that Dubois gave very little information about these fossils and about the structure of the rock layers in which his specimen was found. He finally gave some sketchy information on this subject in 1895, after he came back from Java to the Netherlands. However, he never did publish any detailed information on this subject. Thus, other scientists were unsure whether either Dubois or his helpers carefully determined the rock layer in which Java Man was found.[28] Also, when he first dated the fossil, using the other fossils in the rock layer as a guide, he placed it in the Pleistocene epoch. However, when he realized that it had to be older in order to qualify as a link fossil, he ignored the evidence of the other fossils and described Java Man as belonging to the Pliocene epoch, in the Tertiary period, hundreds of thousands of years earlier. His reason: in his estimation, **such a primitive form belonged to the Tertiary.**[29]

There was also another problem. The first part of the fossil, the skullcap, was found in 1891. A year later and fifty feet away from where the skullcap was found, Dubois' helpers found a human femur (an upper leg bone). Both the skullcap and the femur were found in a formation that had once been river gravel. Such a location implies a great deal of movement and mixing of sediment. **Under these circumstances, there is no reason to assume these two parts belonged together.**

The skullcap appeared to be primitive. Dubois thought it to be ape-like. However, other scientists felt it looked more like Neanderthal man, who is considered human. After returning to the Netherlands and examining newer Neanderthal specimens, **Dubois admitted that his fossil definitely resembled the Neanderthals.**[30] Others, such as Harry Shapiro of the American Museum of Natural History, agree. "When one examines a classic Neanderthal skull, of which there are a large number, one cannot escape the conviction that its fundamental anatomical formation is an enlarged and developed version of the *Homo erectus* skull."[31]

Whatever the opinion of the skullcap might be, the femur was obviously that of a modern human. This was another reason to question whether it should be placed with the Neanderthal-like skullcap. Nevertheless, Dubois continued to insist that the two parts belonged together and that Java Man was truly an intermediate fossil between apes and man.

Dubois also withheld valuable information that could have shed some light on the controversy. When he first came to the Dutch East Indies, before he found Java Man, he was given a skull that had been discovered by a mining engineer who was searching for marble. Dubois visited the site himself and found another skull. These skulls later became known as **Wadjak Man**. Both of them were unmistakably of modern humans. Dubois made mention of them in the reports he periodically made to the government agency which granted him permission to dig. However, he did not publish any news of this find in scientific journals. Instead, he took the skulls home and said nothing about them for thirty years. Although by this time the location where they were found was much harder to pinpoint, **there is some indication that the skulls were found in rock strata that was as old as the rock layers in which Java Man was found**. Therefore, Dubois had found modern human skulls approximately the same age as Java Man.[32] If this is the case, how could Java Man be our ancestor?

However, it was left to a group of scientists that made up the **Selenka-Trinil Expedition** of 1907–1908 to shed some serious scientific light on the whole situation. Frau M. Lenore Selenka, a German professor and scientist led this expedition. All of the expedition members were evolutionists. The expedition's purpose was to get sufficient scientific proof to quiet the controversy about Java Man and thus to prove that he truly was a missing link between apes and man.[33] All of the members of the expedition were scientists, specialists in different fields. They went to the area where Dubois's workers had found **Java Man** (also called **Pithecanthropus** at that time). They began to examine the rocks and fossils nearby but did not find any more fossils of Java Man. However, one expedition member, Dr. Walkhoff, found a human tooth about two miles away. Based on the condition of the fossil, he felt it was older than Java Man. Another expedition member, Dr. E. Carthaus, found traces of man's existence in the same strata where Java Man was found.[34] Also, based on the evidence of other types of fossils in the area, they concluded

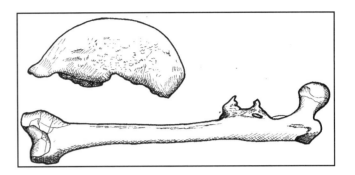

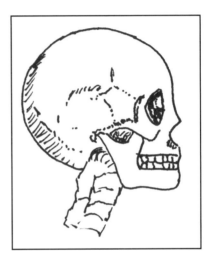

Figure 8-10 *Drawing of bones of Java Man and human skull similar to Wadjak Man. Drawing by A. J. Tersigni.*

that Dubois "seriously overestimated the age of the stratum in which *Pithecanthropus* was found."[35] In fact, they felt it might have been only four or five hundred years old.[36]

Java Man's classification as a true link fossil is thus questionable. Martin L. Lubenow, in *Bones of Contention,* states, "Java Man is not our true evolutionary ancestor but is a true member of the human family."[37] Since the discovery of Java Man, over 200 other specimens have been classified as *Homo erectus.* However, two things prevent them from functioning as true link fossils. **First of all, the structure of the specimens shows them to be very similar to Homo sapiens. Second, the ages of the various Homo erectus fossils, using evolutionists' own dating methods, show that he has lived side by side with other humans.**[38] If he has lived continuously side by side with us, then there is no proof of ancestral relationship.

Questions for Review

1. List two problems concerning Dubois's methods of dating Java Man.
2. List the two parts of the fossil? Why did critics question their being put together?
3. What did Dubois later admit the skullcap resembled?
4. What about the femur? What was it?
5. What information did Dubois fail to report to the scientific community? What effect would it have had on his argument that Java Man was a link fossil?
6. What did the Selenka-Trinil Expedition of 1907–1908 discover about Java Man?
7. What two things prevent the other specimens of Homo erectus from being classified as hominids?

Section 5: The Lake Laetoli Footprints

One of the most important finds of the past thirty years is the Lake Laetoli footprints. In 1978 members of Mary Leakey's expedition found footprints impressed in hardened volcanic ash near Lake Laetoli in northern Tanzania. Ms. Leakey told the story of the find in the April 1979 issue of *National Geographic*. According to the article, two individuals made the footprints before the ash hardened. She mentions that the footprints are "**remarkably similar to those of modern man.**"[39] She also states that "**the form of his foot was exactly the same as ours.**"[40] Virtually every scientist who has examined the footprints agrees. However, potassium-argon dating tests on the hardened ash in which the footprints were found gave an age of 3.6 million years old. Therefore, the evolutionary community believes them to have been made by the hominids known as *A. afarensis*. Why has this occurred? **It is because the age of the footprints agrees with the age ascribed to *A. afarensis* and because of the preconception of evolutionists that modern man could not have been alive that long ago.**

Finally, at Mary Leakey's invitation, Richard R. Tuttle of the University of Chicago made an extensive study of the Laetoli footprints. First, he made casts of them. He then compared them to the footprints of bears, since bear prints are sometimes confused with those of humans. He stated that they could possibly have been made by bears, but there are no fossils of bears anywhere in this area.[41] Thus, he felt it was highly unlikely. He also made casts of

Figure 8-11 *Lake Laetoli footprints. Image taken with permission from* Apes & Ancestors (American Portrait Films); *transferred by Andrew Kee.*

the feet of some Machiguenga Indians of Peru. These Indians habitually go barefoot. He then compared these to the fossil footprints and published his findings in the March, 1990 issue of *Natural History*. In the article he states that "**the 3.5 million-year-old footprint trails at Laetoli site G resemble those of habitually unshod modern humans . . . . If the [Laetoli] footprints were not known to be so old, we would readily conclude that they were made by a member of our genus,** *Homo*."[42] If, in fact, they are identical to modern humans, why not simply accept the evidence as it is? The evidence points to the fact that the Laetoli footprints were made by *Homo sapiens*—modern humans. If this is true, using evolutionary chronology, this puts modern humans here on the Earth before virtually all the hominids mentioned in this book.

What if scientists simply took the evidence and accepted it as it is, without any preconceptions about when modern man appeared on the Earth? It is then possible to set up a chart, **using the evolutionists' own dating system**, that provides powerful proof against the evolution of man. Fig. 8–12 is a chart showing the various fossils of humans and hominids: the amount of the fossil found, the locations, and their ages. The chart demonstrates how each of the various hominids has lived side by side with human beings over long periods of time. The idea that there is a smooth transition in time from *Ramapithecus* through the hominids to modern man has been created for textbooks. In reality, it does not exist. Evidence for the evolution of man is still as elusive as it was one hundred years ago.

Fossil	Amount found	Location(s)	Age/ million years
Ardipithecus ramidus	fragments of 50 individuals	6 kilometers^2	4.4
Kanapoi Hominid	*human upper arm bone*	*1 location*	4+
Laetoli Footprints	*several footprints of bare-foot humans*	*1 location*	3.6
A. anamensis	upper & lower ends of tibia, parts of upper & lower jaw, skull fragments	3 locations 2 rock levels	3.5–4
A. afarensis	40% body found, skull found later	2 locations	3.1
Skull 1470	*complete human skull*	*1 location*	2.8
Homo habilis	cranial fragments hand & foot bones	2 locations	1.8
A. africanus	skull	1 location	.87
Homo erectus (Java Man)	Neanderthal-like skull cap, modern human leg bone	2 locations	.5*
Wadjak Man	*2 modern human skulls*	*1 location*	.5

Figure 8-12 *Modern man and the Hominids: Note that the fossils of modern man are given in italics. *The date for Homo erectus is only for the first specimen, Java man, which was referred to in the text. Later fossil discoveries classified as Homo erectus have closely resembled a smaller version of Neanderthal man. These are only a few of the fossils which have been classified in man's ancestral line. For a much more extensive comparison, see* Bones of Contention *by Martin Lubenow.*

New fossil fragments are constantly being discovered and touted as yet another link in the evolutionary line of man. How can these fossils be properly assessed? It can be done quite well by getting the answers to a few simple questions.

1. How much of the fossil was found?
2. Were all the fossil parts found together, or were they found in several locations?
3. If they were found in different locations, were they found in rocks of the same age?

4. How were they dated? Were radiometric dates "adjusted" to support geologic time scale dates?

Answers to these questions are of vital importance in determining the validity of the evidence for any link fossil. It is important to do serious research and critical thinking before accepting any link fossil as genuine.

QUESTIONS FOR REVIEW

1. According to Mary Leakey, what did the Lake Laetoli footprints closely resemble?
2. How were they dated and what age were they given?
3. Why do evolutionists say they were made by *A. afarensis*?
4. What did Richard Tuttle have to say about the footprints?
5. If these are modern human footprints, where does this put modern humans on the evolutionary time scale – especially in relation to the hominids?
6. What does Figure 8–12 demonstrate about modern man and the hominids?
7. What questions should you ask before accepting a link fossil as genuine?

A COMPARISON OF EVOLUTIONIST AND CREATIONIST VIEWS

EVOLUTIONISTS

Evolutionists believe that man ascended from an apelike ancestor. They also point to several fossils they consider links in man's evolution.

Evolutionists feel they have several fossils that are links in the evolution of man.

Evolutionists early in the twentieth century claimed that Piltdown Man and Nebraska Man were ancestors of humans.

Most evolutionists currently accept *Ramapithecus, A. anamensis, A. afarensis A. africanus, Homo habilis, and Homo erectus* as hominids who are in man's ancestry.

Evolutionists believe the Lake Laetoli footprints were made by the hominid, *A. afarensis* because radiometric dating assigned them an age of 3.6 million years old.

Evolutionists teach in their textbooks that there is a smooth transition in time from *Ramapithecus* through the hominids and ending with modern man.

CREATIONISTS

Creationists believe that man was specially created by God.

Creationists feel that the methods paleontologists use make their findings highly unreliable.

Evolutionists later disproved both Piltdown Man and Nebraska Man. In fact, Piltdown Man was a deliberate fraud.

Creationists point to valid reasons why these species are either members of the ape family or humans.

Mary Leakey, the anthropologist who found the footprints, stated they were identical to those of modern man. This was substantiated by Richard R. Tuttle of the University of Chicago. Creationists point out that since they are identical to those of modern man, it is much more logical to assume that modern man made them.

Creationists point out that using the evolutionists' own dating methods, it can be shown that modern man has co-existed with the so-called hominids, so there is no proof of an ancestor/descendent relationship.

CHAPTER 9
THE PERVASIVENESS OF PERFECTION

INTRODUCTION

Much has been said so far about evolutionary beliefs and why creationists do not share those beliefs. Since there are only two logical possibilities concerning the origin of the Earth, to disprove the one is to prove the other. Because the evidence presented so far indicates that the Earth and all its inhabitants could not have developed "by accident," then it follows that "somebody" must have done it. However, creationists have many more reasons for believing in creation.

Perhaps a discussion of a popular machine of the day would help to illustrate this point. The computer has become a vital part of our everyday life, from controlling the various activities of our space ships and rockets to enabling a student to find information and type a research paper. The typical personal computer has to have several components in order to be useful. First of all, a monitor, keyboard, and mouse are needed for a person to interact with the computer. In addition, the computer itself must have several vital parts. It must have a processor, the "brain," which does the computer's thinking. The computer must also contain a certain amount of RAM that keeps and controls the programs that are working at the moment. A hard drive provides storage for the information contained in the computer. Finally, all these complex parts must be connected to a motherboard, so that they can function together as an even more complex unit. Properly connected, computers can talk to each other, give instructions to each other, and form even more complex, interrelated systems. It is fascinating to note that the Earth is also filled with extremely complex systems much like computers, each system perfectly suited to perform its particular function and also to work together in harmony with other systems to achieve greater goals. How could their existence be a matter of chance?

SECTION 1: PERFECTION IN THE MICROSCOPIC WORLD

When Darwin developed his theory, he realized that much study had yet to be done in many fields. However, he believed that as scientists, with the aid of increasingly better microscopes, were able to study smaller and smaller organic units, they would find that things became increasingly simple. This has not proved to be the case. Instead, scientists have discovered "layer upon layer" of complexity. Everywhere in the microscopic world, scientists have found machines of various kinds working together in perfect harmony, much like computers. One good example of this is the cell, which is filled with **irreducibly complex structures**.

Michael Behe, in *Darwin's Black Box,* gives a clear picture of the meaning of irreducibly complex structures. These are systems that cannot be simplified or they will cease to function. As a man-made illustration, he describes a mousetrap. In order for a mousetrap to work, it must have a platform on which is mounted a spring, a hammer, a catch, and a holding bar. (See Fig. 9-1). All of these parts contribute to and are necessary to its function. In addition, all the parts must be composed of just the right material and in the right shape to enable the mousetrap to work. If the spring is too weak, the hammer it controls will not kill the mouse. If the holding bar is too short or too long, it will not connect properly with the catch, etc. Therefore, in order for the mousetrap to work as a mousetrap, all the parts must be in place and functioning properly together. The mousetrap is thus an irreducibly complex structure

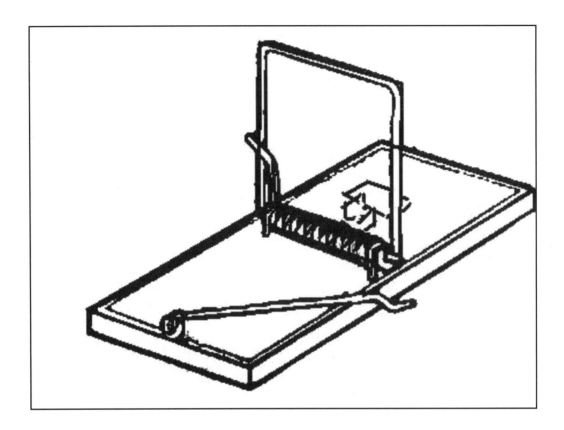

Figure 9-1 *The mousetrap—an irreducibly complex structure. Drawing by Trevor James.*

When studying the cell, it becomes obvious that each cellular machine is an irreducibly complex structure, and that all of them must be present and working in order for the cell to function. In both plants and animals, the cell operates as a factory does. For example, each factory has a head office where individuals decide what product to make. The cell's "head office" is the nucleus, where the DNA resides. Each factory generally has one or more foremen who act as emissaries, carrying instructions from the office to the workmen. The cell's "foreman" is messenger RNA. The factory also will have an assembly line where products are built. This is represented in the cell by ribosomal RNA (the "master" machine), along with the endoplasmic reticulum and the Golgi apparatus. The mitochondria and the cell vacuoles serve as the power plant and the warehouses respectively. The garbage disposal unit of the cell is the lysosome. Not only do these machines manufacture products for use by the cells themselves, but they also produce materials to be used in other locations. In addition, the membranes that surround the various machines (such as the endoplasmic reticulum and the Golgi apparatus), as well as the cell membrane, are "intelligent" enough to recognize various organic particles attempting to move through them and then "open doors" (called pores) to let them enter or leave.

The different functions of various machines in the cell are too numerous to describe. However, an explanation of one cellular activity will serve to illustrate the complexity of cellular activities in general. Michael Behe's explanation of **gated transport** in a cell is a good example. (Dr. Behe classifies transmembrane transport under gated transport for the purpose of his illustration, since they work in essentially the same way.) The primary job of the human cell is to produce various proteins. These proteins then perform thousands of jobs throughout the body. After a protein is made by the cell's ribosomes, it must be transported through the cytoplasm to the site for which it was produced For example, an enzyme (a protein) that is produced by the ribosomal RNA for the lysosome passes through the endoplasmic reticulum and then the Golgi apparatus where modifications are made. Then in the

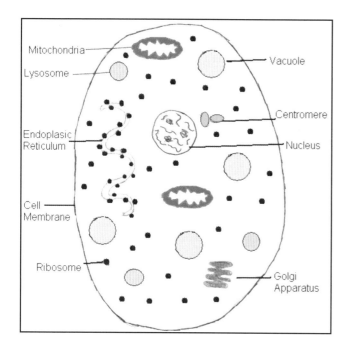
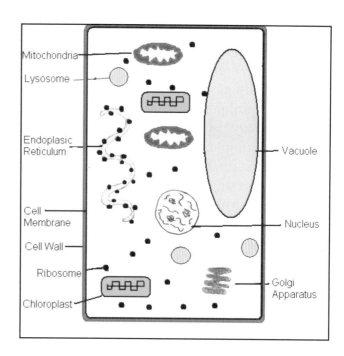

Figure 9-2 *An idealized plant and animal cell. Note: These do not show all the parts of typical cells. The shapes and colors, for the most part, do not attempt to copy exactly the actual organelles. Lysosomes are common in animal cells but rare in plant cells. Drawing by Amy Kochendorfer.*

final compartment of the Golgi apparatus, clathrin vesicles are produced which bind onto the enzyme and transport it to the lysosome.

Dr. Behe focuses on the final part of this complex process, the transport of the enzyme through the lysosome's membrane. He compares it to an automated garage that allows only vehicles with special license plates to enter. Such a garage would require a scanner to read the license plate and, if the barcode is correct, open the garage door to admit the car. The clathrin vesicle performs much like a car in transporting the enzyme. On the vesicle is a v-SNARE protein that acts as the coded license plate. On the lysosome is a t-SNARE protein that corresponds to the scanner. The v-SNARE protein is "scanned," and the enzyme is then allowed through the membrane. Since each of these three parts must be in place and functioning in order for gated transport to occur, we have an example, much like the mousetrap, of an irreducibly complex structure.[1] The question is how could such a system have evolved?

Note: this is an **extremely simplified** explanation of the components of the cell and of one cellular activity. In reality, there are many other cellular machines that perform the jobs that humans and

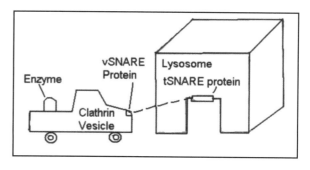

Figure 9-3 *This cartoon drawing demonstrates the interaction of the vSNARE and tSNARE proteins in transmembrane transport, a fully automated system.*

computers do in our factories. This collection of cellular machines allows the cell to function as a fully automated factory. Every day the machines in the individual cells of billions of organisms all over the Earth go about their duties, working in perfect harmony, to allow those organisms to survive and function. Creationists point out that a person would not examine the complexity of an automobile factory and assume it developed on its own. They further assert that it is illogical to assume a fully automated factory, with a complexity man has yet to achieve, has done this.[1]

Dr. Behe gives the **bacterial flagellum**, the extension on the body of a bacteria, as another example of an irreducibly complex structure. Although flagella exist in eukaryotic cells, the prokaryotic (bacterial) flagellum is uniquely different. In spite of the relative "simplicity" of these bacteria, their flagella are extremely complex. Although bacteria can have one, two or several flagella, this text will deal with those having a single flagellum. The long part of the flagellum is the filament that drives the cell through liquids. Its structure is rigid and turned by a motor at its base. This motor comes complete with a series of rings. The M ring is the rotor (the rotating element); the S ring is the stationary element. The base is connected to the filament by a hook which resembles a universal joint in a man-made motor. When energy is applied, the shaft spins counterclockwise inside the S ring, rotating the filament and moving the bacteria forward in a straight line. If the filament rotates clockwise, the bacterium halts and changes direction slightly. In this way, the bacterium uses a "paddling motion" to get to its goal—food! (The movement of bacteria with several flagella is more complex.) Dr. Behe comments, "Because the flagellum is necessarily composed of at least three parts—a paddle, a motor, and a rotor—it is irreducibly complex."[2] The structure of the bacterial flagellum has caused more than one scientist to compare it to an outboard motor. Just as an outboard motor will not run if any of its components are not present and functioning, the bacterial flagellum will not operate if any of its components are missing. All parts must be there and functioning, or there is no purpose for any of them.

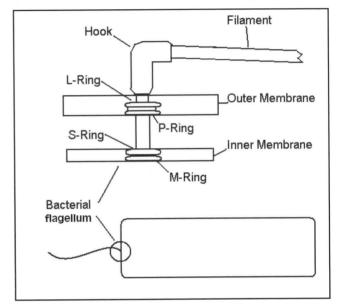

Figure 9-4 *This bacterial flagellum is an example of an irreducibly complex machine. All parts must be present for it to work. Drawing by Trevor James.*

QUESTIONS FOR REVIEW

1. Define *irreducibly complex structure.* Give an example.
2. What can the cell be compared to? Why? Give details.
3. Summarize transmembrane transport, using Mr. Behe's analogy.
4. Why is the bacterial flagellum often called an irreducibly complex structure? Explain

SECTION 2: PERFECTION IN ANIMALS AND BIRDS

Archaopteryx has often been cited as an intermediate form between reptiles and birds because it is assumed by evolutionists that birds evolved from reptiles. However, there are many problems with this theory. Perhaps the biggest problem is the major difference between the reptile and the bird lung. Reptiles, like mammals, have a bellows type of lung. That is, the lungs expand, creating a partial vacuum. The air then rushes into the bronchial tubes and fills ever smaller branching tubes until it reaches little air sacs called the alveoli. In these sacs, which are closely aligned with tiny blood vessels called capillaries, the oxygen in the air is exchanged with carbon dioxide from the blood. Then the reptile exhales, and the lungs contract, creating positive air pressure and sending the carbon dioxide from the body by the *same* pathway. Thus, the reptile and mammal lungs have *two way* passages.

On the other hand, when a bird inhales, there is no lung expansion. Instead, the air flows into its rear air sacs. The rear air sacs then expel the air into the lung where a counter current exchange takes place, insuring maximum efficiency of oxygen and carbon dioxide exchange. The lungs then expel the oxygen-depleted air into the front air sacs, where it is released as the bird breathes out. Thus, the carbon dioxide is expelled from the body by a different pathway: the birds' lungs have one way passages.

Evolutionists have no plausible explanation as to how such a *different* respiratory system could have evolved, especially since birds are believed to have evolved from reptiles, which have two-way lungs like mammals. Birds' lungs are uniquely adapted to their lifestyle. They enhance the bird's endurance and "flight ability." Again, all the parts of the bird's lungs need to be present and functioning as a unit or the bird could not breathe.[3]

Unique characteristics which enable various species to survive and flourish are by no means unusual. The bat's sonar system is another example. Many people think that American scientists created the concept of sonar shortly before World War II, but in reality it was already fully formed and functional in a species of bats called Microchiroptera. These small insect-eating bats use a system of echolocation commonly called "biosonar" that operates on the same principle as the man-made version.

The bat sends out an ultra high frequency sound wave from its specialized larynx. These sound waves are then reflected back to the bat's ears and brain where they are collected and analyzed. The bat's ears and larynx are truly remarkable. The external ears are large while the internal ears are extremely sensitive. The bat's echolocation call can last from less than one up to fifty milliseconds. (A millisecond is a thousandth of a second.) The longer call is used when the bat is hunting insects, while the shorter ones are produced in rapid volleys of about two hundred per second when the bat is closing in for the kill. However, the ability of the bat's brain to analyze the collected information is also extraordinary. In a fraction of a second, the bat must be able to separate the reflected sound of its own pulse from that of other bats around it, and also determine the nature and size of an object and its distance away.[4]

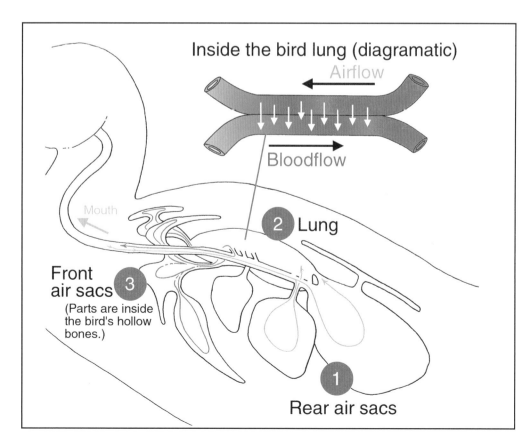

Figure 9-5 *Bird's Respiratory System* Bird's respiratory system diagram courtesy of *Answers in Genesis.*

For this process to be successful requires the rapid and accurate cooperation of the larynx and ears, as well as the vocal and auditory centers of the brain. Without the larynx and ears, along with the bat's brain, working in computer-like precision, there

Figure 9-6 *A bat.*

is no logical reason for the individual parts to develop as they do. Also, how could Microchiroptera survive as an insect hunter without this system in its entirety in place?

The circulatory system of the giraffe is yet another example of a complex structure which must have all its parts present and functioning in order for the giraffe to survive. At first glance, giraffes appear to be some of the more awkward and ungainly creatures of nature. However, nothing could be farther from the truth. Giraffes are really quite graceful and can run at speeds up to thirty-five miles per hour. Because of their height, they are well adapted to reach a food source that is unavailable to other hooved mammals—the leaves of wild apricot, mimosa, and acacia trees. Their height also gives them a "bird's eye" view of the surrounding countryside and any nearby predators.

The giraffe's heart is quite large—weighing close to twenty-six pounds. After all, it would have to be strong to pump blood up the two and one half meters to its brain and also down two and one half meters or more to its legs or even to its head when it bends down to drink.

However, perhaps the greatest feature of the giraffe's body, and the one that poses the greatest challenge from an evolutionary standpoint, is its system of blood vessels. Because the giraffe must be constantly on the lookout for predators, it has to spread its front legs and lower its head rapidly to get a drink. It must also be able to raise its head quickly to keep on the alert and perhaps avoid predators. A powerful heart is needed to pump the blood to its distant extremities. Yet at the same time such a heart could cause the blood pressure to skyrocket in the giraffe's head, literally "blowing its mind" the first time it bent down to drink. If this had occurred in the body of the first long-necked giraffe, it would not have lived long enough to reproduce offspring.

So how does the giraffe survive this great fluctuation in blood pressure? Actually, there is very little change, and the blood pressure of the giraffe is less when its head is lowered. The giraffe's blood travels to the brain through the common and external carotid arteries. Before these arteries reach the brain, there is a connection between them and the vertebral artery. Some of the blood is shunted off through this connection when the head is lowered. The external carotids then divide into a series of smaller arteries just before they reach the brain. These smaller vessels have elastic walls that expand and hold the excess blood that flows toward the brain.

When the giraffe raises its head, why doesn't the blood rush from the brain, causing the animal to lose consciousness? The same vessels that expand to hold the greater flow of blood adjust quickly to retain enough of the fluid in the brain while the blood system's pressure is adjusting.

However, all of this would be of no help to the giraffe if its veins were not also specially adapted. All of the larger veins have valves to counteract the effects of gravity on the giraffe's long legs and neck. These valves prevent part of the blood from receding from the brain. They also prevent it from backflowing when it is returning to the heart from the legs. Without them, blood would collect in the lower extremities instead of returning to the heart to be recirculated. The jugular veins in the giraffe's neck also have valves to prevent the blood's backflow to the brain when the giraffe lowers its head to drink.[5]

How did this unique and complex system come about? Obviously, all parts had to be in place and functioning or a long-necked giraffe would not survive. Yet, without the long neck, there would be no reason for such a blood system to evolve.

Figure 9-7 *The Giraffe*

QUESTIONS FOR REVIEW

1. What is unique about the bird's respiratory system? Why is it difficult to see how it could have evolved?
2. What is unique about the bat's (Microchiroptera's) echolocation system which makes it an irreducibly complex structure?
3. Why would it be necessary for the giraffe's unique circulatory system to have been in place in the first giraffe? Explain.

SECTION 3: PERFECTION IN LARGER SYSTEMS

Perfection is also present in larger systems on the Earth and in the universe as a whole. A good example of this is **oxygen balance.** Many people believe that oxygen is the only important component of the air we breathe. This element presently makes up approximately 20.9% of the Earth's atmosphere by volume. Many might consider the more oxygen the better. However, in reality, the amount of this element in the atmosphere must remain relatively the same. Too little would obviously cause all animal life to suffocate. Too much would lead to widespread, destructive firestorms.

So how is this marvelous balance maintained? First of all, there is a cycle between animal life and plant life that helps to sustain oxygen levels. Animals, during respiration, take in oxygen and give off carbon dioxide. Plants, in turn, take in carbon dioxide and give off oxygen. In fact, billions of tiny algae floating near the ocean surface are responsible for about 70% of the world's oxygen production.

However, there are other mechanisms at work also. For example, chemical weathering of rocks removes oxygen from the atmosphere. Yet at the same time, this weathering releases phosphorous into the Earth's streams that is then carried to the oceans. This phosphorous promotes the rapid growth of more algae, which then produce more oxygen to replace that depleted by chemical weathering.

However, what if the algae growth, stimulated by the extra phosphorous, produces too much oxygen? The oceans also contain bacteria living in the sea floor sediments. The extra oxygen in the seawater stimulates them to remove phosphorus from it. Without the extra phosphorus, the algae on the surface cease to proliferate and oxygen levels go down. If oxygen levels drop too low, the bacteria on the ocean bottom release phosphorus, and surface algae are once again stimulated to grow faster and produce more oxygen.

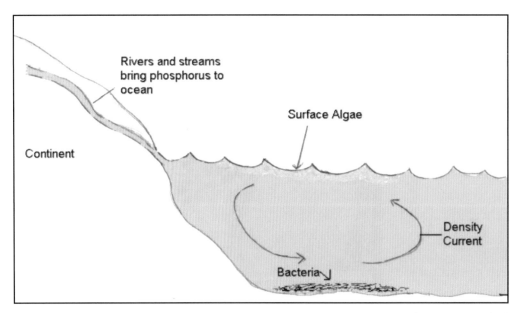

Figure 9-8 *Rivers and streams bring water carrying dissolved phosphorus to the oceans, which stimulates algae to grow and produce more O_2. However, if too much O_2 is produced, bacteria on the ocean bottom absorb phosphorus; the algae growth is curtailed and less O_2 is produced. Illustration by Trevor James.*

The interaction between algae near the ocean surface and the bacteria on the ocean bottom is possible only because there are density currents which carry surface water to the ocean bottom and bottom water to the surface. These currents effectively mix the ocean water and permit these organisms to work together to achieve balance in oxygen production on the Earth.[6]

The question remains, how could such a complicated and multifaceted set of checks and balances have evolved to work so perfectly together? All the parts must be in place and functioning, or it doesn't work at all.

The harmony and perfection of nature go far beyond just oxygen balance. Peter D. Ward and Donald Brownlee in their book, *Rare Earth,* demonstrate this. Although they believe microscopic life may be common in the universe, their book is intended to show how planets capable of sustaining complex life must be rare. In *Rare Earth* they give a list of characteristics which must be in place if complex life is to exist. Some of these are as follows:

1. Right distance from a star
2. Right planetary mass
3. Plate tectonics
4. Jupiter-like neighbor
5. Ocean(s) of the right size
6. Stable planetary orbits
7. Large moon
8. The right tilt
9. The right atmosphere
10. The right galaxy
11. The right position in the galaxy
12. The right amount of carbon
13. Oxygen
14. Few impacts from large asteroids and meteoroids[7]

Dr. Ward and Dr. Brownlee have good reasons for the factors they choose. For example, if the Earth were only five per cent closer to the sun, it would experience "runaway greenhouse heating." On the other hand, if it were only fifteen per cent farther away, it would have "runaway glaciation."[8] In either case, the Earth would be uninhabitable for animal life. These figures are the outer perimeters. Some scientists believe the zone where the Earth would continue to be habitable is much smaller.

A large planet in reasonable proximity is another important factor. In our solar system, Jupiter acts as a planetary "vacuum cleaner," attracting many of the asteroids and meteors that might otherwise hit Earth.

Water is a vital part of living things. Without it, carbon-based life could not exist. Water is also necessary for chemical and physical weathering and for moderating climates. The oceans provide this water, which is circulated in the water cycle.

The earth is tilted on its axis at 23 and 1/2 degrees to the path of its orbit. This position allows the seasons to occur and enables a much larger portion of the Earth to be inhabitable. The Earth also has a stable planetary orbit which is not too elliptical. Its large moon stabilizes the Earth's tilt.[9] This allows for a relatively stable progression of seasons as the Earth circles the sun.

Even the Earth's position in the galaxy is favorable. We are positioned between the arms of a spiral galaxy about 30,000 light years from its center. Because we are in an area of relatively few stars and far enough from the galaxy's center, we are not adversely affected "by too many gamma rays, X-rays or other types of ionizing radiation. The center of the galaxy produces all of these."[10] Because of the large number of special characteristics a planet must have in order to sustain life, the authors feel that other Earth-like planets capable of supporting complex life must be exceedingly rare.

Dr. Ward and Dr. Brownlee are evolutionists; they look upon the Earth's unique location and conditions as brought about by fortuitous chance. They state, "If some god-like being could be given the opportunity to plan a sequence of events with the express goal of duplicating our 'Garden of Eden,' that power would face a formidable task. With the best intentions, but limited by natural laws and materials, it is unlikely that Earth could ever be truly replicated."[11] However, it is precisely the complicated set of circumstances which make the Earth so unique in the universe that leads the creationist to believe that only an intelligent creator could have accomplished this task.

Dr. Michael Denton in his book, *Nature's Destiny,* has also delved into the set of circumstances that must exist in order for the Earth to be inhabitable for higher life forms. Dr. Denton begins his book by discussing the four fundamental forces of nature and how perfectly suited they are for the formation of the universe. However, he goes into greater detail concerning the characteristics of various materials on the Earth which enable it to support life. Two of these, water and sunlight, will be discussed in detail as examples.

The Thermal Properties of Water

Water has five thermal characteristics that make it perfectly suited for the myriad of tasks that it performs on the Earth.

Water:

1. Contracts when the temperature is lowered until it reaches 4° centigrade. However, unlike other substances that continue to contract, water then begins to expand until it reaches freezing point (0° centigrade).
2. When ice melts and liquid water evaporates, heat is absorbed. When ice freezes and gaseous water condenses, heat is released.
3. The specific heat of water (the amount of heat required to raise the temperature of one gram of water 1° centigrade) is higher than most liquids.
4. The thermal conductivity (capacity to conduct heat) of water is four times greater than any other common liquid.
5. On the other hand, the thermal conductivity of ice and snow is very low.[12]

These five thermal characteristics are absolutely necessary for the continued survival of the Earth's climate and of the creatures that inhabit it. For example, if a particular reaction called **hydrogen bonding** did not occur, causing water to expand just before it turned to ice, the denser ice would sink to the bottom, where it would not melt during the ensuing summer. Therefore, all the lakes and streams, and eventually the oceans of the Earth, would slowly freeze up, creating an ice-bound planet incapable of sustaining life. However, because water expands as it is turning to ice, the ice is less dense than water. Thus, it floats. With the coming of spring, the ice on the surface of the lakes and rivers is able to melt, insuring a continuation of the seasons and of life on our planet. Furthermore, because of ice's low thermal conductivity, it provides an insulation of sorts to the water beneath it, allowing marine creatures to continue to function during the winter. The insulating character of ice and snow also enables many animals in higher latitudes to burrow into the winter snows and thus survive the cold season.

A rise in temperature causes ice to melt and water to evaporate; however, the evaporation process absorbs heat. The reverse is also true. A fall in temperature causes ice to form and water to condense, liberating heat. Both events cause a moderation of temperature change. Dr. Denton points out that "without those properties in point two, the climate would be subject to far more rapid temperature changes. Small lakes and rivers would vanish and reappear constantly."[13] These properties also affect humans and animals on a personal level. For example, as a person's body temperature rises, he generally sweats. The evaporation of this perspiration on his skin absorbs heat, cooling his body.

The combination of the larger amount of water on the Earth's surface, and water's high specific heat, helps to moderate our climate greatly. During the summer the Earth's lakes and oceans absorb a great deal of heat. Because of water's high specific heat, it takes time for oceans in the temperate zones to absorb heat. However, water also is very slow to release this heat. Therefore, it continues to surrender heat to adjacent land long after the land has become cooler due to approaching winter. Also, due to the Earth's rotation and to the complex pattern of winds that circle it, several large surface currents move from the tropics to higher latitudes, bringing warmth and moisture to those climates. An opposing set of surface currents bring cooler water south from the higher latitudes, cooling those lower latitudes. Without water's high specific heat, none of this would be possible, and climate extremes would be much more prevalent.

Liquid water's higher thermal conductivity enables cells, which cannot use convection currents, to distribute heat throughout the cell.[14] It also enables the sun's radiant energy to penetrate the oceans sufficiently to warm their surface waters and thus to provide thermal energy to currents such as the Gulf Stream moving through the ocean waters.

Water's Surface Tension

Another physical property of water, its high surface tension, makes possible the existence of large terrestrial plants. "It is the high surface tension of water which draws water up through the soil within reach of the roots of plants and assists in its rise from the roots to branches in tall trees."[15] Water's high surface tension also enables it to be a prime agent of weathering. Because of it, water is drawn into the cracks and crevices of rocks, where it dissolves chemicals. As the weather gets colder, water turns to ice, expands in the crevices, and helps to break the rocks into smaller pieces, causing the formation of soil. Therefore, because of its surface tension, water is able to assist in both chemical and physical weathering. The high surface tension of water also assists in the metabolic processes of man and of other creatures.

Water's Chemical Properties

Several chemical properties of water make it ideally suited for the role it plays in the Earth's biodiversity. First of all, water is a good solvent. Most chemicals dissolve in water. Thus, it is useful in carrying other molecules through the blood and tissues of animals and through the circulatory systems of plants. Dr. Denton points out that water is reactive with other compounds but not too reactive. If it were, it would consume those compounds dissolved in it.[16] However, because it reacts with many substances, it is a common catalyst, and it is also able to assist in chemical weathering. Dr. Denton states, "It seems that, like its other properties, the reactivity of water is ideally fit for *both its biological and its geological role*."[17] Dr. Denton discusses several other traits of water that make it ideally suited to the role it must play in the life of the Earth. However, the details given here clearly demonstrate water's unique character and how each of its properties work together to create harmony in both the Earth as a whole and in each of its creatures.

Solar Energy

Like water, the waves of the electromagnetic spectrum reaching the surface of the Earth make our planet uniquely fit for life. The electromagnetic spectrum is composed of several types of solar energy. The chart below shows the various types of radiation and their wavelengths.

Short Wavelengths				Long Wavelengths		
Gamma Rays	X-rays	Ultraviolet	Visible Light	Infrared	Microwaves	Radio Waves
10^{-16} to 10^{-4}	10^{-4} to 10^{-2}	10^{-2} to .4	.4 to .7	.7 to 10^3	10^3 to 10^9	10^9 and above

Figure 9-9 *The electromagnetic spectrum. Note: the lengths in microns of each type of wave is given directly beneath it. (A micron is one millionth of a meter.)*

It is obvious that the electromagnetic spectrum spans a huge difference in wavelength. The gamma waves are extremely small, below a trillionth of a centimeter, while radio waves can be several kilometers in length. Yet in spite of this broad spectrum of electromagnetic energy, the majority of it is cut off from the surface of the Earth. Seventy per cent of the light energy emitted from the sun's surface lies in an exceptionally tiny band stretching from .3 microns (near ultraviolet), through visible light, to 1.50 microns (near infrared).[18] Because the surface temperature of the sun is approximately 6000°C, it and other stars its size all produce the majority of their radiation in this tiny band. However, what is fascinating about this situation is that energy in this small band is exactly what the plants of the Earth need to photosynthesize.

Dr. Denton also points out that the near ultraviolet light stimulates the skin to manufacture vitamin D, necessary for calcium control and bone formation in all vertebrates, while the infrared is valuable because it provides the heat which makes our world inhabitable.[19]

With the exception of radio waves, the waves lying outside of this narrow band of visible, near infrared, and near ultraviolet light are harmful to living things. What is astounding is that, in addition to the sun producing very little harmful radiation, the Earth's atmosphere acts to block what does reach it. In the upper atmosphere is a layer of a special form of oxygen called ozone. Unlike the oxygen we breathe at the Earth's surface (O_2), a molecule of ozone consists of three oxygen atoms (O_3). The ozone layer blocks much of the harmful ultraviolet rays which do leave the sun. Nearer the Earth, oxygen and other atmospheric gases absorb electromagnetic radiation on either side of the visible and the near infrared waves. Water itself also absorbs harmful radiation. Yet both atmospheric gases and water allow electromagnetic radiation in the visible and near infrared range to pass through. As a result, "virtually no gamma, X ray, ultraviolet, far infrared, and microwave radiation reaches the surface of the Earth."[20]

Thus, once again, a complicated set of special circumstances is set in place; these circumstances then work together to benefit the living things of Earth. It is worth mentioning again that the properties of sunlight and water are only two of these. Many, many more exist. Like Dr. Ward and Dr. Brownlee, Dr. Denton is an evolutionist. However, unlike the others, he concludes from his study that the world looks as if it is a product of intelligent design.

"Whether one accepts or rejects the design hypothesis, whether one thinks of the designer as the Greek world soul or the Hebrew God, there is no avoiding the conclusion that the world looks as if it has been uniquely tailored for life: it *appears to have been designed*. All reality *appears* to be a vast, coherent, teleological whole with life and mankind as its purpose and goal."[21]

The creationist agrees. The evidence of a myriad of complex, interdependent, computer-like systems, ranging from the microscopic to the macroscopic and all working together in perfect harmony, is overwhelming in its reality and its significance. Like the bacterial flagella or the neck of the giraffe, the Earth itself, and perhaps the universe as well, could be considered irreducibly complex structures created by a benevolent God.

QUESTIONS FOR REVIEW

1. Explain the cycle that keeps oxygen in balance on the Earth.
2. List four of special characteristics of a habitable planet mentioned by Dr. Brownlee and Dr. Ward and explain why these characteristics are necessary.
3. List three of the special attributes of water and explain their significance.
4. Explain why the sun's beneficial radiation reaches the Earth's surface, while most of the sun's harmful radiation does not.

"If it could be demonstrated that any complex organ existed which could not possibly have been formed by numerous successive slight modifications, my theory (of evolution) would absolutely break down."

Charles Darwin

CHAPTER 10

ALTERNATE THEORIES OF BEGINNINGS

Vocabulary words to know: Gap Theory, Day-age Theory, Old Earth Creationists, Young Earth Creationists, Intelligent Design Group, Canopy Theory, Hydroplate Theory, circumstantial evidence, "ring of fire," subduction zone, Runaway Subduction Theory, supercontinent, subduction, polystrate fossils, and ice age

SECTION 1: NON-EVOLUTIONIST GROUPS

Much has been said in evolutionist's circles about creationists criticizing evolutionary theories but having nothing to replace them. It is true that creationists have much to say about current scientific beliefs. As has been demonstrated in the past four chapters, there are many valid scientific reasons to question them. However, in the larger scheme of things, there are only two possibilities: both the universe and all its inhabitants are the result of random mechanistic processes or the result of intelligent action. To prove that it is impossible for the former to occur is to offer strong evidence for the latter. Creationists also have specific theories about the beginning of life on Earth. Because some of them do not attempt to offer scientific proof as their support, they will be mentioned only briefly here. Three theories do attempt to offer a scientific explanation for the formation of the fossil record. For this reason they will be described in detail.

However, before attempting to discuss these theories, it is necessary to explain that even those scientists who believe in a "creator" are not totally in agreement on all the evidence. Some scientists simply recognize that the production of all the living things on Earth is, as one put it, "beyond the reach of chance."[1] They recognize that it cannot be scientifically determined which "designer" is responsible for all the complexity they see, and they do not attempt to deal with the issue. Put simply, they believe "somebody" had to do it. These individuals might be called the **Intelligent Design Group**.

Some creationists believe that the Earth is billions of years old. They are called **Old Earth Creationists**. One group of Old Earth creationists is

called **Day-age theorists**. These individuals are generally Christians who believe that God created the inhabitants of the Earth over a long period of time. They look to II Peter 3:8 for support for their beliefs. This verse states, "With the Lord a day is like a thousand years, and a thousands years are like a day."[2] Day-age theorists feel that God is outside of time, and the days mentioned in Genesis are really ages—long periods of times. There are also Old Earth creationists who believe that there was an earlier creation which was destroyed when Satan was put out of Heaven. They use Isaiah 14:12–16 and Ezekiel 28:12–17 as support for their beliefs. This belief is referred to as the **Gap Theory**. It is important to point out that these two theories developed only after scientists generally had accepted a uniformitarian explanation of geology and believed the Earth to be billions of years old. Thus, it is likely they came about because Christians were trying to explain the Scriptures in light of an old Earth.

Since both the day-age theorists and the gap theorists rely on some scriptures to support their theories, it is important to demonstrate that other scriptures cast serious doubt on them. For example, the Gap Theory states that there was an earlier creation that was destroyed when Satan was driven from heaven. They claim that the fossil record was created at that time. Yet Romans 5:12 states that through Adam sin entered the world and death came about as a result of sin. If death did not occur until after Adam sinned, how can we have the millions of dead things in the fossil record? Likewise, the Day-age Theory proposes that the days mentioned in Genesis were ages rather than twenty-four hours. Yet the Hebrew word used for *day* in Genesis refers to a twenty-four hour period. In addition, the phrase, "And there was evening and there was morning," follows the events of each day. This indicates that the term *day* was to be taken literally as a twenty-four hour period. In view of this, coupled with the fact that current scientific dating methods are unreliable, it seems much more reasonable to accept the first chapter of Genesis as written.

Finally, there are **Young Earth Creationists** who believe that the Earth is thousands rather than billions of years old. These individuals take the first chapter of Genesis literally. They believe the six days of creation refer to twenty-four hour days. It is important to remember that each of these theories is a matter of **belief**, not scientific fact. **From a scientific standpoint, it is impossible to know positively what happened at the beginning, since no one was there to witness it.** However, creation scientists currently discuss three theories that attempt scientifically to explain ancient conditions that could have had an influence on the modern Earth. For this reason they will be described in detail.

NON-EVOLUTIONIST	BELIEF	BASIS
Intelligent design Group	Someone had to do it.	Exclusively scientific evidence from nature
Old Earth Creationists (Day-age Theorists)	God did it over millions of years of time	The Bible—II Peter 3:8; possibly currently accepted old Earth beliefs
Old Earth Creationists (Gap Theorists)	God did it; fossils are from an earlier creation millions of years ago.	The Bible—Isaiah 14:12–17 and Ezekiel 28:12–17; also possibly currently accepted beliefs in an old Earth
Young Earth Creationists (including Canopy, Hydroplate, and Runaway Subduction Theorists).	God did it; fossils are from Noah's flood. Earth is thousands of years old.	The Bible (Genesis) & scientific evidence from nature

Figure 10-1 Non-evolutionists' beliefs.

QUESTIONS FOR REVIEW

1. Describe the gap theory and the day-age theory. Is there any reason to question them?
2. Contrast the beliefs of the old-Earth and young-Earth creationists. Which groups fall under each category?
3. Describe the attitude of the intelligent design group.

SECTION 2: THE CANOPY AND HYDROPLATE THEORIES

A canopy refers to a layer of gases and water vapor that can entirely surround a planet. Creation scientists have looked at the other planets of our solar system and noticed that Venus has a canopy of gases which holds in the heat, creating a greenhouse effect. This canopy is so efficient that Venus has the highest average surface temperature of any planet in the solar system, 470 degrees Celsius – even higher than Mercury, which is fifty million kilometers closer to the sun! Figure 10-2 illustrates this.

The Earth's atmosphere also produces a mild greenhouse effect. A portion of the heat reaching the surface of our planet is reflected back. However, our atmosphere retains some of this reflected heat

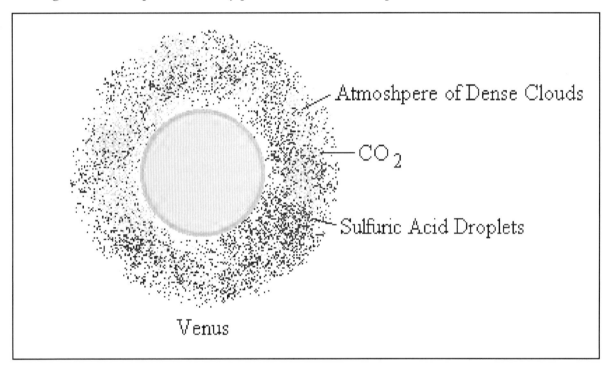

Figure 10-2 *The canopy causes an intense greenhouse effect; the average daily temperature on the surface of Venus is 470⁰ C. Drawing by A. Margetic.*

and does not permit it to return to space. Scientists theorize that at one time in the Earth's early history a more efficient canopy of water vapor surrounded the Earth. This canopy would act in much the same way that a greenhouse does in the winter, creating a uniform, mild climate over most of the Earth. These scientists also consider the description of the early Earth which is given in the Bible. Genesis 2:6 states that "the Lord God had not sent rain on the Earth . . . but streams came up from the earth and watered the whole surface of the ground."[3] They also take into account the description of a worldwide flood that is given in Genesis 6–8.

Canopy theorists envision an Earth that was made up of only one continent with one ocean surrounding it. They believe the temperature varied only slightly over the entire supercontinent. (Like evolutionists, creationists believe that all the continents were once joined in one large continent. It is often called Pangaea.) There was no rain. Instead, the Earth's surface was watered by springs that gushed from the ground. They also believe the collapse of this canopy precipitated the rains of Noah's flood. However, scientists at the Institute for Creation Research have done computer simulations testing the canopy theory. **They have found that a canopy large enough to hold all the waters** of Noah's flood would have held in so much heat that the Earth would have been too hot to support life, in much the same way that Venus is today. Therefore, if there was a canopy around the early Earth, it would not have been able to generate all the water needed for Noah's flood.

Another explanation of Noah's flood is the **hydroplate theory**. Hydroplate theorists believe that the early Earth had a layer of water beneath the Earth's crust. This water would have been under great pressure because of the rock layers above pressing down upon it. If for some reason the crust were to crack, the water trapped below would spray out of the ground under tremendous pressure. It would shoot high into the atmosphere, adding millions of gallons of water to it. Some scientists believe that this is what did occur. They feel both the Canopy and the Hydroplate theories are correct and that the critical addition of water from the hydroplates collapsed the canopy and started the first rain.

Many suggestions have been made about what caused the crack in the Earth. Some scientists believe that a large meteorite hitting the Earth could have damaged its crust and made the crack. Others hypothesize that the pressure of the underlying water layer could have caused the Earth's crust to split. Once the crack began, however, it would continue around the Earth. Anywhere the crack appeared, it would allow the underlying water to spurt out under high pressure, causing massive erosion of the rock on either side of the split. This eroded rock would then create abundant sediments which would trap plants and animals and form the fossil record.[4] Hydroplate theorists believe that at this time rapid continental drift occurred, creating the seven continents and forming many of today's landforms, such as the Himalayan Mountains.

Genesis 7: 11–12 states, "on that day all the springs of the great deep burst forth, and the floodgates of the heavens were opened. And rain fell on the Earth forty days and forty nights."[5] This supports the description given above. **However, no strong scientific evidence exists to suggest that this, in fact, is what did occur. In fact, there are serious scientific problems with the hydroplate theory which make it an unlikely explanation of the cause of Noah's flood.**

QUESTIONS FOR REVIEW

1. Describe the canopy that may have covered the ancient Earth.
2. Describe the structure of the continents and the climate of the pre-flood Earth, as pictured by canopy theorists and hydroplate theorists.
3. What have creation scientists learned about the effects of a heavy canopy? Could the canopy have held all the waters of Noah's flood?
4. Where do hydroplate theorists suggest the main source of water come from in Noah's flood and how do they feel it may have been released? Are there any problems with this theory?

Like many other scientists, Dr. Steve Austin became fascinated with science at an early age. He grew to be so knowledgeable that while he was still in elementary school, he spoke about scientific subjects on local television in California. One of the subjects he discussed was evolution, which he accepted as truth. Dr. Austin went to church and describes himself as a theistic evolutionist during his early years. He became a committed Christian at the age of eighteen, but this did not change his mind about evolution. However, while he was doing his undergraduate study at the University of Washington, he read several books by both evolutionists and creationists and became convinced that the creation model was the scientifically accurate one.

Dr. Austin received a master's degree in geology from San Jose State University and a doctorate in geology from Pennsylvania State University. He joined the staff of the Institute for Creation Research in 1979 and has published extensive material on creation research since that time. He is also an associate professor of geology at Christian Heritage College. Dr. Austin is married and lives in California.

SECTION 3: THE RUNAWAY SUBDUCTION THEORY

Creation scientists in general are quick to point out that although a canopy may have surrounded the pre-flood Earth, it could not have been very heavy. If it existed, it could have been heavy enough to cause a mild greenhouse effect. However, scientists from the Institute for Creation Research propose another theory to explain where the majority of the floodwaters originated.[6] In order to comprehend this theory, it is necessary first to understand some basic facts about the structure of the Earth. Through the study of earthquake waves, scientists have learned a great deal about the Earth's internal structure. For example, there is evidence that the inner core of the Earth is made up primarily of solid iron and nickel and is approximately 1200 kilometers thick. The outer core, in contrast, is believed to be made of liquid iron and nickel and is about 2300 kilometers thick. Then there is the mantle, which is made up mostly of silicon and oxygen, along with some magnesium and iron. Its average thickness is 3550 kilometers. Most scientists believe the mantle to have a plasticlike consistency, much like "silly putty." Therefore, it has many characteristics of a solid, but if put under enough pressure, it can flow like a liquid. Finally, the outermost and thinnest layer is the crust, which varies in thickness from five to thirty-five kilometers. (See Figure 10-4.)

The **Runaway Subduction Theory** is based on plate tectonics. Modern geologists point to the fact

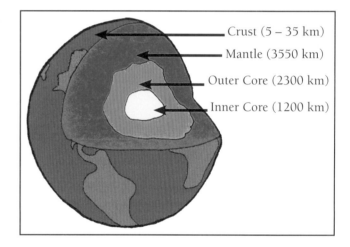

Figure 10-3 *A cross section of the Earth showing the different layers and their depths. Drawing by A. Margetic.*

that the crust of the Earth is cracked into various plates. Each of the continents rests on a plate, and the ocean floors are also broken up into several plates. (See Figure 10-4.) It is interesting to note that the present-day continents are made up primarily of granites and have an average density of 2.7 grams per cubic centimeter, while the ocean plates are made up of basalts with an average density of 3.5 grams per cubic centimeter.[7] Because of this difference in density, scientists believe that where the ocean plates collide with the continental plates,

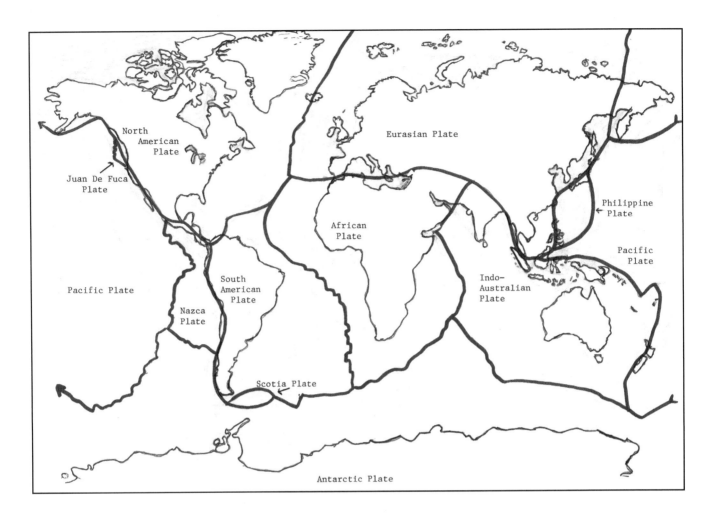

Figure 10-4 *The crust of the Earth is broken into several sections. Volcanic activity and/or movement occur at all plate boundaries.*

the denser ocean plates dive under the continental plates, forming a **subduction zone**. (See Figure 10-5.) This subducting process is thought to be occurring very slowly today. As the ocean plate descends into the mantle, it tends to melt, and the magma that is produced often finds its way to the surface through cracks in the crust, forming volcanoes. This is believed by many scientists to be the reason that the Pacific Ocean is encircled by a "**ring of fire**," a string of volcanoes that has formed all around the edge of the Pacific plate where it collides with the continental plates.

ICR scientists propose that the early Earth's ocean floor was made up of rock similar to the material in the underlying mantle. However, this crust would be much cooler than the mantle. Thus, the average density of the crust of the ocean floor would be greater than the density of both the continental crust and the mantle. It would also be denser than today's ocean plates. Under these circumstances, the ocean plates would descend more rapidly, and a phenomenon known as **runaway subduction** could occur. As the denser ocean crust descended into the mantle, friction between the plate and the mantle would cause heating which would allow the subduction to accelerate. Under these conditions, the rate of subduction could eventually reach 2.6 meters per second.[8]

Divergent plate boundaries also exist between some plates, particularly some ocean plates. For example, a divergent plate runs down the middle of the Atlantic Ocean. Lava coming from this diver-

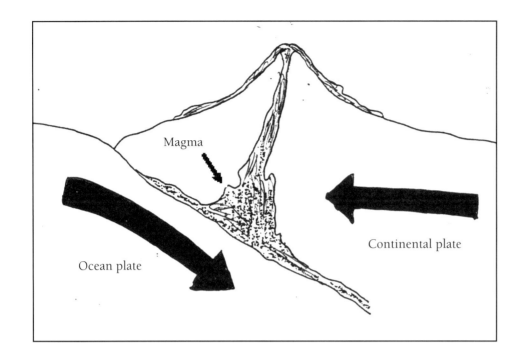

Figure 10-5 A
subduction zone.
The denser ocean
plate subducts
beneath the less
dense continental
plate. Drawing by
A. Margetic.

gent boundary has formed an underwater mountain chain thousands of miles long. It has also formed the island of Iceland and is continuing to create islands in that area. There are divergent plates in the other oceans also. Scientists from the Institute for Creation Research postulate that as the ocean plates subducted beneath the continental plates, the divergent boundaries would spread apart, releasing basaltic magma from the mantle. This magma would form the new ocean crust. Thus, a convection current would be at work in the mantle, with downward movement at the subduction zones and upward movement at the divergent boundaries.[9] (See Figures 10-5 and 10-6.)

As the hotter, less dense basaltic lava spread across the ocean floor, replacing the denser ocean plate, the ocean crust would start to rise, displacing much of its water onto the continents. Undersea earthquakes caused by the rapid subduction and divergence would also produce huge tsunamis which would add to continental flooding.[10] Scientists believe these created much of the water of Noah's flood and provided the sediments for most of the sedimentary rock we see today.[11]

Later, while the lighter continental crust rose, cooling of this new ocean crust would increase its density. The ocean floor would sink and once again accommodate the water it had displaced.[12]

Runaway subduction theorists also agree with the idea of one large continent existing in the past. During the time of the flood, the original super-continent that once existed on the Earth separated because of the intense tectonic activity and formed the seven continents that we know today. The Earth then settled into a new state of relative geologic balance, with earthquakes and volcanic activity dropping to the present state.

The mechanisms that have been described here are widely accepted as occurring within the mantle and the crust. Most creationists and evolutionists accept plate tectonics, subduction, and plate divergence. Even the idea of convection currents flowing within the mantle is widely accepted. The only difference is the predicted speed with which this occurred in the past. ICR scientists have done computer simulations on their theory and have found that under the postulated conditions, the computers predict that events would occur exactly as they hypothesized. **For these reasons, the Runaway Subduction Theory seems the best explanation yet proposed by creation scientists.**

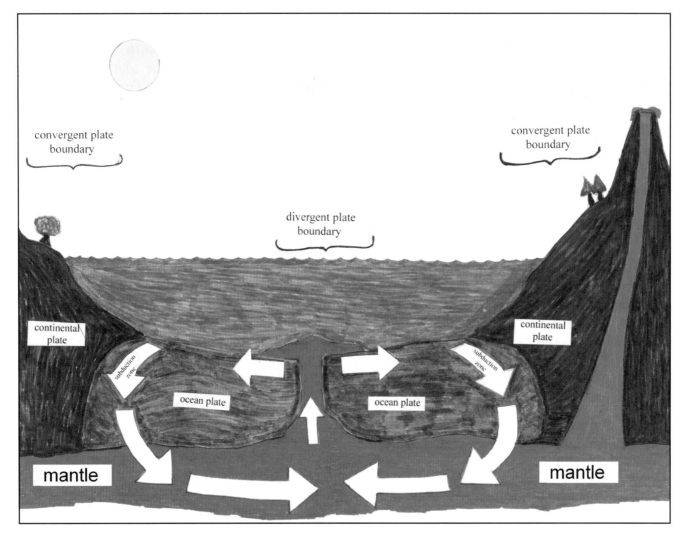

Figure 10-6 *The runaway subduction theory proposes that in the past the ocean plates were denser than they are today. This would cause rapid subduction of these plates under the continental plates. A convection current would carry the subducted material to the mid ocean where it would rise through a crack in the crust. The rapid movement of the Earth's plates would have caused the destruction of Noah's flood. Mantle and lava are colored in red. Drawing by K. Bartley and S. MacFarlane.*

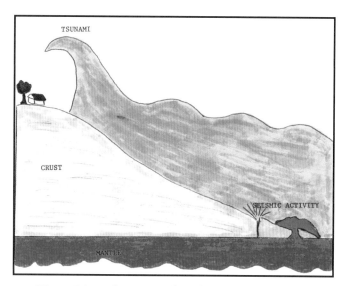

Figure 10-7 *When an earthquake occurs in the ocean floor, energy is released into the water. This energy moves through the water and creates a huge wave called a tsunami as it reaches nearby shores.*

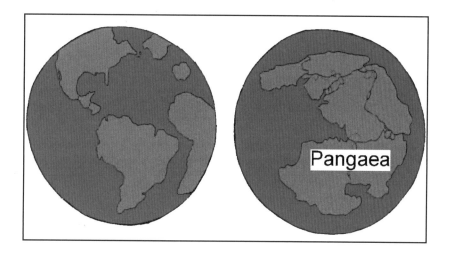

Figure 10-8 *Most scientists believe that the continents of the Earth were once joined together into one supercontinent as in the drawing at the far right. They have named this ancient supercontinent Pangaea. Drawing by A. Margetic.*

QUESTIONS FOR REVIEW

1. What is subduction? Define, please.
2. Describe the Runaway Subduction Theory.
3. What would cause the ocean to subside to its present level, according to this theory?
4. What happened to the super continent that once existed? When did this occur?
5. What were the results of the scientists' computer simulations?

Formation of Coal and Polystrate Fossils

Plants growing in swamps and buried there are generally transformed into peat, a coal-like substance. Many scientists believe that this peat is then turned into coal by heat and pressure. Since the accumulation of peat in swamps is a slow process, conventional scientific thought is that coal formation is a very slow process, requiring up to a thousand years per inch of thickness.

However, Dr. Steve Austin of the Institute for Creation Research has developed another model of coal formation. Dr. Austin points to Spirit Lake, the body of water just north of Mt. St. Helens, a volcanic mountain in Washington State. Because the lake was directly in the line of the blast when the volcano erupted, a hot, hurricane force wind knocked down a forest growing around it. A huge wave of water also caused by the eruption then carried the uprooted trees down into the lake.

For many years, thousands of trees have floated in the lake, creating a log mat. The wind has constantly moved these logs back and forth across the lake, scouring the bark from their sides. As a result, the sunken bark has accumulated into peat at the bottom of the lake. This peat resembles many coal beds of the eastern U.S. where the layers are quite easily distinguished. (Normally, peat formed in swamps has a homogenized texture.) The peat at the lake's bottom needs only to be buried and slightly heated to turn into coal. Therefore, the floating log mat theory of coal formation seems to be one that more accurately explains the observed facts.

In addition, because many of the trees in the lake still have their heavier roots attached, these trees float upright in the water, with the roots hanging down beneath the surface. Interestingly, many of these trees have now sunk, still in upright position, creating a "forest" on the bottom of the lake. These trees are being buried at different levels. Therefore, if they were to be buried quickly enough to be fossilized, they would appear to be "multiple forests which grew on different levels over periods of thousands of years."* This is the way the petrified forests of Yellowstone Park have been interpreted. Yet when the roots of the petrified trees of Yellowstone were examined, they were found to be broken off a few feet from the trunk in much the same way the trees in Spirit Lake are. This indicates they were violently uprooted and then deposited in their current positions and brings into question the standard interpretation of how the petrified forest of Yellowstone came into being.

*Steve Austin, "Mt. St. Helens and Catastrophism," Impact No. 157, El Cajon, California: Institute for Creation Research, July, 1986, p. 3.

Figure 10-9 *Floating logs on Spirit Lake, Washington.*
Photo courtesy of U.S. Geological Survey.

SECTION 4: NOAH'S FLOOD AND THE ICE AGE

Circumstantial evidence is evidence left behind at the scene of an event that points to a logical conclusion. It is often considered more valuable than eye witness testimony; many criminal cases are decided on circumstantial evidence alone. In discussing origins, the argument can be made that since there were no scientists there at the beginning to provide eye witness testimony, what we must look at is circumstantial evidence left behind and determine the most logical conclusion. In doing this, we find that there is a great deal of circumstantial evidence that points to a world-wide catastrophic event.

Although creation scientists may disagree as to the cause of Noah's flood, they generally agree that there was a worldwide flood as recorded in Genesis. There are several phenomena which have not been explained by any evolutionist theory but which are logically explained by such a catastrophe. For example, **polystrate fossils** have long posed a difficulty for those who believe that the geologic column was laid down slowly over millions of years. Polystrate fossils are usually plants (especially trees) which extend through several layers of sedimentary material. These fossils are found in coal seams and sedimentary rock, often extending through thirty or forty feet of strata.[13] Rapid burial and sedimentation are necessary for organisms to be fossilized. Otherwise they will decompose. This would indicate that these layers of sediment were deposited relatively rapidly. Yet, to an evolutionist, forty feet of rock strata would represent millions of years of time. A much more logical explanation would be that the rock strata were laid down rapidly by a catastrophic flood.

The structure of the fossil beds is another factor that supports a catastrophic flood. If Darwinian evolution were true, the fossil record should show a few fossils in many widespread locations. After all, evolutionists believe that the fossil record was gradually laid down over millions of years as organisms died and were buried. However, this is not what the fossil record reveals. Instead, thousands of fossils are usually found together.

For example, in a quarry in Ohio, thousands of trilobites and brachiopods have been found together. In Dinosaur National Park the bones of thousands of dinosaurs can be found. At Ghost Ranch, New Mexico, about 50 miles north of Santa Fe, is an area where over 1,000 small dinosaurs have already been extracted, and it is estimated there are thousands more to be removed. Likewise, in the Green River Formation in Wyoming, thousands of fish and bird fossils have been discovered.[14] In fact, it is far more commonplace to find the fossils of thousands of organisms together than it is to find only a few. Often they are distorted as if caught in some violent current. In one rock formation, a fossil fish is seen in the very act of eating another fish! This is what we would expect if these organisms were buried in a worldwide catastrophic event.

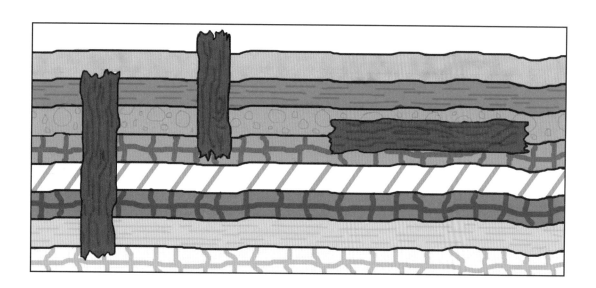

Figure 10-10 *Note how two of the logs extend upward through five or more sedimentary rock layers. These are polystrate fossils. They are common around the Earth. Drawing by A. Margetic.*

Figure 10-11: *Fossilized big fish eating a smaller fish. Photo courtesy of Joachin Sheven, photographer and owner. Fossil in Creation Museum in Germany.*

The Ice Age

Perhaps one of the most interesting phenomena that cannot presently be explained by any evolutionist theory is the ice age. There is abundant geological evidence to support one ice age having occurred in the past. However, conditions on today's Earth are not right for another ice age. It is true that our current winters are already sufficiently cold, but cold winters are not enough. Abnormally cool summers are also needed so that most of the ice and snow will not melt. In addition, the oceans must be abnormally warm to provide extra moisture. Today, in polar regions the temperature is often very cold —**so cold that there is not enough moisture in the air to produce the prodigious amounts of snow needed to create the continental glaciers.** However, after Noah's flood, conditions would have been right for such an ice age. First of all, the cracking of the crust and runaway subduction would have caused intense volcanic activity. This would have released a great deal of volcanic ash into the atmosphere. Volcanic ash reflects much of the sun's energy back into space. This would lead to cooler summers. Also, the post-flood oceans would have been warmer than today's oceans. Those who consider the runaway subduction theory to be the best explanation for the flood would point to all the underwater volcanic activity which would heat up the oceans. They would also say that the water that came from deep within the ground during the flood would have been very warm or even hot. This water would have mixed with the ocean waters and resulted in much warmer oceans just after the flood.[15] There is evidence to support this theory of a warmer, shallower ocean in the past. For example, off the coast of Norway there is a fossil coral reef at a depth of 1500 feet. Although the corals themselves are gone from these northern latitudes, the reefs they left behind are very hard to explain, unless the waters in this region were much warmer and shallower at some time in the past. Coral is a subtropical creature. It grows at depths of one hundred and fifty feet or less and only in warm waters. Today, coral reefs exist off the coast of East Africa, in the warm waters of the Pacific, and in the West Atlantic from Bermuda to Brazil.[16] There are no active coral reefs closer to the poles than these.

Thus, the unusual conditions of warm oceans combined with abnormally cool summers would have been ideal for the formation of the continental glaciers that spread across North America, Europe, and Asia. The ice age cannot be explained by uniformitarian principles. Conditions must have been very different in the past. The catastrophic events of Noah's flood provide an excellent explanation of the causes of the ice age.

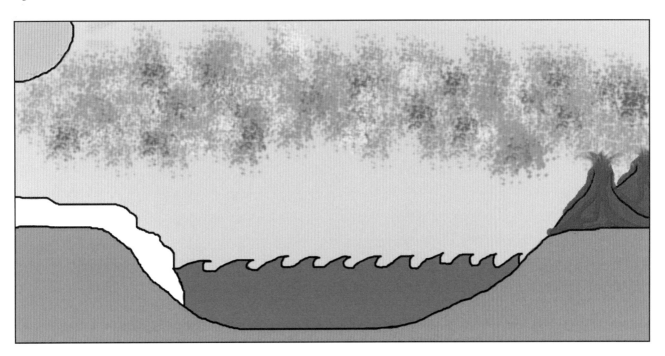

Figure 10-12: *If the runaway subduction theory is correct, post-flood conditions of an abnormally warm ocean, combined with colder summers due to volcanic ash in the atmosphere, would have caused massive continental glaciers. Drawing by A. Margetic.*

QUESTIONS FOR REVIEW

1. Give at least two examples of supporting evidence for Noah's flood.
2. What two conditions are necessary for an ice age to occur?
3. What events may have created the conditions necessary for an ice age immediately after Noah's flood?
4. What exists off the coast of Norway today which gives evidence for a warmer, shallower ocean? Why?

CHAPTER 11

THE EFFECTS OF A BELIEF IN EVOLUTION

INTRODUCTION

Ideas are powerful things. Some ideas seem to take on a life of their own, apart from the intent of their creator. For example, Darwin's theory has had effects that have gone far beyond what Darwin originally intended. In the 19th century, those of the Western world who were exposed to his theory and accepted it reacted in one of several ways. Some continued to accept a creator God but, because they believed parts of the Bible to have been proven false, held to the tenets of their faith less strongly, For others, evolution scientifically reinforced what they had already come to believe—that there is no God. Still others lost their faith completely. These attitudes, in turn, caused them to react in various ways. Some continued to live their lives as before, although their worship of God might have been less devoted. Others abandoned the religious teachings of their faith, choosing to live by their own rules instead. Still others used the theory of evolution, particularly natural selection, to justify all kinds of evil behavior. Today, the response remains much the same, though evolution's effects are greater and more widespread.

Figure 11-1 *Charles Darwin.* Photo from public domain.

SECTION 1: THE POLITICAL RAMIFICATIONS OF DARWINISM

Karl Marx

Although Darwin might not have fully understood the political effects of his work, there were others who did. One of them was Karl Marx, the father of communism. Marx was an atheist. He viewed religion as "the opiate of the people." Marx felt that the ruling classes used religion to control the working classes. If life was hard for them, they always had hope of a better life after death, and this hope would help to compensate them for their misery on Earth. Thus, the wealthy and powerful people could maintain control over the lower classes and keep them working for them. Marx stated, "The mortgage the peasant has on heavenly possessions guarantees the mortgage the bourgeois has on peasant possessions."[1] Although Marx did not believe in God, and atheism was a basic principle of communism, he had no explanation for how the Earth and all its inhabitants got here. This made it

Figure 11-2 *Karl Marx.* Photo from public domain.

difficult for him to convince others that atheism was practical and logical. However, after reading Darwin's *Origin of Species*, Marx was quick to realize that an evolutionary explanation for the origin of life was exactly what he needed to make atheism scientifically acceptable. He was so impressed and grateful to Darwin that he offered to dedicate his book *Das Kapital* to him. "Darwin hastily declined the honour in a polite, cautiously phrased letter, saying that he was unhappily ignorant of economic science, but offered the author his good wishes in what he assumed to be their common end —the advancement of human knowledge."[2]

Lenin

Vladimir Ulyanov, better known as Lenin, was a Russian disciple of Karl Marx. It was he who led the communist revolution in Russia in 1917 and established the communist dictatorship which ruled Russia for over seventy years. Lenin was deeply influenced by the theory of evolution. In the winter of 1888–1889, when he was in his late teens, Lenin read Karl Marx's *Das Kapital*. He also read some of Darwin's books.[3] Both these men were to have an enormous effect on his thinking for the rest of his life. Lenin "was a staunch supporter of the idea of

evolution: he accepted Darwin wholeheartedly and laid great stress on the dynamic and dialectical nature of the universe."[4] It has been argued that Lenin's belief in natural selection and social Darwinism led to every form of extremism and violence. "Merciless violence that strove for the destruction of every actual and potential opponent, was for Lenin not only the most effective but the only way of dealing with problems."[5] As Richard Piper points out in *A Concise History of the Russian Revolution*, "Marxism and Bolshevism, its offspring, were products of an era in European intellectual life that was obsessed with violence. The Darwinian theory of natural selection was promptly translated into a social philosophy in which uncompromising conflict occupied a central place."[6] This belief in the right of the strong to conquer and kill or enslave the weak became an abiding principle of Russian communism throughout its period of dominance.

Figure 11-3 *Lenin.* Photo from public domain.

Joseph Stalin

Another disciple of both Marx and Darwin was Joseph Stalin, Lenin's successor as the leader of communist Russia. Official Soviet biographers early recognized the importance of Darwin's theory in the shaping of Stalin's life. In fact, they claim that he first read Darwin in his early teens and became an atheist.[7] One of his English speaking biographers, Isaac Deutscher, doubts this is true but believes he may have read summaries of Darwin's ideas and thus been influenced against religion.[8] There is no doubt, however, that Stalin read Darwin's books while he was at the seminary where he received an education from 1894 till 1899. Although these books were not part of the seminary's curriculum, the seminary students secretly read and shared them.

"He [Stalin] treasured all his life the knowledge that had been so bold in his youth—that men have evolved in Darwinian fashion from the primates."[9] He used his belief in social Darwinism to justify many of his actions during his time in power. In 1928 he introduced the first of several five-year plans. This one was an attempt to eliminate the kulaks (peasants who owned their farms), convert their land into large collective farms, and begin the enforcing of grain quotas which the peasants had to meet. In the Ukraine, Stalin had an additional motive. He wanted to crush the peasant resistance he felt existed there. During the next few years 120 million people were forcibly removed from their land.[10] Many of these families were shot or deported to work camps in Siberia. Often family members perished on the way to the camps, while others did not survive the cruel winters and

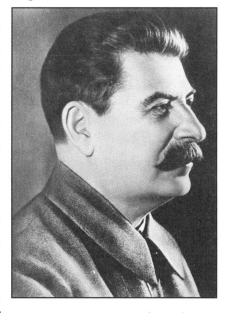

Figure 11-4: *Stalin.* Photo from public domain.

lack of food and shelter once they arrived. "The Soviet economist, V. A. Tikhonov, estimates that about three million peasant households were liquidated between 1929 and the end of 1933, leaving not fewer than fifteen million people without shelter or any place in the future rural society."[11]

In addition, the communists mounted an intensive campaign against the Orthodox churches and monasteries, and thousands of monks and nuns were deported to Siberia.[12] The peasants responded by killing millions of their livestock rather than give them up to the state. "Stalin was impervious to human suffering; but the loss of so valuable an asset as farm animals was a different matter."[13] Because of the high grain quotas, so much food was taken from the peasants that famine broke out, taking the lives of millions more. Altogether, 14.5 million people died. The number dying in Stalin's "war against the peasants" was greater than the number of lives lost in World War I.[14] Later, in the nineteen thirties, Stalin's purges of so called "enemies of the people" took at least three million more lives.[15] This does not include those who died under Stalin's rule from 1939–1953. In order to maintain his position as ruler and the communist party's control over the Soviet Union, he, along with other important members of the communist party, officially sanctioned the use of torture, terrorism, and execution to control the people. In Stalin's eyes, the right of the strong to deal with the weak as they saw fit was totally acceptable.

Adolph Hitler

Adolph Hitler was also deeply influenced by evolution. In fact, his entire justification for conquering and annihilating non-Germanic people was that Germanic people were at the top of the evolutionary scale. They were the most fit. Therefore, since the basic principle of life was "survival of the fittest," the German people had a right to take what they wanted and treat other people as slaves. "Politics is nothing more than the struggle of a people for its existence. It is an iron principle," [Hitler] declared, "the weaker one falls so that the strong one gains life."[16] He reiterated, "The right to possess soil can become a duty if without extension of its soil a great nation seems doomed to destruction."[17] Although his racial beliefs were also influenced by other individuals such as Gottfried Feder, Hitler used the evolutionary

Figure 11-5: *Adolph Hitler.* Photo courtesy of Archives + Library of Canada.

theory to justify racial dominance and destruction, especially of the Jews. It is interesting to note that Hitler did not look on Judaism as a religion but as a race. "He wrote that anti-Semitism should be based not on emotion, but on 'facts', the first of which was that Jewry was a race, not a religion . . . . Anti Semitism based on 'reason' must . . . lead to the systematic removal of the rights of Jews. 'Its final aim,' he concluded, 'must unshakably be the removal of the Jews altogether.'"[18] Hitler also used his belief in Darwinism as an excuse to dominate and destroy many other races besides the Jews. Peter Hoffman perhaps says it best in his book, *Hitler's Personal Security.* "Hitler believed in struggle as a Darwinian principle of human life that forced every people to try to dominate all others; without struggle they would rot and perish. In case of success the victorious people would have to become divided against itself to be able to continue the struggle so vital for human existence."[19] In 1945, when he realized the Russians would be victorious, Hitler still believed in this "principle" and declared the Russians had proven themselves stronger and therefore had a right to conquer Germany.[20] The basis of his cohesive, yet totally inhumane and destructive worldview was heavily dependent on Darwinism.

Benito Mussolini

According to a major biographer, Benito Mussolini, dictator of Italy from the 1920's until 1944, was deeply influenced by the theory of evolution. The biographer noted that Mussolini regarded Darwin as one of the two greatest thinkers of the nineteenth century.[21] Other writers agree. "Mussolini's attitude was completely dominated by evolution. In public utterances, he repeatedly used the Darwinian catchwords while he mocked at perpetual peace, lest it should hinder the evolutionary process."[22]

Mussolini emulated Hitler in his theory of the superiority of the Aryan race. He considered Italians to be Aryans, along with the Germans. Other races, especially Blacks, were definitely inferior. He felt so strongly about this that after he conquered Ethiopia, he instituted racial laws that made it a crime to marry or have sexual relations with an Ethiopian. In 1937 he extended these laws to include Libya, which was also an Italian colony. Two young Arabs were sentenced to eight years in prison after they "touched" an Italian girl in the street. Their crime was "having insulted racial prestige."[23] He also ordered the slaughter of thousands of Ethiopians and Libyans.

Finally, in 1938, Mussolini published an article in which he stated that the Jews were racially inferior. Although the article was supposed to have been written by a group of scientists, Mussolini had actually told a young scientist what to write.[24] In the article, now often called "The Manifesto of the Racist Scientists," he condemns the intermarriage of "racially pure" Italians with the Jews. Although

Figure 11–6: *Benito Mussolini.* Photo from public domain.

many Italians opposed this attitude, from that point on, the Jews were under official attack in Italy.

Like Hitler, Lenin, and Stalin, Mussolini also glorified war. He considered it right and natural for the strong to use force to subjugate the weak. Obviously, "survival of the fittest" was Mussolini's policy also.

It may be argued by some that Lenin, Stalin, Hitler, and Mussolini were all evil tyrants who would have killed and enslaved people anyway. However, others point to a connection between a belief in Darwin's theory and the behavior of many of the twentieth century's dictators. "From the 'preservation of favoured races in the struggle for life,' it was a short step to the preservation of favored individuals, classes, or nations—and from their preservation to their glorification. Social Darwinism has often been understood in this sense: as a philosophy, exalting competition, power and violence over convention, ethics and religion. Thus it has become a portmanteau of nationalism, imperialism, militarism, and dictatorship, of the cults of the hero, the superman, and the master race."[25]

QUESTIONS FOR REVIEW

1. Describe Darwin's attitude toward Christianity.
2. Why was Karl Marx so pleased with Darwin's theory of evolution? What did he offer to do?
3. What effect did a belief in evolution have on Lenin?
4. What effect did a belief in "survival of the fittest" have on Stalin?
5. How did Hitler justify Germany's conquering and enslaving nearby countries?
6. How did Mussolini justify his treatment of other countries and peoples?

SECTION 2: THE SOCIAL EFFECTS OF DARWINISM

Charles Darwin

Although Darwin looked upon his theory as applying primarily to biological evolution, he was also aware of the social ramifications. For example, in *The Descent of Man*, he points out:

> With savages, the weak in body or mind are soon eliminated; and those that survive commonly exhibit a vigorous state of health. We civilized men, on the other hand, do our utmost to check the process of elimination; we build asylums for the imbecile, the maimed, and the sick; we institute poor-laws; and our medical men exert their utmost skill to save the life of every one to the last moment. There is reason to believe that vaccination has preserved thousands, who from a weak constitution would formerly have succumbed to smallpox. Thus the weak members of civilized society propagate their kind. No one who has attended to the breeding of domestic animals will doubt that this must be highly in-jurious to the race of man. It is surprising how soon a want of care, or care wrongly directed, leads to the degeneration of a domestic race, but excepting in the case of man himself, hardly any one is so ignorant as to allow his worst animals to breed.[26]

Darwin's belief in the beneficial effects of natural selection led him to believe that helping the weak and the sick was a bad idea for the human race. Many individuals have accepted this viewpoint and used it to justify such things as abortion, infanticide, and euthanasia, as well as the denying of help to the poor and the sick.

Herbert Spencer

One of the individuals who was quick to apply natural selection to human society was a contemporary of Darwin, a man named Herbert Spencer. Spencer had already come to a belief in evolution before he read Darwin's *Origin of Species*. He applauded Darwin's work because he felt it explained evolution scientifically. His application of evolutionary principles to human society became known as "social Darwinism." It was Herbert Spencer who coined the phrase "survival of the fittest." He stated in his book, *Social Statistics*, that "the forces which are working out the great scheme of perfect happiness, taking no account of incidental suffering, exterminate such sections of mankind as stand in their

Figure 11-7: *Hebert Spencer.* Photo from public domain.

way, with the same sternness that they exterminate beasts of prey and useless ruminants."[27] Spencer felt the victory of the strong over the weak was not only logical but also acceptable. In *Man Versus the State*, Spencer argued that "London's 'good-for-nothings' ought not to be kept alive by charity but allowed to perish, for this was the universal law of nature."[28]

Effect on Literature

Such a worldview became commonplace over the next decades. It is even demonstrated

in some literature, influencing the works of such well-known American writers as Jack London and Stephen Crane, as well as English writers such as George Bernard Shaw. For example, Jack London wrote a short story entitled "The Law of Life." In it, Koskoosh, an old, blind Alaskan Indian who is no longer able to care for himself is left by his tribe to die. His granddaughter gives him a small supply of wood and seats him by a tiny fire. Then the tribe breaks camp and leaves him to die alone. Soon, the wolves find him and begin to close in. At first, Koskoosh uses burning sticks from the fire to hold them off. However, he realizes it is only a matter of time until the fire burns out and the wolves have him. The story ends, "Koskoosh dropped his head wearily upon his knees. What did it matter after all? Was it not the law of life?"[29]

In a current novel by the well-known mystery writer, Jonathon Kellerman, entitled *Survival of the Fittest,* a psychologist attempts to catch a serial killer who is preying on the handicapped. At the climax of the story, the psychiatrist and the killer discuss his motives.

[Killer] "How many ants have you stepped on in your lifetime? Millions? Tens of Millions? How much time have you spent regretting the fact that you committed ant genocide?"

Figure 11-8: *Authors, Jack London (above left).* Photo courtesy of California Parks and Recreation Dept. *Stephen Crane (above right).* Photo in public domain.

[Psychologist] "Ants and People . . ."

[Killer] It's all tissue, organic material – jumbles of carbon. So simple, until we elevated apes come along and complicate things with superstition. Remove God from the equation and you're left with a reduction as rich and delicious as the finest sauce: It's all tissue, it's all temporary."

[Psychologist] "Survival of the Fittest."

[Killer] "Spare me the sloppy compassion. Without the fittest there will be no survival. Retardates don't discover cures for diseases. Spastics don't steer jumbo jets. Too many of the unfit, and we'll all be enduring, not living."[30]

The killer later explains that he considers the handicapped to be experiencing what Hitler called "lives not worth living."[31]

It may be argued that these statements are the ravings of a madman. It must also be emphasized that the book's hero in no way shares the killer's views. However, the killer's reasoning, although warped and distorted, is a generally **logical** outcome of the application of natural selection to human society. This is demonstrated in the next section by some real-life attitudes and actions based on an evolutionary worldview.

QUESTIONS FOR REVIEW

1. According to Darwin, what effect do vaccination and caring for society's weak have on the human race?
2. How did Herbert Spencer's belief in evolution affect his view of human society?
3. Describe two instances of evolution's effect on literature.

SECTION 3: DARWINISM'S EFFECTS ON ETHICS

The effects of evolutionary beliefs have gone beyond the social and political realms. A belief in evolution has also affected the ethics of many throughout the twentieth century. For example, Hitler's application of natural selection to society led to the forced sterilization of thousands of mentally and physically handicapped persons in Germany because of their "racial impurity."[32] Many of these people later perished in the death camps. The Nazis also killed older people who were no longer able to contribute to society.

Today, many philosophies and practices based on, or influenced by an evolutionary worldview are becoming increasingly popular throughout the world. For example, Peter Singer is an Australian-born philosopher who is a professor at Princeton University. Many individuals consider him reputable and "moderate." In fact, he was recently asked to write the essay on ethics for the *Encyclopedia Britannica*. Singer's belief system comes directly from his evolutionary worldview. In his book, *Rethinking Life*

and Death, Singer demonstrates the importance of Darwin's theory to his way of thinking.

> Darwin's theory, embodied in these two great works [Origin of Species and Descent of Man], undermined the foundations of the entire western way of thinking on the place of our species in the universe. He taught us that we too were animals, and had a natural origin as the other animals did. As Darwin emphasized in The Descent of Man, the differences between us and nonhuman animals are differences of degree, not of kind. Nor did he rest his case on physical similarities alone. The third and fourth chapters of The Descent of Man show that we can find the roots of our own capacities to love and to reason, and even of our moral sense, in the non-human animals.
> The difference Darwin makes is more momentous than many people appreciate . . .

—if we are an animal, rather than a specially created being made in the image of God – how can this not reduce the gulf between us and them?[33]

Based on this worldview, Mr. Singer has rewritten five of the traditional commandments. Below is a brief summary of them

Traditional Commandment (based on Christian ethic)	New Commandment (based on evolutionary humanism)
Treat all human life as of equal worth.	Recognize the worth of human life varies.
Never intentionally take innocent human life.	Take responsibility for the consequences of your decisions; allowing or helping others to die may be appropriate.
Never take your own life and always try to prevent others taking theirs.	Respect a person's desire to live or die.
Be fruitful and multiply.	Bring children into the world only if they are wanted.
Treat all human life as always more precious than any nonhuman life.	Do not discriminate on the basis of species.[34]

Dr. Singer assumes that evolution is a fact. **His system of ethics shows a logical progression of thought, based on this assumption.** If evolution were true, why wouldn't the things he advocates be reasonable?

Mr. Singer is a founder of the animal-rights movement. He wants to elevate the moral status of animals to that of humans. He considers a "person" to be "a being with certain characteristics such as rationality and self-awareness."[35] Singer states, "There are other persons on this planet. The evidence of personhood is at present most conclusive for the great apes, but whales, dolphins, elephants, monkeys, dogs, pigs and other animals may eventually also be shown to be aware of their own existence over time and capable of reasoning. Then they too will have to be considered as persons."[36] Singer advocates the abortion of all defective fetuses, as well as the killing of defective newborn babies.[37] In addition, he advocates infanticide of healthy babies in countries where there are more infants than people willing to care for them. He says, "In regarding a newborn infant as not having the same

Figure 11-9: *Peter Singer.* Photo provider: AP Wide World Photos.

right to life as a person, the cultures that practised infanticide were on solid ground."[38] He goes on to state, "Since neither a newborn human infant nor a fish is a person, the wrongness of killing such beings is not as great as the wrongness of killing a person."[39] In other words, it is not as wrong to kill a newborn baby as it is to kill an ape. Singer also advocates assisted suicide of the terminally ill and euthanasia of those too ill to make this decision. Apparently, an individual too sick to think rationally is no longer to be considered "a person" and thus does not have the right to life that a healthy ape does.

Singer is not the only prominent secular humanist whose belief system leads him to promote euthanasia in the United States. His point of view is shared by many. For example, Derek Humphry's acceptance of Singer's beliefs is obvious. His comment, written on the jacket cover of Singer's book, *Rethinking Life and Death,* states that Singer "brilliantly debunks old concepts and introduces honesty to modern medical ethics." Humphry, a well-known author, has written several books on euthanasia. In 1980 he also founded The Hemlock Society, an organization dedicated to making assisted suicide and euthanasia legal. Humphry assisted in the suicide of his first wife, who had cancer. He later was alleged to have pressured his second wife to commit suicide after she also was diagnosed with the same disease and to have divorced her when she refused.[40]

Many of Singer's and Humphry's beliefs are shared by other secular humanists. For example, The American Humanist Society actively promotes atheism and accepts evolution as the sole basis for origins.[41] Prior to Darwin, humanism had many advocates who believed in God. However, once Darwin's theory became popular, humanist societies were largely made up of atheists and agnostics.

Since humanists generally feel that human existence is restricted to the present life, they feel mankind's goal should be to make this life as pleasant, convenient, and fulfilling as humanly possible. Because its members usually do not accept Christian principles concerning the sanctity of life, they generally favor abortion, assisted suicide and euthanasia.

Dr. Jack Kevorkian, a well-known humanist, is also a Michigan pathologist who has assisted in at least twenty suicides and has euthanized one patient. He has presented a detailed plan for assisted suicide and euthanasia, which he calls "medicide." He has even proposed a new medical specialty that he calls "obitiatry." This specialty would require four years of training in "medicide."[42]

There are dozens of others who have written books advocating euthanasia or assisted suicide. In each case, supporting this position requires a belief in Singer's first and third "commandments"—commandments based on evolutionary humanism and in direct opposition to Christian ethics.

Although assisted suicide and voluntary euthanasia are not yet legal in the United States, they are already being carried out in the Netherlands today. Dr. Herbert Hendin, an American, did a detailed study of this practice and wrote a book describing its consequences. He points out that the Dutch have set up elaborate guidelines to protect the patient from being killed without his knowledge or consent. However, in practice, the guidelines are often ignored. The Dutch organized a government commission to study the problem. The results were published in 1991. The commission found that in over 1,000 cases, "physicians admitted they actively caused or hastened death without any request from the patient."[43] In over 5,000 other cases, decisions were made which were intended to shorten *competent* patients' lives without consulting them.[44]

Figure 11-10: *Jack Kevorkian.* Photo provider: AP Wide World Photos.

(*Emphasis added by author.*) Dr. Hendin concludes, "The Netherlands has moved from assisted suicide to euthanasia, from euthanasia for people who are terminally ill to euthanasia for those who are chronically ill, from euthanasia for physical illness to euthanasia for psychological distress, and from voluntary euthanasia to involuntary euthanasia."[45] In spite of these problems, euthanasia and assisted suicide continue to be practiced in the Netherlands today.

What caused this abrupt change in the sanctity of human life in the Netherlands? Many observers attribute it to moral relativism, which they say is common in Dutch society. One observer describes the Dutch as "relatively uninterested in moral philosophy . . . and as unwilling to accept any moral absolutes and lacking in moral passion. The Dutch, he points out, tend to equate morality with religion, seeing themselves as non-religious."[46] Yet this has not always been the case. At the beginning of the twentieth century, almost 98% of the Dutch were members of Christian churches.[47]

Others point out that humanists have waged a long and successful battle in the Netherlands since World War II. Dr. Peter Derkx, professor of humanism and world views at the Zingeving University for Humanistics in the Netherlands, states, "In the period 1946–1965 it [the Dutch Humanist Association] waged a successful emancipation struggle as a worldview organization on behalf of non-Christian humanists, and atheists and agnostics in general. In 1965 one can say that it had completed this mission."[48] During this time Dutch humanists also "crusaded in favor of the legalization of abortion and euthanasia."[49] Their opinions seem to have prevailed. Evidently, the values of the Dutch population have changed.

Dr. Hendin points out that euthanasia is also being advocated by a large number of people in the United States. He attributes this to our increasing lack of connection to "family, religion, country, and work."[50] Hendin states, "In a culture in which *life has no continuity, in which life lacks significance beyond itself,* death becomes more threatening and intolerable."[51] (*Emphasis added by author.*) He later adds, "In such a society, dying can be a terribly lonely and desperate experience. Therefore, many attempt to control this fear by hastening the process."[52]

If there is no creator God, life obviously has no significance beyond itself. Nor are humans under any obligation to follow what they may consider outdated rules of conduct.

QUESTIONS FOR REVIEW

1. Who is Peter Singer?
2. How does his belief in evolution affect his ethical beliefs concerning the old and the ill?
3. Whom does Singer consider to be a person?
4. What does Singer consider a fetus or a newborn baby to be? How does he feel about abortion and infanticide?
5. How is euthanasia being practiced in the Netherlands today? Who is being affected by it?
6. Why does Dr. Hendin believe euthanasia is being advocated by many in the U.S. today?

SECTION 4: THE MORAL CONSEQUENCES OF A BELIEF IN DARWINISM

It is evident that the Christian society that was once established in the Netherlands has been replaced by a secular society in which many of the things Mr. Singer advocates are being practiced. During World War II Dutch doctors refused to help the Nazis with euthanasia. Yet, now they are in the forefront of such practices. However, this trend is not restricted to the Netherlands. Abortion is already legal in many nations once considered Christian. Euthanasia is encouraged in many. The "personhood" of many humans is being questioned. Why? Because as Peter Singer points out, a belief in evolution logically leads to the creation of a new set of "commandments" to replace those of the Bible. This was recognized in the latter half of the nineteenth century—very soon after Darwin's theory was publicized—with the "birth" of the "God is Dead" philosophy which was "resurrected" in the 1960's.

Paul A. Carter wrote of this philosophy in an article in the magazine, *American Scholar*, in 1973. In the article he traces the "battle" between science and Christianity. He also emphasizes the contribution of Darwinism to this struggle.[53] He shows how this has caused many Christians to retreat from their beliefs because of the claims of science. Carter points out that God can be considered "dead" in a social sense because "the political, economic, and educational institutions which used to convey and confirm the presence of God no longer do so."[54] Finally, he says that God may be theologically dead, and "that Christian . . . theology has become only a somewhat novel mode of atheist humanism."[55]

Nevertheless, God is not dead as far as many Christians are concerned. Numerous Christian believers still have faith in the existence of a personal Creator and attempt to follow the moral imperatives outlined in His word. However, what is being spoken of here is a **trend** that seems to be affecting Christian churches. Mr. Carter recognized that evolution is at least one important source of the problem. After all, if all living things evolved from a single-celled creature which spontaneously arose, there is no need for a creator God. At the very least, the Genesis account of creation must be false. If Genesis is false, the reliability of the Bible as the true word of God is in question. If the Bible is unreliable, even if a person believes in God, he may feel he has no reliable access to God's will for his life and thus has no moral absolutes to guide him. Moral relativism is a logical outgrowth of such a situation.

It has been rightly stated that many belief systems have fostered evil acts by some of their advocates. For example, all manner of evil behavior has been justified in the name of Christianity. The so-called "Christian" Crusades are but one example. **What is often ignored in the case of Christianity is the fact that such evil behavior is in direct opposition to the teachings of Christ and that those who practice it should not be considered Christians.** Such people are obviously not living according to Christian principles.

However, with a belief in evolution, this is not the case. **If a secular humanist practices moral relativism or Social Darwinism, it is a logical outcome of his beliefs.** It is unquestionably true that millions of individuals accept evolution as true and yet lead decent and productive lives. Yet many fail to see where a belief in this theory logically leads.

Ideas truly are powerful things. If a belief in evolution had been restricted to science, it would have caused few problems. As scientific knowledge expanded and scientists came to realize that this knowledge pointed to an intelligent designer, those beliefs would have been changed. However, the theory of evolution has fostered a philosophy that has gone beyond the realms of science to have far-reaching effects on the political, social, ethical, and moral climate of the world. This fact was recognized as early as 1965:

> Most enlightened persons now accept as a fact that everything in the cosmos—from heavenly bodies to human beings—has developed and continues to develop through evolutionary processes. The great religions of the west have come to accept a historical view of creation. Evolutionary concepts are applied also to social institutions and to the arts. Indeed, most political parties, as well as schools of theology, sociology, history, or arts, teach these concepts and make them the basis of their doctrines. Thus, theoretical biology now pervades all of Western culture indirectly through the concept of progressive historical change.[56]

That these effects are based on a belief that has little or no scientific support is one of the great ironies of history.

QUESTIONS FOR REVIEW

1. What is the "God is Dead" philosophy, and what is the reasoning behind it?
2. According to Paul A. Carter, in what sense is God dead?
3. Explain the pattern of reasoning that can develop from a belief that evolution is true.

GLOSSARY

A

Adaptations Certain traits organisms generally have that help them to survive in a specific environment. For example, the white coat of the polar bear helps it to blend in with its environment and thus more easily capture prey.

Adaptive radiation Evolutionists define it as the process by which members of a species adapt to different ecological "niches."

Adenine One of the four nitrogen-carrying bases of DNA.

Adolph Hitler The dictator of Germany from 1932 until 1945. He was responsible for the deaths of millions of civilians in concentration camps, including five million Jews.

Agricultural revolution This refers to a time, dated by evolutionists at about 10,000 to 11,000 years ago, when people stopped hunting and gathering as their primary source of food and began to domesticate animals and plant crops.

Ambulocetus. This fossil, a proposed ancestor of the whales, was found in Pakistan and is described as a "walking whale" about 3 meters long, with sharp teeth and short, broad legs.

The fossil consists of a partial skeleton with skull, vertebrae, ribs, and partial limbs. The hind limbs have hooves.

Anaerobic bacteria Bacteria that cannot exist in the presence of free oxygen.

Analogous structures Body parts in different species that are different in structure but are used in the same way. For example, the wings of birds and butterflies are different in their basic structure but are both used for flight.

Archaeopteryx A proposed link fossil between reptiles and birds. It is considered to be this by evolutionists because it possesses teeth, claws on wings, and flat breastbone (so-called reptilian features), along with wings and feathers (bird features).

Ardipithecus ramidus A fossil paleoanthropologist Timothy White discovered at a site in Ethiopia. The fossil consists of teeth and arm bones of an animal he thinks is bipedal. He dated it at 4.4 million years old. He has decided it is more primitive than the australopithecines and has created a new genus as well as a new species for it.

Articulated skeletons Skeletons that are all together in one location, with the bones in roughly the correct proximity to one another.

Assumptions Ideas that are accepted without proof.

ATP Adenosine triphosphate, an energy carrier in many living cells.

Australopithecines Genus believed by evolutionists to have included the earliest known hominids.

Australopithecus afarensis This species is based on a fossil discovered by Donald Johanson in East Africa in 1974. Forty per cent of the fossil was found. It is believed to have been an erect-walking female about three feet tall and weighing fifty pounds.

Australopithecus africanus This species is based on a fossil discovered by Raymond Dart in southern Africa. The original specimen consisted of a cast of a brain, along with the front portion of a skull. Dart created the genus *australopithecus* based on this fossil.

Australopithecus anamensis This species is based on a fossil discovered by Meave Leakey in Africa. Its parts were found in three different locations and two different rock strata.

Australopithecus robustus An australopithecine which is often considered a link fossil in the evolution of the ape family but not in the evolution of man.

B

Basilosaurus Yet another proposed link fossil in the ancestry of the whale, *Basilosaurus* was a marine creature that had a long, slender body. It also had flippers, small flukes on its tail, tiny hind legs, and a flexible backbone.

Bipedalism The ability to walk on two legs.

Broca's area The part of the brain that controls muscles for speech in humans.

Brontosaurus A dinosaur that did not exist. Scientists assembling dinosaur skeletons mistakenly put the wrong head on the body of an *Apatosaurus* and created Brontosaurus.

C

Cambrian explosion This refers to the fact that there is a sudden "explosion" of fossils in rocks dated to be very old. In fact, representatives of 95% of all the phyla found in the fossil record show up suddenly in Cambrian rock.

Canopy theory This theory proposes that the Earth was once surrounded by a canopy of water vapor and other gases in much the same way Venus is today. The canopy then collapsed, signaling the beginning of Noah's flood. The canopy theory has been largely discounted by most creationists today.

Carbon film fossil This fossil occurs when an organic structure, such as a leaf, becomes buried in sediments, and the weight of the upper sediments causes it to turn to carbon.

Casts These form when other materials fill in molds, which are hollows in rocks shaped like the organism trapped in them.

Circular reasoning Using two ideas to validate each other; for example, making the assumption that idea A is true because of idea B and that idea B is true because of idea A, without validating either idea through an independent source.

Circumstantial evidence Evidence left behind at the scene of an event that points to a logical conclusion. At a crime scene, for example, a murder weapon with fingerprints or DNA left behind would be circumstantial evidence.

Codons Groups of three nucleotides; they are the "words" of DNA.

Coelacanth The coelacanth was once believed to be a transitional form between the fish and the amphibians because of a bone structure that was slightly different from present-day fish. However, when a fisherman caught two living coelacanths off the eastern coast of Africa, it was easy to determine that the coelacanth was merely a fish and not a transitional form at all.

Comparative embryology The study of similarities between the embryos of different species, such as fish, birds, dogs, and humans, to prove evolutionary similarities and common ancestry.

Convergent evolution Evolutionists define it as the process by which widely different organisms become more alike as a result of adapting to similar environments.

Correlating the rocks This refers to scientists examining rock strata in different locations and determining through the character of the rocks, and the fossils that they hold, that they are of the same age.

Cro magnon A "variety" of humans based on five fossils found in a cave in France in 1868. Since that time, many other camps with similar fossils have been discovered. Physically, the Cro-Magnon people were identical to modern humans.

Crossover During meiosis, a process in which homologous chromosomes (those that contain genes from each parent for the same traits) come together and trade genes.

cytochrome C A protein in the mitochondria of all eukaryotes which is used in aerobic respiration.

Cytosine One of the four nitrogen-carrying bases of DNA.

D

Daughter or decay element The stable element into which a radioactive element decays.

Day-age theorists These individuals are generally Christians who believe that God created the inhabitants of the Earth over a long period of time. They look to II Peter 3:8 for support.

Decay element See "daughter element."

Dendrochronology Tree ring dating.

Devolution Change which comes about primarily through a loss of information.

Divergent evolution The process of organisms becoming less alike due to adaptation to different environments.

Dominant The genes that are expressed in the phenotype of an organism.

Dynamo Theory A theory which suggests that the Earth's magnetic field has a self-exciting dynamo which produces electricity and adds to the Earth's magnetic field from time to time.

E

Electron transport chain This refers to "supercharged" electrons moving from one chlorophyll molecule to another in the light phase of photosynthesis. As each transfer is made, some energy is released.

Embryonic tail This so-called tail is nothing more than the end of the spine before the legs begin to grow. It becomes the tailbone, which is "an important point of muscle attachment required for our distinctive, upright posture."

Euthanasia So-called "mercy" killing. Taking the life of a critically ill or very old person because he or she can no longer "contribute" to society and is thus a "burden."

Evolution Evolutionists define it as change over time.

F

Fossils The remains of once living organisms.

G

Gap Theorists Old Earth creationists who believe that there was an earlier creation that was destroyed when Satan was put out of Heaven. They use Isaiah 14:12–16 and Ezekiel 28:12–17 as support.

Gene pool All the genes of all the organisms in a given population.

Genetic drift The elimination of genes from a population due to chance.

Genetic isolation The separation of members of a population into two or more groups so that they no longer can interbreed freely.

Geographic isolation Occurs any time a natural barrier such as a river or a mountain range comes between members of the same population of animals and prevents them from freely interbreeding; it leads to genetic isolation.

Geologic column A chart which attempts to correlate all the sedimentary rocks of the Earth into one continuous sequence of layers; it designates the bottom layers as the oldest and the subsequent layers as progressively younger as one moves from the bottom to the top. There are also geologic columns that chart only a local area.

Geologists Scientists who use fossils (and other methods) to help determine the history of the Earth.

Gill slits The pharyngeal pouches (neck portion) of various embryos. The term is also used in reference to human pharyngeal pouches, even though the human embryo does not develop gill slits there.

Glucose The sugar which the bodies of humans and many other organisms use for energy.

Guanine One of the four nitrogen-carrying bases of DNA.

H

Half-life The half-life of an isotope is the time it takes for one half of its atoms to break down into its daughter element.

Hardy-Weinberg principle The main point of this principle is that although a population's gene frequencies can be affected by outside influences such as genetic drift or natural selection, the proportion of various genes within a population tends to remain the same over long periods of time.

Heterozygous Carrying a dominant and a recessive gene for a particular trait.

Hominids "Human-like" species; evolutionists believe them to have been bipedal but to have retained many ape-like characteristics.

Homo erectus This species is based on a fossil discovered on the island of Java by an expedition working under the leadership of a Dutch medical doctor named Eugene Dubois. This fossil consisted of a skull plate and a femur. It became known as Java man and later, *Homo erectus* because it was believed to have walked upright. Several more complete skeletons have since been found and assigned to this species.

Homo habilis A fossil found by Lewis and Mary Leakey consisting of a mandible, some skull parts, a foot and some finger bones. The scientists also found some primitive tools nearby. Believing the fossil to have at one time used the tools, they named this new species *Homo habilis*, which means "handy human."

Homo sapiens The genus and species to which humans belong. Generally, Neanderthals, Cro magnon, and modern humans are all classified as *Homo sapiens*. The term literally means "wise human beings."

Homologous chromosomes Chromosomes which have genes for the same trait, but they are not identical because they are inherited from different parents.

Homologous genes Corresponding genes on the chromosomes of different organisms of different species.

Homologous structures Structures in different species, such as the arms of humans and the front legs of dogs, the wings of birds and the flippers of whales, which are similar in structure but different in use; to an evolutionist, this structural similarity indicates a common ancestor.

Horse series Several fossils scientists have found that they believe demonstrate the evolution of the horse from a tiny, dog-like creature to the modern horse we have today.

Hydrogen acceptor In the light phase of photosynthesis, this bonds with hydrogen ions that are left when light energy splits water molecules.

Hydroplate theory Hydroplate theorists believe that the early Earth had a layer of water beneath the Earth's crust. This water would have been under great pressure because of the rock layers above pressing down upon it. If for some reason the crust were to crack, the water trapped below would spray out of the ground under tremendous pressure. It would shoot high into the atmosphere, adding millions of gallons of water to it and these waters would have been part of Noah's flood. This theory has been largely discounted by creationists.

I

Igneous rock Rocks formed when processes within the earth melt existing rock.

Imprints fossils These occur when soft body structures, such as leaves or feathers, are pressed into developing rock and leave an impression of their shape.

Index fossils In order to be classified as an index fossil, a particular fossil species must be found in rock strata in a number of areas. It is particularly helpful if it is found on several continents. However, these fossils must also be distributed only in a few rock layers. To the evolutionary geologist, this means that the species was wide spread but existed during a geologically short period of time. Thus, they believe it can be used to date rocks in which it is found.

Inheritance of acquired traits Lamarck believed that organisms adapted to their environment by changing their existing organs or developing new ones and that these acquired traits could then be passed on to the organisms' offspring.

Intelligent design group Scientists that have determined scientifically that spontaneous generation and evolution are not possible. They recognize that it cannot be scientifically determined who did the creating, and they do not attempt to deal with the issue. Put simply, they believe "somebody" had to do it.

Intrusion An intrusion occurs when magma forces its way up through a crack in sedimentary rock and then hardens.

Isochron dating This is simply a variation of Rubidium-Strontium or Uranium-Lead dating. However, instead of measuring the ratio of only the initial radioactive and the final, stable elements, scientists also check the amount of intermediate isotopes that is present.

Isotopes Two or more forms of an element that have the same number of protons but different numbers of neutrons.

K

Kanapoi hominid A human upper arm bone, found in one location, and dated using evolutionists' methods, to be over 4 million years old, older than all the hominids mentioned except *Ardipithecus Ramidus.*

Kevorkian, Jack A former Michigan pathologist who is an outspoken advocate of assisted suicide.

L

Lake Laetoli Footprints Footprints members of Mary Leakey's expedition found. They were impressed in hardened volcanic ash near Lake Laetoli in northern Tanzania in 1978. They have been dated using the evolutionists' own method (radiometric dating) to be 3.6 million years old. Mrs. Leakey mentions that the footprints are "remarkably similar to those of modern man." She also states that "the form of his foot was exactly the same as ours." Thus, the most logical explanation is that they **are** the footprints of man.

Leaching Materials being washed out of rocks by groundwater.

Left—and right-handed amino acids Amino acids come in two forms that are identical except that they are "mirror images of each other." Because their shapes look slightly similar to the two human hands, they are often referred to as "left-handed" and "right-handed" amino acids. Living things use exclusively left-handed amino acids.

Lenin, Vladimir First communist dictator of the Soviet Union. He ruled during the early twentieth century.

Link fossil A fossil of an organism that appears to be intermediate between two species. For example, *Archaeopteryx* has some characteristics which are bird-like and some which evolutionists consider "reptile-like." Thus some evolutionists consider this fossil to be a link or intermediate fossil between reptiles and birds.

Long-range radiometric dating methods Dating methods using radioactive isotopes whose half-life is measured in millions of years; i.e. uranium-lead dating.

M

Marx, Karl The father of communism, Marx was an atheist. He viewed religion as "the opiate of the people." Marx was quick to realize that an evolutionary explanation for the origin of life was exactly what he needed to make atheism scientifically acceptable.

Meiosis The process which allows for the separation and inheritance of specific genes. It is also the process by which the chromosome number is divided in half.

Mesonychid A land dwelling carnivore that is usually described as walking on four legs, and having sharp teeth, fur, and long tails; it is believed by evolutionists to be an evolutionary ancestor to the whale.

Metamorphic rock Rocks that have been subjected to further pressure by upper rock layers. This pressure, along with heat, causes them to undergo physical and chemical changes while remaining solid.

Migration The movement of organisms into or out of a population.

Missing Links Thousands of link fossils between all the species on the Earth, which should exist if evolution is true, but which have not been found.

Molds These are formed when hard body parts or pieces of wood are completely covered by sediments and then decompose, forming a hollow that is shaped like the original organism.

Moral relativism With moral relativism, what is right depends on the circumstances, not on moral absolutes.

Mussolini, Benito Fascist dictator of Italy during the 1930's and most of World War II, he was responsible for the deaths of thousands of Libyans and Ethiopians.

Mutation A random change in a gene or chromosome which usually leads to a loss of genetic information; a "typing error" in the genetic code.

Mutation theory. A theory proposed by Hugo DeVries that the random changes in genes and chromosomes were what provided the genetic variety on which natural selection could work to cause evolution.

N

Natural selection Those organisms best adapted to their environment will survive and reproduce more often than those that are not well adapted. Darwin's expanded definition is as follows. Traits vary among individuals of the same species. There are limited natural resources to support these individuals. Organisms tend to produce more offspring than can survive. The environment selects for survival those organisms that are best adapted to it.

Neanderthals A series of fossils, the first of which was discovered in a cave in the Neanderthal valley of Germany in 1856.

Because the skeletons of the first specimens were bent, many scientists believed they had found a link fossil between the apes and human beings. However, later specimens were shown to have straight skeletons, and the earlier individuals were then believed to have suffered from some sort of disease.

Nucleotides. "Letters" which make up DNA, the cell's genetic code.

O

Old Earth creationists Creationists that believe the Earth and its species are millions of years old.

Original remains Organisms that have been preserved in ice, tar, or amber which prevents their decay.

P

Pakicetus A fossil found in eastern Pakistan, it has teeth that resemble some mesonychids. *Pakicetus* is believed to have been a land animal that spent a great deal of time in the water, and it is also believed to be a link fossil in the evolution of the whale.

Paleontologists Scientists who study fossils of all kinds.

Parent element The radioactive element in a decay series is often called the parent element.

Petrified fossils These are created when minerals gradually replace the hard parts of an organism, such as bones. The shape and texture of the bone remain, but the bone is then made of rock.

PGA Phosphoglyceric acid; this compound, formed during the dark phase of photosynthesis, reacts with hydrogen from the light phase to form PGAL.

PGAL Phosphoglyceraldehyde; this organic compound forms during the dark phase of photosynthesis.

Physical anthropologists Scientists who study primarily human fossils. (also known as **paleoanthropologists**).

Pithecanthropus Another name for Java Man.

Pleiotrophy The phenomenon of individual genes affecting more than one structure. It is species-specific and quite common.

Polystrate fossils These fossils are usually plants (especially trees) which extend through several layers of sedimentary material. They are found in coal seams and sedimentary rock and often extend through thirty or forty feet of strata.

Principle of biogenesis This states that living things can arise only from other living things. At first, this principle of biogenesis was called the **law** of biogenesis.

Principle of dominance This states that if the factors for a trait in an organism are different, one factor may prevent the other factor from being expressed.

Principle of segregation This states that when hybrids are crossed, the recessive factor separates or "segregates" in some of the offspring.

Principle of uniformity This states that "the present is the key to the past." In other words, the processes that shape the world today are the same processes that shaped the world in the past. Since erosion and sedimentation are generally slow processes at the present time, it is assumed that the thick layers of sedimentary rock which cover the Earth took vast periods of time to form.

Protoavis A fossil found in 1986 by well-known paleontologist, Sankar Chatterjee. He states that it is the skeleton of a modern bird in a rock layer that appears to be older than the layer in which *Archaeopteryx* was found.

Protocell According to evolutionists, the first cell to have arisen spontaneously from organic molecules.

Punctuated equilibrium. Proponents of punctuated equilibrium propose that drastic environmental changes can occur which threaten to cause the extinction of entire populations. They believe that in the past these catastrophic events led to very rapid genetic changes followed by long periods of stasis. Thus, there would be very few intermediate species because evolution occurred very rapidly over a relatively short period of time.

R

Radiocarbon dating Another term for Carbon 14 dating

Ramapithecus A small, monkey-like primate dated to be 8 to 17 million years old and believed to be an ancestor of both the human and the ape families.

Rapid Decay Theory A theory which suggests that the Earth's magnetic field is decaying at a steady and relatively fast rate.

RDP Ribulose diphosphate

Recessive The genes that are not expressed in the phenotype of an organism. They do not disappear but rather are masked by the dominant genes.

Reducing atmosphere. An atmosphere that contains little or no free oxygen.

Right-handed amino acids See "left—and right-handed amino acids."

Ring of fire A string of volcanoes that has formed all around the edge of the Pacific Ocean plate where it collides with the continental plates.

Runaway subduction Very rapid subduction of ocean plates under continental plates.

Runaway Subduction Theory This theory is based on plate tectonics. Because the average density of ocean plates is greater than that of continental plates, most scientists (both evolutionists and creationists) believe that ocean plates subduct under continental plates. Runaway subduction theorists propose that in the past there was a greater difference in ocean and continental plate densities. This would cause rapid subduction to occur, as well as rapid continental drift, tsunamis, and the general destruction of Noah's flood.

S

Sedimentary rock Rocks formed when rock particles gradually build up under water. The upper layers of material can force much of the water out of the lower layers. Gradually the lower layers of material can harden, forming a rock very much like concrete.

Selenka-Trinil Expedition The expedition took place in 1907–1908. Its purpose was to get sufficient scientific proof to quiet the controversy about Java man and thus to prove that he truly was a missing link between apes and man. However, the expedition actually proved that Java Man could not have been a link fossil (hominid).

Sexual dimorphism This refers to the male members of a species being much larger than the females—a phenomenon that occurs among the gorillas, as well as other species.

Short period comet Those that have an orbital period of 200 years or less.

Short-range radiometric dating method Dating method using radioactive isotopes whose half-life is measured in thousands of years; i.e. Carbon 14 dating.

Situational ethics Another term for moral relativism.

Skull 1470 A fossil skull the Leakeys' son Richard found that he labeled KMN-ER 1470. The skull was of particular interest because it was obviously so human in nature and was found in rock strata which Richard Leakey dated, using the evolutionists' own methods, to be at least 2.8 million years old, making it older than the *Homo habilis* specimens.

Singer, Peter An Australian-born philosopher who is a professor at Princeton University. Many individuals consider him reputable and "moderate," even though he advocates abortion, infanticide, and euthanasia. According to his own words, his beliefs are a natural outgrowth of his acceptance of evolution.

Spencer, Herbert One of the individuals who was quick to apply natural selection to human society, Spencer had already come to a belief in evolution before he read Darwin's *Origin of Species*. He applauded Darwin's work because he felt it explained evolution scientifically. He developed a theory that became known as "social Darwinism." It was Herbert Spencer who coined the phrase "survival of the fittest."

Stable element One that remains the same element throughout its existence.

Stalin, Joseph A former communist dictator of Russia, he took power when Lenin died. He was a brutal leader, responsible for the deaths of millions of his own people.

Start and stop codons The "punctuation" of the genetic code.

Stasis A state of equilibrium with little or no change.

Subduction zone An area where an ocean plate goes under a continental plate.

Supernova Remnant (SNR) A huge expanding cloud of dust created by a supernova.

T

Taung skull Another term for the original specimen of *A. Africanus*.

Theory of use and disuse According to Lamarck, if an environmental change led to the **disuse** of an organ, it gradually would disappear because it was no longer needed. On the other hand, if an organ was gradually used more heavily, it would become more prominent in succeeding generations.

Thermoluminescence A method used to date archaeological materials such as flint or pottery.

Thymine One of the four nitrogen-carrying bases of DNA.

Transitional forms Another term for link fossil or intermediate fossil.

U

Unstable element Radioactive elements that decay into other, more stable elements. Elements are usually unstable for one of three reasons: they have more neutrons than protons. (this is most common.); their nuclei are too large for stability, or they have an excess of protons.

V

Vestigial Organs that appear to be reduced in size and have no obvious function.

W

Wadjak Man Skulls of unmistakably modern humans. Although the location where they were found was hard to pinpoint, there is some indication that the skulls were found in rock strata that was as old as the rock layers in which Java Man was found, indicating that Dubois, Java Man's founder, had found modern human skulls approximately the same age as the first specimen of *Homo erectus*.

Y

Yolk sac A sac that is attached to the early embryo, which in the past was referred to as vestigial. It has been cited as existing because our common ancestor with the birds needed this organ to supply food. In reality, it is the source of red blood cells until the embryonic bone marrow takes over this function.

Young Earth Creationists Creationists who believe that the Earth is thousands rather than billions of years old. These individuals take the first chapter of Genesis literally. They believe the six days of creation refer to twenty-four hour days.

A QUESTION OF ORIGINS NOTES

Chapter Four : Spontaneous Generation: What Scientists Proved

[1]"Aristotle," *Encyclopedia Britannica,* 15th Edition, 1994, Volume 14, P. 1119.

[2]Percival Davis & Dean H. Kenyon, *Of Pandas and People,* Dallas, Texas: Haughton Publishing Co., 1989, P. 47.

[3]Michael Behe, *Darwin's Black Box,* New York: The Free Press, 1996, P. 274.

[4]Davis & Kenyon, P. 3.

[5]E.J. Ambrose, *The Nature and Origin of the Biological World,* Chicester, England: Ellis Horward Limited, P. 35.

[6]Davis & Kenyon, P. 5.

[7]Davis & Kenyon, P. 5.

[8]Harry Clemmey & Nick Badham, "Oxygen in the Precambrian Atmosphere: an Evaluation of the Geologic Evidence," *Geology,* March, 1982, P. 141.

[9]Clemmey & Badham, P. 145.

Chapter Five: The Scientific Facts about Genetics and Comparative Embryology, etc.

[1]Percival Davis and Dean H. Kenyon. *Of Pandas and People.* Dallas, Texas: Haughton Publishing Co., 1989, P. 7.

[2]Ernst Mayr. *Population, Species, and Evolution.* Cambridge, Massachusetts: Harvard University Press, 1970, P. 93.

[3]Mayr, P. 93.

[4]Davis & Kenyon, P. 65.

[5]E. J. Ambrose, *The Nature and Origin of the Biological World.* Chicester, England: Ellis Horwood Limited, 1982, P. 120.

[6]Ambrose, P. 120.

[7]Ambrose, P. 121.

[8]Elizabeth Pennisi. "Haeckel's Embryos: Fraud Rediscovered." *Science.* Vol. 277. September 5, 1997. P. 1435.

[9]Michael K. Richardson, et. al., "There Is No Highly Conserved Embryonic Stage in the Vertebrates." *Anatomical Embryology,* 1997, Volume 196, P. 105.

[10]Gary Parker, *Creation Facts of Life,* Green Forest, Arkansas: Master Books, 1994, P. 51.

[11]Parker, P. 49.

[12]Parker, P. 53.

[13]Sir Gavin de Beer, "Homology: an Unresolved Problem," *Oxford Biology Readers* (Eds. J.J. Head & O.E. Lowenstein) P. 8.

[14]Michael Denton. *Evolution: A Theory in Crisis*, Bethesda, Md.: Adler & Adler, 1985, P. 146.

[15]Denton, P. 147.

[16]De Beer, P. 15.

[17]Charles Darwin. *Origin of Species*. Volume 49. *The Great Books*. Chicago: William Benton, Publisher, 1952, P. 247.

[18]Denton, P. 280.

[19]Davis & Kenyon, P. 143

[20]Davis & Kenyon, P. 143.

[21]Carl Weiland, "Goodbye Peppered Moths," *Creation Ex Nihilo*, 21(3) June-August, 1999, P. 56.

Chapter Six: What Does the Fossil Record Really Say?

[1]*See Sediment and Transport in the Lower Missouri and the Central Mississippi Rivers*, (June 26-September 14, 1993) U.S. Geological Survey Circular 1120–1.

[2]Andrew Snelling, "Stumping Old-age Dogma," *Creation Ex Nihilo* Vol. 20, No. 4, September-November 1998, P. 49.

[3]See William R. Corliss, "Baby Oil," *Science Frontiers Online*, August 25, 1999. (Taken from *Science Frontiers*, No. 76, July-August, 1991.)

[4]J. Madeleine Nash, "When Life Exploded," *Time*, Vol. 146, No. 23, December 4, 1995, Pp. 64–74.

[5]Michael Denton, *Evolution: a Theory in Crisis*, Bethesda, Md.: Adler & Adler, 1986, P. 187.

[6]Gary Parker, *Creation Facts of Life*, Green Forest, AR.: Master Books, 1997, P. 138.

[7]Charles Darwin, *The Origin of Species*, Vol. 49, The Great Book Series, Chicago: William Benton, publisher, 1952, P. 152.

[8]Darwin, P. 152.

[9]See Stephen Jay Gould, *Dinosaur in a Haystack*, New York: Harmony Books, 1995, Pp. 135–136.

[10]Michael Denton, P. 180.

[11]Percival Davis & Dean H. Kenyon, *Of Pandas and People*, Dallas, Texas: Haughton Publishing, 1989, P. 104.

[12]Davis & Kenyon, P. 105.

[13]Denton, P. 177.

[14]Davis & Kenyon, P. 105.

[15]See "The Lonely Bird: Claims of the Earliest Avian Fossil Launch a Paleontologic Flap," *Science News*, Vol. 140, No. 7, August 17, 1991, pp. 104–108. See also "Early Bird Threatens Archaeopteryx's Perch,' *Science*, Vol. 253, No. 5015, July 5, 1991, P. 35.

[16]Duane T. Gish, *The Challenge of the Fossil Record*, El Cajon, California: Master Books, 1988, P. 85. See also Luther D. Sunderland, *Darwin's Enigma*, Santee, California: Master Books, 1988, P. 81.

[17]For further information on the horse series, consult Jonathan Sarfati, "The Non-evolution of the Horse," *Creation Ex Nihilo* 21(3) June-August, 1999, Pp. 28–31.

[18]Sarfati, P. 30.

[19]Annalisa Berta, "What is a Whale?" *Science*, Vol. 263, No. 5144, January 14,1994, P. 181.

[20]Angela Meyer, "The World of Whales," *Creation Ex Nihilo*, Vol. 19, No. 1, December 1996–February 1997, P. 26.

[21]Colin Patterson as quoted in Davis & Kenyon, P. 113.

[22]Darwin, P. 232.

Chapter Seven: Radiometric Dating

[1]John Morris, Ph.D., *The Young Earth*, Colorado Springs: Master Books, 1994, P. 52.

[2]"Radioactive Dating," *MacMillan Encyclopedia of Physics*, Volume 3, New York: Simon & Schuster MacMillan, 1996, P. 1326. See also, John Daintith, ed., *A Dictionary of Chemistry*, New York: Oxford University Press, 1996, P. 501.

[3]"Radio Isotope Dating," *Encyclopedia Americana*, 1999 ed., Vol. 23, P. 189.

[4]Karen Liptak, *Dating Dinosaurs and Other Old Things*, Brookfield, Connecticut: Millbrook Press, 1992, Pp. 27–28.

[5]Liptak, P. 26.

[6]"How Old is the Earth?" Answers in Genesis Online, August 23, 1999.

[7]John G. Funkhouser and John J. Naughton, "Radiogenic Helium and Argon in Ultramafic Inclusions from Hawaii," *Journal of Geophysical Research*, Volume 73, No. 14, July 15, 1968, Pp. 4601–4606.

[8]*MacMillan Encyclopedia of Physics*, P. 1326 See also John Daintith, Pp. 428–429.

[9]Y.F. Zheng, "Influence of the Nature of the Initial Rb-Sr System on Isochron Validity," *Chemical Geology* (Isotope Geoscience Section) Volume 80, 1989, P. 13.

[10]Morris, p. 59.

[11]Morris, P. 59.

[12]Zheng, Pp. 1–14.

[13]Dr. Alexander Wilson as quoted in Liptak, P. 40.

[14]Robert E. Lee, "Radiocarbon, Ages in Error," *Anthropological Journal of Canada*, Volume 19, No. 3, 1981, P. 27.

[15]Lee, P. 9.

[16]"Thermoluminescence," *New Encyclopedia Britannica*, 15th edition, 1998, Volume 11, P. 702.

[17]Morris, P. 86.

[18]Morris, P. 75.

[19]Morris, P. 75.

[20]For a more detailed treatment of this subject, see Danny R. Faulkner, "Comets and the Age of the Solar System" *Creation Ex Nihilo Technical Journal*, 11(3):26, 4–273, 1997. The article is also available on line at answersingenesis.com.

[21]Jonathon Sarfati, "Exploding Stars Point to a Young Universe," *Creation Ex Nihilo*, 19(3) June-August, 1997, P. 46.

[22]Sarfati, P. 46.

[23]Sarfati, P. 46.

[24]Morris, P. 83.

[25]Morris, P. 89.

Chapter Eight: Evolution of Man?

[1]John Evangelist Walsh, *Unraveling Piltdown*, New York: Random House, 1996, P. 51.

[2]Walsh, Pp. 67–68.

[3]Walsh, Pp. 79–80.

[4]Michael Hornsby and Tim Jones, "Old Bones Crack Riddle of Piltdown Man," *The Times* (London), May 23, 1996, Britain page.

[5]Peter Andrews, "Ecological Apes and Ancestors," *Nature*, Vol. 376, August 17, 1995, P. 556.

[6]Meave Leakey, "The Farthest Horizon," *National Geographic*, Vol. 188 No. 3, September, 1995, P. 49.

[7]Meave Leakey, P. 47.

[8]Meave Leakey, p. 47.

[9]Andrews, P. 555–556.

[10]Meave Leakey, P. 44.

[11]Donald C. Johanson, "Face to Face with Lucy's Family," *National Geographic*, Vol. 189, No. 3, March, 1996, P. 101.

[12]D. Johanson. p. 101.

[13]D. Johanson. p. 101.

[14]D. Johanson. p. 102.

[15]Marvin L. Lubenow, *Bones of Contention*, Grand Rapids, Michigan: Baker Books, 1992, P. 53.

[16]Phillip V. Tobias, "Implications of the New Age Estimates of the Early South African Hominids," *Nature*, Volume 246, November 9, 1973, P. 82.

[17]Alan Walker & Pat Shipman, *The Wisdom of the Bones*, New York: Alfred A. Knopf, 1996, P. 93.

[18]Bruce Bower, "Hominid Headway: Scientists have used modern technology to scour the inside of an ancient child's skull, but the youngster's growth patterns remain controversial," *Science News*, Vol. 132, No. 25–26, December 19, 1987, P. 408.

[19]T. C. Partridge, Geomorphological of Cave Openings at Makapansgat, Sterkfontein, Swartkrans, and Taung, *Nature*, Volume 246, November 9, 1973, P. 78.

[20]Lubenow, P. 159.

[21]Richard E. Leakey, "Skull 1470," *National Geographic*, June, 1973, P. 819.

[22]Lubenow, P. 162.

[23]Richard Leakey, p. 820 (also *Science News*, Vol. 102, November 18, 1972, P. 324.)

[24]R. Leakey, P. 819.

[25]Lubenow, P. 164.

[26]Lubenow, P. 165.

[27]Lubenow, P. 90.

[28]Lubenow, P. 91.

[29]G. H. R. Von Koenigswald as quoted in Lubenow, P. 88.

[30]Lubenow, P. 96.

[31]Harry Shapiro, *Peking Man*, New York: Simon & Schuster, 1974, P. 125.

[32]Lubenow, P. 102.

[33]Lubenow, P. 115.

[34]A. Keith, "The Problem of Pithecanthropus," *Nature*, Vol. 87, No. 2176, July 13, 1911, P. 50.

[35]Lubenow, P. 115.

[36]Lubenow, P. 116.

[37]Lubenow, P. 87.

[38]Lubenow, Pp. 120–121.

[39]Mary Leakey, "Footprints in the Ashes of Time," *National Geographic*, Vol. 155, No. 4, April, 1979, P. 446.

[40]Mary Leakey, P. 453.

[41]Russell H. Tuttle, "The Pitted Pattern of Laetoli Feet," *Natural History*, March, 1990, P. 62.

[42]Tuttle, P. 64.

Chapter Nine: The Pervasiveness of Perfection

[1]Michael Behe, *Darwin's Black Box,* New York: The Free Press, 1996, Pp. 108–109.

[2]Behe, P. 72.

[3]For a more detailed discussion, please see Michael Denton, *Evolution: a Theory in Crisis,* Bethesda, Maryland: Adler & Adler, Publishers, 1986, Pp. 210–213.

[4]Paula Weston, "Bats: Sophistication in Miniature," *Creation Ex Nihilo,* December 1998–February 1999, P. 29.

[5]For further information see Anne Innis Dagg & J. Bristol Foster, *The Giraffe, Its Biology, Behavior, and Ecology,* New York: Van Nostrand Reinhold Co., 1976. Much of the information for this section was gleaned from its pages.

[6]For further information, see "How the Seabed Saves the World," *New Scientist,* February 3, 1996, P. 15. Much of the information for this section was taken from it.

[7]Peter D. Ward & Donald Brownlee, *Rare Earth,* New York: Springer-Verlag, New York, inc., 2000, Pp. xxvii -xxviii.

[8]Ward & Brownlee, P. 19.

[9]Ward & Brownlee, P. 223.

[10]Ward & Brownlee, P. 28.

[11]Ward & Brownlee, P. 37.

[12]Michael Denton, *Nature's Destiny,* New York: The Free Press, 1998. P. 28.

[13]Denton, P. 28.

[14]L. J. Henderson as quoted in Denton, P. 29.

[15]Denton, P. 30.

[16]Denton, Pp. 31–32.

[17]Denton, P. 32.

[18]Denton, P. 51.

[19]Denton, P. 59.

[20]Denton, P. 55.

[21]Denton, P. 389.

Chapter Ten: Alternate Theories of Beginnings

[1]Michael Denton. *Evolution: A Theory in Crisis.* P. 308.

[2]The Bible, New International Version.

[3]The Bible, New International Version.

[4]Refer to the film, *The Search for Noah's Ark,* produced by Dr. John Morris, Institute for Creation Research, 1988.

[5]The Bible, New International Version.

[6]See Steven A. Austin, Ph. D. Et. Al. Catastrophic Plate Tectonics; *A Global Flood Model of Earth History.* (Slides with explanatory data) Santee, California: Geology Education Materials, 1996.

[7]Austin. *Catastrophic Plate Tectonics notes.* P. 6.

[8]Austin. Notes. P. 11.

[9]Austin. Notes. Pp. 7–8.

[10]Austin. Notes. P. 7.

[11]Austin. Notes. P. 11.

[12]Austin. Notes. P. 16.

[13]John D. Morris, *The Young Earth*, Colorado Springs: Master Books, 1994, P. 100.

[14]Morris, P. 102.

[15]Carl Wieland, "Tackling the Big Freeze," *Creation Ex nihilo*. Volume 19, Number 1, December, 1996–February 1997, P. 42.

[16]"Coral," *Encyclopedia Americana*, 1999 edition, Volume 7, P. 777.

Chapter Eleven: The Effects of a Belief in Evolution

[1]Karl Marx. *On Revolution,* (Volume 1, *The Karl Marx Library*) New York: McGraw – Hill Book Co., 1971, P. 195.

[2]Isaiah Berlin. *Karl Marx, His Life and Environment*. New York: Time Incorporated, 1963. Pp. 204–205.

[3]Robert Service. *Lenin: A Political Life*. Bloomington, Indiana: Indiana University Press, 1985. Vol. 1. P. 33.

[4]Michael Morgan. *Lenin*. Dayton, Ohio: Ohio University Press, 1971. P. 221.

[5]Richard Piper. *A Concise History of the Russian Revolution*. New York: Alfred A. Knopf, 1995. P. 394.

[6]Piper, P. 393.

[7]Isaac Deutscher. *Stalin: A Political Biography*. New York: Oxford University Press, Inc., 1969. P. 8.

[8]Duetscher, P. 8.

[9]Francis B Randall. *Stalin's Russia*. New York: The Free Press, 1965. P. 71.

[10]Alan Bullock. *Hitler & Stalin: Parallel Lives*. New York: Alfred A. Knopf, 1992. P. 264.

[11]Bullock. P. 276.

[12]Bullock. P. 264.

[13]Bullock. P. 264.

[14]Bullock. P. 277.

[15]Bullock. P. 507.

[16]Ian Kershaw. *Hitler 1889–1936 Hubris*. New York: W.W. Norton & Co., 1998. P. 289.

[17]Kershaw. P. 249.

[18]Kershaw. P. 125.

[19]Peter Hoffman. *Hitler's Personal Security*. Cambridge, Massachusetts: The M.I.T. Press, 1979. P. 264.

[20]Hoffman. P. 264.

[21]Denis Mack Smith. *Mussolini*. New York: Alfred A. Knopf, 1982. P. 15.

[22]Robert E.D. Clark, PhD. *Darwin: Before and After*. London: Paternoster Press, 1958. P. 115.

[23]Joseph Ridley. *Mussolini*. New York: St. Martin's Press, 1997. P. 285.

[24]Ridley. P. 288.

[25]Gertrude Himmelfarb. *Darwin & the Darwinian Revolution*. Chicago: Ivan R Dev, Publisher, 1959. P. 416.

[26]Alexander Alland, Jr, Ed. *Human Nature: Darwin's View*. New York: Columbia University Press, 1985. P. 112.

[27]"Herbert Spencer." *Encyclopedia Americana*. 1999 Ed. Vol. 25. Pp. 480–481.

[28]"Spencer." P. 481.

[29]Jack London. To *Build a Fire and Other Stories*. New York: Bantam Books, 1986. P. 79.

[30]Jonathon Kellerman. *Survival of the Fittest*. New York: Bantam Books, 1997. Pp. 499–500.

[31]Kellerman. P. 504.

[32]Kershaw. P. 411.

[33]Peter Singer. *Rethinking Life and Death*. New York: St. Martin's Press, 1994. Pp. 171-172.

[34]Singer. Pp. 190-202.

[35]Singer. P. 180.

[36]Singer. P. 182.

[37]Singer. P. 215.

[38]Singer. P. 215.

[39]Singer. P. 220.

[40]See Derek Humphry, *Dying With Dignity: Understanding Euthanasia*, Secaucus, N. J.: Carol Publishing Group, 1992. See also Derek Humphry, *Final Exit: Practicalities of Self Deliverance and Assisted Suicide for the Dying*, New York: Dell Trade Paperback, 1996. See also Rita Marker, *Deadly Compassion: The Death of Ann Humphry and the Truth about Euthanasia*, New York: William Morrow & Co., 1993.

[41]See Humanist Manifesto I, Principles 1–4.

[42]Jack Kevorkian. "A Failsafe Model for Justifiable Medically Assisted Suicide." *American Journal of Forensic Psychiatry*. Volume 13. 1992. Pp. 7–81.

[43]Herbert Hendin, M.D. *Seduced by Death*. New York: W.W. Norton, & Co., 1997. P. 75.

[44]Hendin. P. 76.

[45]Hendin. P. 23.

[46]Hendin. P. 142.

[47]Peter Derkx. "Modern Humanism in the Netherlands." Internet article, July 6, 2004. P. 9. Based on Chapter 3 of his book, *Empowering Humanity: State of the Art in Humanities,* 2002.

[48]Derkx, P. 10.

[49]Derkx, P. 7.

[50]Hendin. P. 151.

[51]Hendin. P. 150.

[52]Hendin. P. 152.

[53]Paul A. Carter. "Science and the Death of God." *American Scholar*. 42:407. Summer, 1973. P. 407.

[54]Fred M. Hudson as quoted in Carter. P. 420.

[55]Fred M. Hudson as quoted in Carter. P. 421.

[56]R. Dubos. "Humanistic Biology." *American Scientist*. Vol. 53. March, 1965. P. 6.

To order additional copies of

A Question of

Created or evolved? # Origins

Have your credit card ready and call

Toll free: (877) 421-READ (7323)

or send $26.95* each plus $6.95 S&H** to

WinePress Publishing
PO Box 428
Enumclaw, WA 98022

or order online at: www.winepressbooks.com

*WA residents, add 8.4% sales tax

**add $1.50 S&H for each additional book ordered